INSIGHT ⊙ GUIDES

SAN FRANCISCO
CITY GUIDE

www.insightguides.com/USA

◉ Walking Eye App

YOUR FREE DESTINATION CONTENT AND EBOOK AVAILABLE THROUGH THE WALKING EYE APP

Your guide now includes a free eBook and destination content for your chosen destination, all for the same great price as before. Simply download the Walking Eye App from the App Store or Google Play to access your free eBook and destination content.

HOW THE WALKING EYE APP WORKS

Through the Walking Eye App, you can purchase a range of eBooks and destination content. However, when you buy this book, you can download the corresponding eBook and destination content for free. Just see below in the grey panels where to find your free content and then scan the QR code at the bottom of this page.

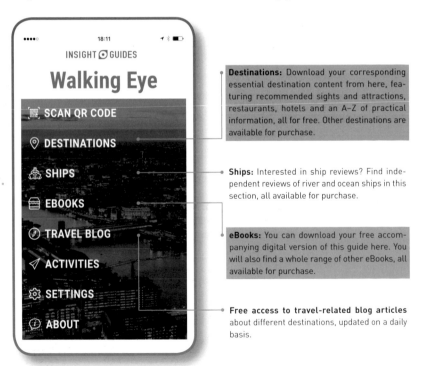

Destinations: Download your corresponding essential destination content from here, featuring recommended sights and attractions, restaurants, hotels and an A–Z of practical information, all for free. Other destinations are available for purchase.

Ships: Interested in ship reviews? Find independent reviews of river and ocean ships in this section, all available for purchase.

eBooks: You can download your free accompanying digital version of this guide here. You will also find a whole range of other eBooks, all available for purchase.

Free access to travel-related blog articles about different destinations, updated on a daily basis.

HOW THE DESTINATION CONTENT WORKS

Each destination includes a short introduction, an A–Z of practical information and recommended points of interest, split into 4 different categories:

- Highlights
- Accommodation
- Eating out
- What to do

You can view the location of every point of interest and save it by adding it to your Favourites. In the 'Around Me' section you can view all the points of interest within 5km.

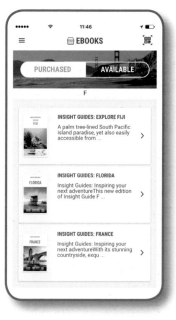

HOW THE EBOOKS WORK

The eBooks are provided in EPUB file format. Please note that you will need an eBook reader installed on your device to open the file. Many devices come with this as standard, but you may still need to install one manually from Google Play.

The eBook content is identical to the content in the printed guide.

HOW TO DOWNLOAD THE WALKING EYE APP

1. Download the Walking Eye App from the App Store or Google Play.
2. Open the app and select the scanning function from the main menu.
3. Scan the QR code on this page – you will then be asked a security question to verify ownership of the book.
4. Once this has been verified, you will see your eBook and destination content in the purchased ebook and destination sections, where you will be able to download them.

Other destination apps and eBooks are available for purchase separately or are free with the purchase of the Insight Guide book.

THE BEST OF SAN FRANCISCO: TOP ATTRACTIONS

At a glance, everything you can't afford to miss when you visit San Francisco, from world-class bridges, parks, and neighborhoods to iconic monuments and historic missions.

▷ **Mission Dolores.** The city's oldest building, established in 1776 just days before the signing of the Declaration of Independence. See page 188.

△ **Golden Gate Bridge.** Opened in 1937, four years after construction began. Painted international orange (not gold), the bridge is San Francisco's most powerful image. See pages 200 and 204.

▽ **Golden Gate Park.** The park entertains the city with playgrounds, windmills, lakes, museums, a Japanese tea garden, and the 19th-century Conservatory of Flowers. See pages 176 and 184.

UNITED STATES PENITENTIARY
ALCATRAZ ISLAND | AREA 12 ACRES
1½ MILES TO TRANSPORT DOCK
ONLY GOVERNMENT BOATS PERMITTED
OTHERS MUST KEEP OFF 200 YARDS
NO ONE ALLOWED ASHORE
WITHOUT A PASS

◁ **Alcatraz.** The island is a former prison that was home to some of America's most notorious criminals. See page 104.

▷ **The Ferry Building.** Opened in 1898 as a busy passenger terminal before becoming a market for California's freshest produce. See page 82.

▽ **Chinatown.** San Francisco's Chinatown is one of the largest outside Asia, and with its temples, statues, and squares, is really a city within a city. See page 123.

△ **Coit Tower.** On top of Telegraph Hill, Coit Tower was bequeathed to the city by an eccentric heiress who was also a passionate firebuff. See page 120.

▷ **Fisherman's Wharf.** A busy waterfront, boisterous sea lions, and terrific seafood restaurants. See page 97.

▽ **San Francisco Museum of Modern Art.** The distinctive museum was designed by Swiss architect Mario Botta. See page 148.

▽ **North Beach.** Low-key, low-rise and home of the Beat generation, North Beach has bars, bookstores, and some of the best nightlife in the city. See page 107.

THE BEST OF SAN FRANCISCO: EDITOR'S CHOICE

Stunning places and unique attractions...
Here are our recommendations, plus some
tips even San Franciscans won't always know.

BEST BARS, PUBS, AND CAFÉS

The Buena Vista. Irish coffee was introduced to the United States here. The mayor of SF was employed to source the correct cream. www.thebuenavista.com.

Caffé Trieste. Rich in literary history with a distinctly Italian accent, this landmark is an essential North Beach stop. Drop by on Sunday morning for the opera jam session or any other day for exceptional coffee and people-watching. See page 114.

John Folley's Irish House. Warm and inviting, this isn't your regular seedy pub. Enjoy excellent Irish food, friendly staff, and live music weekends. www.johnnyfoleys.com.

Tonga Room. A classic example of tiki-kitsch, this bar in the Fairmont Hotel features an indoor rainstorm, a Don Ho-type band, and cute cocktails in coconuts. www.tongaroom.com.

Tosca Café. Style and substance collide in this classic lounge, hinting of a time when crooners ruled the airwaves and people drank sidecars and old fashioneds. It's a favorite hangout for celebrities. See page 113.

Vesuvio Café. The tattered romance of the Beat era lingers on at this funky corner bar overlooking Jack Kerouac Alley. Stop here for a drink on your way to or from City Lights Bookstore, which is most conveniently right next door. See page 112.

CLASSIC SAN FRANCISCO

City Hall. This handsome Beaux Arts building with a rotunda is well worth visiting. See page 141.

Great American Music Hall. A stunning rococo-style music venue with bands nearly every night. See page 144.

John's Grill. The quintessential San Francisco steakhouse, visited by Sam Spade in *The Maltese Falcon*. See page 68.

The Palace Hotel. Take a look at the glass ceiling in the dining room for a glimpse into the city's opulent past. See page 136.

Sutro Baths. Explore the remains of these 19th-century swimming pools. See page 199.

BEST PLACES FOR A LITTLE ROMANCE

Land's End. This hiking trail winds its way along the coastline revealing pocket beaches, secret coves, and dramatic vistas. See page 199.

The Top of the Mark. A martini from the bar complements the near 360-degree view of the city from atop Nob Hill. See page 152.

Japanese Tea Garden. This lush garden offers a perfect respite to savor a moment of serenity and a cup of tea in the middle of gorgeous Golden Gate Park. See page 180.

The Bimini Twist. This modern and inviting restaurant uses the finest locally sourced ingredients to create an inspiring menu. The seafood is a speciality and the bread is homemade. www.thebiminitwist sanfrancisco.com.

Sunset cruise to Angel Island. The wind in your hair, the glittering waters of the bay, and the sunset silhouetting the skyline – what's not to love? See page 220.

Cocktails at Tonga Room.

BEST ARCHITECTURE IN SAN FRANCISCO

Transamerica Pyramid. The pyramid has been described as an upside-down ice-cream cone, but also a dunce cap. Luckily time has softened San Francisco's opinions, and it is now one of the beloved icons of the city. The building has 48 floors and was built in 1970 by William L. Pereira and Associates. See page 137.

Fabulous architecture.

Painted Ladies. These stately, ornate Victorian homes can be found all over town, but some of the most famous border the east side of Alamo Square. See page 170.
Sentinel Building. The handsome Sentinel Building was completed in 1907 and is currently the headquarters of film director Francis Ford Coppola's company, Zoetrope. See page 113.

Academy of Sciences. The award-winning, Renzo Piano-designed eco-house houses the Academy of Sciences and features a rain-forest exhibit and a living roof. See page 185.

Contemporary Jewish Museum. In the art enclave of the SoMa area, this is a fresh example of mixed-use design, incorporating the city's architectural past with the present. See page 147.

Conservatory of Flowers. Golden Gate Park's fabulous greenhouse dates from 1879, it was built to hold rare plants, flowers, and towering palms. See page 178.

Palace of Fine Arts. The palace is a lovely, romantic relic of the 1915 Panama Pacific International Exposition. See page 202.

de Young Museum. The museum's monolithic, bold design is so different from the building it replaced, not everyone is convinced that it works. Go to Golden Gate Park and make up your own mind. See page 179.

The Transamerica Pyramid and Flatiron building.

FREE IN SAN FRANCISCO

Barbary Coast Trail. This fun activity is a self-guided tour through Union Square, Chinatown, North Beach, and beyond. Keep your eyes on the sidewalk on Columbus and Broadway for markers, or pick up a map at the Visitor Center. See page 112.

Golden Gate Promenade. Bayside near the Palace of Fine Arts is a lovely pathway that leads from the boat docks to the Golden Gate Bridge. Sit on a bench and watch the water sports or rent a bike and ride across the bridge. See page 202.

Sea Lions. San Francisco's most famous residents entertain captive audiences as they tussle, roll, bark, and bask in the sun beside Pier 39. See page 103.

Bay to Breakers. Billed as the biggest footrace in the world, this event (held every May) starts near the Ferry Building and ends at Ocean Beach. Most participants wear outrageous costumes, although some might wear nothing at all. Jump in and join the fun if you're in town. www.zapposbayto breakers.com.

Stern Grove Music Festival. Every summer Sunday at 2pm, the Grove hosts an outdoor concert. Bring a snack and a beverage and enjoy the music. Check the local free papers for details. Concerts are held regularly from June to August, but check out www.sterngrove.org for more information.

Grace Cathedral. This Gothic gem on Nob Hill was inspired by Notre Dame Cathedral in Paris. Note the gilded bronze doors, replicas of the great Doors of Paradise in Florence's Baptistery. The Keith Haring altarpiece and the soaring rose window are great, too. See page 156.

Wave Organ. A magical piece of environmental art, this is a wave-activated acoustic sculpture on a spit of land jutting into the bay. The jetty itself was constructed from old stones taken from a local Gold Rush-era cemetery; it contains a wonderful assortment of carved granite and marble. See page 163.

Lose yourself in nature.

BEST WITH KIDS

Pier 39. The closest thing to an amusement park in San Francisco, Pier 39 has a vintage carousel, aquarium, arcade, street performers, sea lions, and lots of shopping. The Musée Méchanique nearby on Pier 45 is packed with salvaged penny-arcade machines. See page 103.

San Francisco Zoo. Take a walk on the wild side in the Outer Sunset and cavort with lions, tigers, and bears, as well as lemurs, penguins, giraffes, and zebras. There is also a steam train, a carousel, and a Children's Zoo. See page 198.

Yerba Buena. This place has all kinds of attractions for kids – ice-skating, a carousel, bowling, playgrounds, and the Children's Creativity Museum, a hands-on space with workshops and performances. See page 146.

Laid back on Pier 39.

Residents of San Francisco Zoo.

BEST EXCURSIONS

Big Sur. Highway 1 south of San Francisco through the Monterey Peninsula to Big Sur may be the most spectacular route in America, hugging the coast in a series of sharp switchbacks. At the end of the journey, Big Sur is a consummate reward. See page 243.

Muir Woods. San Francisco in the morning; redwoods in the

Ripe for the picking.

afternoon. Take a stroll under grand trees and stop at the Pelican Inn at Muir Beach for a spot of tea or a cold mug of beer. See page 222.

Mendocino. The four-hour drive north to arrive at this lovely, arts-oriented town is so diverting you may never make it. See page 234.

Sausalito and Tiburon. Hop on a ferry and cross the bay to experience bars, galleries, and the finer elements of the hot-tub lifestyle. See pages 217 and 220.

Wine Country. Take your pick: Napa or Sonoma counties. Both are just an hour and a half north of the city, but eons away in pace and landscape. See page 245.

Scenic coastal roads made for driving.

FESTIVALS

Chinese New Year. This parade is the largest outside Asia; usually in February. See page 127.

Haight Street Fair. In June, the city's main street shuts down for a weekend of music and dancing. www.haight ashburystreetfair.org.

SF Sketchfest. Warm your winter blues with January's festival of comedians. See page 63.

Pride Week. A week-long gay-fest in June, climaxing in the world's biggest Pride Parade. See page 192.

BEST WALKS IN SAN FRANCISCO

Dolores Park. Dubbed "Dolores Beach" by locals, this is a hangout for everyone from moms with babies to hipsters with dogs, to the GLBT crowd. Situated between the lively Mission and the Castro districts, it owes it's monikor due to the sunny location. Sit under a palm tree here and enjoy the people watching. The café on the corner makes a great latte. See page 190.

The Embarcadero. This promenade extends all the way from Fisher man's Wharf past the

Ferry Building and toward AT&T Park. It is a great place for a stroll. For an in-depth experience, look out for signs and kiosks that have detailed historic facts. See page 136.

Filbert Steps. These steps (see left) run in three sections from Telegraph Hill to Montgomery Street near Coit Tower. Admire the gardens, Art Deco buildings, and wonderful views, and take a break at the top before climbing the tower. See page 118.

Buses. For frequent travel on buses, it's worth buying a pass; these can be bought to cover one, three, or seven days, or a month. If you are making just one trip which involves a change of buses, remember to ask the driver for a transfer, which is valid for up to two

hours. Go to www.sfmta.com for details. **BART from the Airport.** Taxis are expensive and shuttles take forever. The BART airport extension allows you to get downtown cheaply and quickly. **Tickets.** Discount tickets can be bought for shows and other events from the tix kiosk at Union Square.

CityPass. CityPass saves time and money on attractions, cruises, cable cars, and more. www.citypass.com. **Museum Discounts.** Many San Francisco museums have one day a month when the entrance is free; call for details. Some also offer student and senior discounts.

An early morning cable car ride on Lombard Street.

View of Bay Bridge.

Cable car ride with views of Bay Bridge.

THE STREETS OF SAN FRANCISCO

**"Arrival in San Francisco is an experience in living"
observed writer William Saroyan in the 1930s;
most modern visitors would agree.**

San Francisco is an enchantingly beautiful city, one of the most distinctive in the world, with panoramas from 43 different hills, watery vistas, and a verdant park that seems to go on forever. The man-made landscape is mostly low-rise, with wooden houses that delight the eye as they have since they were built a century or more ago.

The Golden Gate Bridge

The "city by the bay" is what many call it, and although there must be scores of cities beside scores of bays, almost everybody knows this reference to mean San Francisco. It's a big bay, too, 50 miles (80km) around and crossed by no fewer than five bridges. One, the Golden Gate Bridge (perhaps the most famous bridge in the world), is as evocative of the city as the cable cars, Fisherman's Wharf, and, yes, Tony Bennett's timeless song. Even before he left his heart here, San Francisco was one of the favorite cities for tourists – and that includes all the people who haven't even been here yet.

San Francisco is a city with a strong sense of neighborhood, each with its own distinct identity, overlapping and interrelating so that people mix and mingle and travel through communities instead of bypassing them on the highway when they want to visit some other part of town – which is the more familiar pattern in the United States.

Small as it is (pop. 864,000 in San Francisco County), the city has featured many times on the world's front pages: the discovery of gold, the 1906 earthquake and fire, the founding and first home of the United Nations, the Beat Generation poets and writers, the Bay Area tech revolution, the fierce battles of the gay community to be awarded equal rights. Most famously, perhaps, was the Haight-Ashbury commune that became an international magnet for 1960s hippies and the renowned attitude of tolerance that has served as a sort of metaphorical welcome mat for unorthodox lifestyles.

The city will welcome you, too, whatever your tastes and inclinations, and will doubtless be everything you want it to be. You'll absorb the ambiance, be entranced by the sights, delight in the food, and sleep well at night. You might even learn to appreciate the fog; some people think it quite romantic. But, of course, those tend to be the people who live here.

Salesgirl in flower shop on Union Street.

SAN FRANCISCANS

**First came the peaceful missionaries, followed by the
rough-and-tumble gold-seekers. San Franciscans have
developed into a friendly bunch who welcome visitors
with open arms, regardless of vice or virtue.**

Cars pause at crossroads, unprompted, to allow pedestrians to cross the street. San Francisco is the only town in the United States, probably the world, to have issued credit-card swipes to beggars, because of the lack of cash in the pockets of generally wealthy locals. This is the place that legalized gay marriage.

San Francisco is keen to accommodate and to include. Truly, it has grown and evolved through waves of migration, but there's another explanation for its enduring popularity: for most, the City by the Bay is not a way-station – it's where they want to be. It's beautiful, the climate is pleasant, food is good, and almost every kind of outdoor activity is available. Most tastes for indoor recreation are also catered for. People like it here. And once they arrive, they want to stay.

Besides being west, as in "Go West, young man, and grow up with the country" (a quote

Views from a cable car.

> While most residents will tell you they are at home here, few actually are: only 35 percent were born in California, and native San Franciscans are even harder to find.

originally from an 1851 editorial by John Soule in the Indiana Terre Haute Express, but usually attributed to Horace Greely), the very landscape has offered hope and the promise of opportunity to countless generations.

Statistics

San Francisco is the United States' 14th- largest city, with 864,000 people dwelling snugly in an area only 7 by 7 miles (11 by 11km). According to the US Census Bureau , the population is 53.6 percent white, 35.3 percent Asian (most of whom are Chinese), 15.3 percent Latino, and 5.7 percent African-American. In recent years, the city has also drawn increasing numbers of Filipinos and Southeast Asians, and a certain proportion of eastern Europeans.

The city's demographic mix includes a high percentage of young unmarrieds, with the number of single people between 25 and 34 years of age having increased dramatically in the past few decades. Only 15 percent of San Francisco households include children, fewer

Sorority sisters at the University of California.

A hippie with headgear.

than one-fifth of adults under 45 own their own home, and nearly 100,000 people – almost one in seven residents of the city – live with a friend, lover, or with roommates.

San Francisco is a decentralized metropolis, where many of its inhabitants root themselves in cozy neighborhood enclaves; where their distinct cultures and identities grow and thrive; and where each is characteristically tolerant of the other. The LGBT (lesbian, gay, bisexual, and, transgender) population crosses all ethnic divisions, and wields cohesive political power in the city. Demographic estimates of the gay population range between one in five and one in seven city residents.

All that glitters

People of almost every state, nation, and race were caught up in the rush for gold; by 1850, immigrants from Mexico, Ireland, Germany, and France made up four-fifths of the foreign-born population. Once the miners arrived, as historian James Adams wrote, "…every type of citizen of every social grade or profession came, not to hew forests, farm, and make homes, but to get as rich as possible as quickly as possible."

San Francisco became an overnight boomtown. Between 1848 and 1851, the population jumped from 1,000 to 40,000 – a staggering growth. Among those who made their way here in search of riches were thousands of free blacks from the old South, who quickly organized and took action to secure their civil rights.

A Franchise League campaigned for the repeal of a law forbidding blacks the right to testify in trials involving white people. Five hundred white San Franciscans signed the petition in 1860, and by 1863 the campaign had succeeded and a course of integration had, at least, been set. One black pioneer, J.B. Sanderson, famously founded city schools for poor Indian, Asian, and black children, many of whom had been barred from local institutions. Sanderson himself picked up a piece of chalk and taught lessons until he was able to recruit more teachers.

(DON'T) CALL IT FRISCO

Newspaperman Herb Caen, chronicler of things San Franciscan, felt strongly enough to name his book *Don't Call It Frisco*. Unpopular with locals since the 1930s, the name is not a corruption of *Francisco*, but is thought to be from an old English word, *frithsoken*, meaning refuge, and was used by sailors to refer to a port with repair yards. Recently there has been a resurgence: the term is reappearing on the hooded tops, caps and T-shirts of young residents, particulartly native Latinos and African American males. And the folks who run Frisco Tattoo in the Mission District say that Frisco is one of their most popular indelible etchings.

San Francisco's finest.

Italian New World

Genovese sailors had been trading along the western shore for years, but the remote towns and harbors offered little to interest the worldly seafarers. When the shout rang out that there was gold in the Sierra foothills, the Genovese were the first Italians to settle. Within months, tales of streets paved with gold spread to the old country, and people from the northern Italian provinces soon followed their pioneering cousins. Rural Ligurians, Luccans, Florentines, and Venetians all made the grueling five-month journey from the old world to the new. Not all their dreams came true, but California was a land rich in possibilities. The soil was fertile, the bay was filled with fish, and the town was starved of commerce. For diligent people, San Francisco was close enough to paradiso.

By the 1860s, Italians had established a strong presence in North Beach. The new San Franciscans called their relatives over, and whole families – sometimes entire villages – arrived in the New World. People of different regions brought distinct dialects and customs; their provincial differences traveled with them. The battles that rocked the newly unifying Italy

> *St Patrick's Church conducts mass in Tagalog, the Filipino language. At North Beach's Saints Peter and Paul, the faithful can hear mass in English, Italian, and Chinese.*

were fought with equal vigor in the New World. The seafaring Genovese mostly stuck to trade and fishing; Ligurians grew and sold produce; and the others opened stores or established street-corner businesses.

By 1851, 25,000 Chinese worked in the mines, the majority of them later settling in San Francisco. These Chinese fortune-seekers shared a common dream that Gum San, the Gold Mountain, would provide them with healthy fortunes with which they could return home and rejoin their anxious families. The first Chinese who came to San Francisco were called "coolies" – although the term is now considered derogatory, it originates from the Chinese phrase ku li, meaning "bitter strength." They were willing to do hard labor in the mines and on the railroads for significantly lower wages than whites. This new life was unimaginably

Painting a historic Victorian building.

harsh: a newspaper of the time reported that 20,000lbs (9,000kg) of bones were collected from shallow graves along the railroad tracks where Chinese workers had died. The bones were sent home to China for burial.

In the first decade of the 20th century, the number of Japanese people in the US increased from 6,000 to 25,000. Most of these immigrants settled in California, with many choosing San Francisco as their new home. Local trade unions protested against the hiring of Japanese workers and, after the earthquake of 1906, many fled south to Los Angeles.

Down south

An astonishing 10 percent of the population of Mexico migrated to the southwestern US in the first 30 years of the 20th century, the majority of whom went to Texas and California. In California, their numbers swelled enormously,

ALTERNATIVE OUTLOOKS

San Franciscans are known the world over for their fascination (some say obsession) with the health of their bodies, souls, and environment. In terms of legislation, Marin County was the first place to zone itself as "scent-free," and California introduced some of the world's first and most progressive anti-smoking laws.

California led the world on emissions standards for automobiles, in spite of the continuing enthusiasm for gas-guzzling SUVs.

On the spiritual side, the city is home to the first Buddhist training monastery outside of Asia, and

40,000 of the city's residents use bicycles as their main mode of transportation. San Francisco has more yoga studios, acupuncturists, natural food stores, and vegetarian restaurants per capita than any other American city of its size and, collectively, spends the most on organic food.

None of this is to the exclusion of having a good time, though. The city lays claim to the first espresso on the West Coast and to the origin of the Martini. Residents also spend more per head on clothes, books, and alcohol than anywhere else in the United States.

Cafe life in San Fran.

from 8,000 to 370,000. Most harvested cotton, cantaloupe, and lettuce crops during the season and returned to their families across the border as soon as they could. But some stayed.

Urban centers

In the 1930s (the Dust Bowl years), many poor white farmers fled from Louisiana, Oklahoma, and Texas, memorably chronicled by author John Steinbeck in *The Grapes of Wrath*. They headed for the urban centers of the west coast and the thriving war industries. During World War II, a huge influx of blacks also came from the South, to work in shipyards and the increasingly popular defense businesses.

The Navy contributed a migration of gay men during the war, discharging them from the ships when they berthed at the San Francisco docks. These men formed communities, establishing the liberal haven for gays that draws people from around the globe. These wartime migrations all fueled a housing shortage in San Francisco.

While many Japanese men fought for the United States against Japan during World War II, on the side of the United States, thousands

Bastille Day draws a boisterous crowd of Francophiles to the alleyways of downtown San Francisco – home to many French immigrants since the Gold Rush.

more had their possessions confiscated and/or were detained in concentration camps. Japanese people, returning from this long, harsh internment, came back to find they could no longer afford homes. Reparations from the federal government 40 years later did little to erase the bitter memories.

After the Republic of the Philippines was established in 1946, strong economic and military ties to the United States were established and the immigration quota was raised. Revised immigration laws in 1952 brought a wave of Filipino immigration; recent census figures show the Filipino community to be among the city's fastest-growing Asian-Pacific immigrant groups. Lacking the regional and family organization of the Chinese and the Japanese to establish settlements, Filipinos, many from

All dressed up for a night on the town.

The city streetscape has many bookstores.

A guide to the city published a few decades ago advised that when you got tired of walking San Francisco and its hills, you could always just stop and lean on it.

remote islands, finally found unity through the American labor movement. They ultimately merged with Mexican-American union members to form the United Farm Workers Union.

More recent arrivals from the Philippines have been professional people, who tend to specialize in fields like engineering and medicine. Today, a huge Filipino community occupies the area just south of San Francisco in Daly City.

Refugees from Kampuchea, Vietnam, and Laos have recently settled in record numbers, too, and, predictably, have faced some discrimination. There have been clashes between Vietnamese fishermen and local white fishermen, who feel threatened by the newcomers. A number of strong-advocate legal groups have emerged to serve the interests of the vulnerable Vietnamese people.

Conversely, the African American population of San Francisco is shrinking, having dropped below 49,000. Most of those who leave are moving to the suburbs that have begun to push the Bay Area's outer limits into the San Joaquin Valley and others parts of central California.

Wired community

The most recent gold rush (the massive internet rush of the 1990s) has been a major factor in shaping the modern San Francisco landscape. Boutiques, wine bars, chic restaurants, and computer stores began to spring up, seemingly on every street corner. Everything, and everyone, became wired. New media companies moved into old warehouses, and districts like South Beach became trendy overnight.

Another more recent rush of technology has creeped into the city from Silicon Valley. Companies like Twitter and AirBnB maintain headquarters in San Francisco now, as opposed to the San Jose area. "Google" buses with tinted windows crawl across the city picking up and dropping off emplyoyees, who finally figured out that living in San Francisco offers much more than the Valley.

This boom has caused a massive increase in home prices and rents. Applicants line up with printouts of their credit reports and financial portfolios, and apartments are rented within hours, sometimes even mere minutes. Unfortunately, artists, teachers, and working class people are getting priced out as a result.

AT&T Park breathed new life into McCovey Cove, as techies spent their leisure hours frequenting the new ball park and the watering holes that opened in the neighborhood. Sleek

Twilight near Golden Gate Park.

sailboats cruised into the Marina and Fort Mason districts.

The Californian body/spirit culture is accompanied by personal and ecological development, which has led to social and environmental pioneering; in the nation that pollutes the planet's atmosphere the most, San Francisco has some of the world's toughest anti-pollution laws. Tolerance of cultural, religious, racial, and gender divergences are hard-wired into the city's civic codes and legislation.

Tech toys

While there is no shortage of personal wealth in San Francisco, prosperity is not displayed so much in clothes and accessories as in discreet displays of what can best be described as tech toys. Status is quietly conveyed with the latest cell phones, computers, and vehicles, although parking is such a trial that most cars spend much of their time standing in garages.

The tech that drives the toys is clearly from the hottest tip of the cutting edge. The first internet café was established across the bay in Berkeley, and a sizeable portion of the world's foremost technology and communications companies is headquartered in the Bay Area. Groovy gadgets show up here first.

A bright future

Immigration still surfaces as an issue in political campaigns, as politicians will often inflame the emotive issues as an easy way to further their own agendas, and discrimination does occur here, as it does everywhere. The difference is that the city usually meets these challenges head-on, positively, and proactively. San Francisco's cultural atmosphere is bright, confident, accommodating, and optimistic. Much like its people and its landscape.

CHILDREN

In spite of having the lowest proportion of children of any large American city (13.4 percent), San Francisco is as child- and family-friendly as a town could be. Restaurants often offer attractive selections for children on their menus, and crayons, too. Many of the city's charms are outdoors, such as a walk or bicycle ride across the Golden Gate Bridge or walking down "the crookedest road in the world" – Lombard Street. Golden Gate Park has the oldest playground in the United States, with a carousel that was built in 1912. The visual arts facility, Children's Creativity Museum, is geared toward older kids. And since this is California, they have both an animation and production studio.

DECISIVE DATES

Stained-glass window of Mission Dolores.

Pre-1500s
The Miwok, Ohlone, and Wituk tribes occupy much of the land now known as northern California.

1535
Spain's Hernando Cortés sets foot on California's shore, followed later by Portugal's Juan Rodriguez Cabrillo.

1579
Sir Francis Drake lands at Port Reyes, reporting to Europe that California is an island.

1769–1823
The Spanish establish a chain of 21 missions along or near the coast between San Diego and Sonoma: the "string of pearls."

1776
Both the Presidio of San Francisco and Mission Dolores, located nearby, are founded.

1792
British explorer Captain George Vancouver sails into San Francisco Bay.

1834
Governor Figueroa assigns boundaries to the pueblo of San Francisco.

1846
John Fremont christens the entrance to the Bay the "Golden Gate."

1848
Gold is discovered in the nearby Sierra Nevada foothills, precipitating a boom in the city's economy that would put San Francisco on the map.

1850
San Francisco is almost completely destroyed by fire, but the town rebuilds.

1854
The first US Mint in the state of California opens on Commercial Street.

1859
There are more discoveries in the Sierra Nevadas – this time a boom following a silver strike.

1862
The San Francisco Stock Exchange opens.

1869
The transcontinental railroad is completed.

1873
The world's first street cable railroad begins its run along Clay Street.

1880
George Hearst pours huge sums of money into the *San Francisco Examiner*, turning it over to his son, William Randolph *(below)*, seven years later.

Influential publisher William Randolph Hearst.

1901
First publication of *The Octopus* by Frank Norris, a devastating criticism of the Southern Pacific Railroad.

1906
An earthquake estimated at 8.25 on the Richter scale, followed by fire, levels much of the city.

1907
Destroyed by the earthquake, the Fairmont Hotel (Nob Hill's first) is rebuilt.

1909
The third, and current, Cliff House is built, after the

The Palace of Fine Arts dates from 1915.

first two (constructed in 1894 and 1907 respectively) are destroyed by fire.

1911
Formation of the San Francisco Symphony Orchestra.

1914
The first transcontinental telephone conversation takes place: Alexander Graham Bell in New York talks to Thomas Watson in San Francisco.

1915
The Panama Pacific International Exposition celebrates the opening of the Panama Canal; the centerpiece is the Palace of Fine Arts in the Presidio.

1920
The first transcontinental airmail flight is completed, and mail begins to arrive from New York.

1923
The opening of the San Francisco Opera.

1924
The Palace of Legion of Honor is dedicated.

1933
Construction of the Golden Gate Bridge begins.

1934
US Government converts Alcatraz island into a federal prison.

1936
The Bay Bridge opens, linking San Francisco and the East Bay.

1937
Pan American begins flights between San Francisco and New Zealand.

1938
Herb Caen's column begins in the *San Francisco Chronicle* and runs for nearly half a century, earning him the nickname "Mr San Francisco."

1939
The Golden Gate International Exposition opens on Treasure Island.

1942
San Franciscans of Japanese ancestry are rounded up and sent to internment camps for the duration of World War II.

1945
The United Nations' first headquarters is established in the city.

1950s
The "Beats," a bohemian literary group that originated in and was centered in North Beach.

1951
The Japanese premier signs a peace treaty (at the SF Opera House) that officially ends World War II.

1965
Entrepreneur Bill Graham opens The Fillmore, a premier music venue.

1966
The Beatles play their last live concert at Candlestick Park in San Francisco.

Alcatraz island was a federal penitentiary from 1934 to 1963.

City Hall was the scene of mass protests in the 1960s.

1967
The "Human Be-In" gathering of hippies takes place in Golden Gate Park during the Summer of Love. Jimi Hendrix makes his US debut at the Monterey Pop Festival.

1969
Activists from the American Indian Movement (AIM) take over the island of Alcatraz.

Alcatraz was taken over by the National Park Service in 1973.

1972
The first Gay Pride parade takes place in the Castro.

1973
The National Park Service takes over the decommissioned Alcatraz, and Park Rangers begin tours.

1977
Harvey Milk makes headlines by becoming the first openly gay person to be elected to public office in California when he won a seat on San Francisco's Board of Supervisors. The Gay and Lesbian Film Festival is established.

1978
Milk and Mayor George Moscone are assassinated by conservative political opponent Dan White. Dianne Feinstein, with massive support from the gay movement, begins a 10-year stint as mayor.

1980s
The local computer industry booms: Silicon Valley and the Apple computer become household words.

1986
The Names Project Memorial Quilt, commemorating HIV and Aids victims, is started in the Castro.

Silicon Valley made a splash in the 1980s.

1989
An earthquake measuring 7.1 on the Richter scale hits the Bay Area, killing 62 people and injuring thousands.

1993
The city's Board of Supervisors votes to ban smoking in the workplace.

1994
The Presidio army base, with its views of the Golden Gate Bridge, is turned over to the Park Service.

1995
The new San Francisco Museum of Modern Art opens in the South of Market (SoMa) area;

The South of Market area (SoMa).

shops, restaurants, and other museums soon follow.

1998
A city-wide smoking ban in restaurants and bars is introduced.

2000
Baseball's Pacific Bell Park (now AT&T Park) opens in South Beach, spearheading gentrification of the area. It is home to the San Francisco Giants.

2002
The dot-com bubble bursts, leading to a crash on the stock market.

2003
Protests over America's

BART, the San Francisco transit system, established WiFi in the tunnels.

invasion and subsequent involvement in Iraq lead to the arrest of hundreds.

2004
Mayor Gavin Newsom authorizes the city clerk to issue marriage licenses to same-sex couples, sparking a national debate. BART becomes the first transit system in the nation to offer wireless communication to its passengers as they travel underground.

2008
The California Academy of Sciences moves back to Golden Gate Park and into a new building designed by Renzo Piano.

2010
San Francisco mayor Gavin Newsom is elected Lieutenant Governor of California and heads to Sacramento. Ed Lee steps in as mayor, making him the first Asian-American to fill the mayoral post. The San Francisco Giants, recognized as the underdog, win baseball's World Series.

2013
After a long battle samesex marriages finally become legal. SFJAZZ Center opens in Hayes Valley.

2014
The San Francisco Giants win World Series for the third time in five seasons. Levi's Stadium in Santa Clara becomes the new home of the San Francisco 49ers football team.

The Civic Center's Asian Art Museum.

2015
The Brooking Institution report states that San Francisco has the wealthiest people of any major U.S. city, and the fastest growing income inequality. The 27 story 535 Mission Street skyscraper opens in the South of Market district. Murder of Kathryn Steinle who is killed by a homeless illegal immigrant resonates across the country starting a debate on the city's liberal immigration regulations. Golden State Warriors basketball team wins their first NBA title since 1975.

2016
San Francisco becomes the first US city to require employers to offer six weeks of fully paid leave for new parents. The San Francisco Museum of Modern Art (SFMOMA) reopens after a three-year extension. Golden State Warriors are defeated by Cleveland Cavaliers in the NBA finals.

EWS' & STOCKWELL'S

GRAND OPERA HOUSE

THE LARGE COMMODIOUS AND ELEGANT THEATRE.

MAGNIFICENT PRODUCTION

OF THE NEW REALISTIC SCENIC, SENSATIONAL AND DOMESTIC DRAMA IN 7 TABLEAUX

ENTITLED

YOUTH

REGULAR SUNDAY EVENING PERFORMANCES.

MATINEES WEDNESDAY & SATURDAY.

OUR POPULAR PRICES

15 cts   25 cts   50 cts   & 75 cts

THE MAKING OF SAN FRANCISCO

In the early days California was a peaceful place. Then came the Europeans, followed by the discovery of a precious metal at Sutter's Mill that would change the landscape forever.

The Miwok, the Ohlone, and the Wituk tribes occupied much of northern California with the most rudimentary technology; or in ecological harmony with the land, depending on your view. Then the Spaniards arrived. Europeans settled the land and regarded the tribes as little more than animals. The decline of the Native Americans was inevitable. Within a century "the people of reason" had virtually obliterated the cultures and ravaged the environment. The city of San Francisco was built from the companionship of greed and gold.

Early explorers

Precisely what Sir Francis Drake discovered in 1579 during his voyage around the world in the *Golden Hind* has not been established with certainty. Drake had a mission from Elizabeth I to "annoy" the Spanish provinces; he obediently caused havoc up and down the west coast of Mexico. In his gentlemanly manner of operation, though, not one person was killed.

Apparently Drake passed by the entrance to the San Francisco bay without venturing inside or even noticing the opening, but his log shows that he did anchor just north of the bay and sent several landing parties ashore. It was believed that one of these groups left behind the small brass plate discovered in 1936 near Drake's Bay, though debate over its origin continues.

Tales of riches enticed the Spaniards from the beginning. The early explorers sought a Northwest Passage that would lead them to the Orient and the valuable spice trade. Hernando Cortés, the conqueror of Mexico, ordered a series of expeditions up the coast of Baja California

Sir Francis Drake sailed near the bay in 1579.

Prayer Book Cross, a monument to Sir Francis Drake, sits on a hill in Golden Gate Park above a cascading waterfall.

– at the time thought to be an island – but it was not until 1542 that Juan Rodriguez Cabrillo discovered the land to the north, though he too passed by without noticing the immense natural harbor now called San Francisco Bay. Perhaps fog concealed it, as is so often the case.

Later, Gaspar de Portolá, on his northern expedition to find a suitable harbor, also missed

Miwok and Ohlone Native Americans settled in northern California long before the Europeans arrived.

> *San Francisco was originally named Yerba Buena (the good herb) for the abundance of mint, the aromatic plant that grew wild on the sandy hills.*

its significance, thinking it to be an open gulf. A later explorer, José Francisco Ortega, reported the bay as "a great arm of the sea extending to the southeast farther than the eye could see." Discovery was slow, and it wasn't until Captain Juan Bautista de Anza's visit six years later that plans were made for a mission at Yerba Buena.

San Francisco de Assisi

Captain José Moraga and Fray Francisco Palóu founded the mission with a handful of settlers in 1776, just days before the Declaration of Independence was signed on the far side of the country. The church was dedicated to San Francisco de Assisi, but became known as Mission Dolores, probably for the small lagoon on which it was built: Nuestra Senora de los Dolores.

Palóu acted for the renowned "Apostle of California," Father Junipéro Serra, who was responsible for founding nine of the eventual 21 Californian missions, and personally baptized thousands of American Indians. Presidios (garrisons), like the one nearby, were built at strategic points to protect each mission against attack from hostile tribes or foreign colonists.

The garrison was strong enough to withstand forays by hostile Indians, but would have easily fallen to an attack from the sea. Northern California was still a remote outpost then, and held little appeal for foreign adventurers. Ironically, the Gold Rush might have come a century earlier; the Spanish padres were shown a find of gold, but advised silence, reasoning that knowledge of its existence would bring an influx of invaders.

By the end of the 18th century foreign officials were taking an interest in the region. In 1792, the English sailor George Vancouver scouted the coast, bringing with him the first American visitor, John Green, to the shores of California. The Russians also arrived. Their trading post and garrison only 50 miles (80km) north at Bodega Bay made the Californians nervous, but they departed in 1841. By this time Mexico had declared independence from Spain and the secularization of the missions had begun – a process intended to turn over

Mission Dolores, founded in 1776.

The Presidio was established in 1776.

the land and livestock to Native American families, but which mostly resulted in their further exploitation by new owners.

When a certain Captain Beecher visited this part of northern California in 1826, five years after Mexican independence from Spain, he noted among the residents only ennui. "Some," he wrote, "were ingenious and clever men but they had been so long excluded from the civilized world that their ideas and their politics, like the maps pinned against the wall, bore the date 1772, as near as I could read for fly specks."

It wasn't until 20 years after his visit that the US flag was raised, the year (1846) that Samuel Brannan arrived with 230 Mormons to colonize what was then renamed San Francisco. There was apprehension about the growing signs of interest in the west by France and Britain, and especially the value to a foreign power of San Francisco Bay, which an American diplomat described as, "capacious enough to receive the navies of all the world."

Stars and stripes

In May 1846, President James Polk engaged the United States in war with Mexico. Even before news of the declaration reached California, an independent group of nationalists at Sonoma, led by Ezekiel Merritt and William B. Idle, awoke the Mexican authority, General Vallejo, from his bed and obliged him to sign articles of surrender.

The action was encouraged by the presence of a US expedition led by a cartographer and explorer, Captain John Charles Fremont. As he declined to allow the rebels to raise the Stars and Stripes, they created a new flag depicting a grizzly bear racing a red star – the Bear Flag, as it became known. Accepting his acclamation as

President of the Californian Republic, Fremont led a mission to capture the state capital at Monterey, but found Commodore John Sloat had sailed from Mazatlan to arrive there first. Whatever Mexican resistance there was crumbled. Across California, people raised the Stars and Stripes and claimed the territory.

The war ended and California was ceded to the United States with the signing of the Treaty of Guadalupe in January, 1848. One week before, James Marshall, who had just built a mill for John Sutter, discovered gold in the Sierra Nevada foothills. Sutter was an immigrant from Switzerland, whose 49,000-acre (19,800-hectare) Sacramento Valley ranch had

1822 California became part of the territory of Mexico.

The Bear Flag, raised in Sonoma in 1846.

been granted to him by the Mexican governor of California. He tried to keep the find secret, but the news, of course, changed the landscape of this peaceable pastoral region forever.

Gold fever

Early arrivals made instant fortunes simply by washing nuggets out of a stream, or scraping gold dust from easily accessible veins in the rock. It was estimated that the area was yielding as much as $50,000 of the precious metal each day. But once the easily accessible gold was stripped, the risks increased, the supply dried up, and prices of everything skyrocketed. The real necessities of life were buckets, shovels, rockers, dippers, and pans. Miners – called '49ers because of the year of their arrival – mainly lived in tents, sleeping on blankets atop pine needles. For a roof overhead, the rental of a hut in town ran to as much as $3,000.

It wasn't long before those who serviced the prospectors grew considerably richer than most of the prospectors themselves. Levi Strauss arrived from Germany to sell tents, but riveted his supply of canvas into durable work trousers. In 1850, a gold digger wrote home: "You can scarcely form a conception of what a dirty business this gold digging is… A little fat pork, a cup of tea or coffee, and a slice or two of miserable bread form the repast of the miners."

Prostitutes, merchants, miners, and adventurers – all saw in San Francisco an opportunity. Edwin Markham later compared the city to Venice and Athens "in having strange memories," but found it unique "in being lit from within by a large and luminous hope."

Already in debt and lacking funds to keep law and order, much less provide shelter or health care for the newcomers, officials of San Francisco cast around for ways to raise funds. They hit on the idea of a steep tax on gamblers, of whom there seemed to be an unlimited and growing supply. "Gambling saloons glittering like fairy palaces … suddenly sprang into existence, studding nearly all sides of the plaza and every street in its neighborhood," an historian recorded in 1855. "All was mad, feverish mirth where fortunes were lost and won on the green cloth in the twinkling of an eye." As much as $50,000 could ride on the turn of a card.

New gaming licenses paid for policemen and the upkeep of a brig – moored at Battery and Jackson streets – used as a city jail. Virtual anarchy reigned in the streets, where gangs of hoodlums prowled, some operating with almost military precision. The depredations of

> Before the discovery of gold, John Fremont named the Bay's entrance Chrysopylae (Greek for Golden Gate) because he believed it resembled Istanbul's Golden Horn.

a group known as the Hounds were so outrageous that citizen volunteers armed themselves, rounded up the criminals, tried and sentenced them, though they were soon released for lack of facilities to confine them. Two years later, in 1851, the citizens again took control by forming a 200-member Committee of Vigilance.

"Whereas… there is no security for life and property," they declared they were "determined

After gold was found in 1848, San Francisco went from a backwater to a boom town.

that no thief, burglar, incendiary or assassin shall escape punishment either by the quibbles of the law, the insecurity of the prisons, the carelessness or corruption of the police or a laxity of those who pretend to administer justice." This group caught, tried, and hung a trio of burglars before a regular law-and-order policy could be brought into effect.

Water rights

The gold was beginning to peter out, and disputes over water rights arose, which continue to this day. Miners whose claims were far from stream beds collaborated to build ditches funneling water from sources whose riparian rights (i.e. ownership of the adjoining land) conflicted with appropriation rights. The introduction of hydraulic mining, bringing streams of water to bear on hillsides, intensified the problem. The network of canals and flumes that brought water long distances from its source came to be worth more than the claims they served, but the arguments over who had a prior right to the water were never fully resolved. In *California as It Is and as It May Be*, the first book published in San Francisco (in 1849), author F.B. Wierzbicki wrote that the city looked like it had only been built to endure for a day, so fast had been its growth and so flimsy its construction.

Rapid expansion

For most of the '49ers, the town was rough, ready, and very expensive. Eggs from the Farallone Islands sold for $1 apiece. Real-estate speculation reached epidemic proportions. Each boatload of new prospectors represented another batch of customers. As the burgeoning city burst out from the confines of Yerba Buena Cove, "water lots" sold for crazy prices on the expectation that they could be made habitable with landfill. The practice continued for decades, and many of today's downtown San Francisco neighborhoods are built on landfill.

GOLD! GOLD! GOLD!

By the end of May, 1848, word of the discovery at Sutter's Mill spread all over California: the editor of *The Californian* newspaper announced the suspension of publication because his entire staff had quit.

"The whole country from San Francisco to Los Angeles and from the seashore to the base of the Sierra Nevada," he wrote, "resounds with the sordid cry of gold! gold! gold! – while the field is left half-planted, the house half-built and everything neglected but the manufacture of shovels and pick-axes." Before the year was out, more prospectors arrived from Mexico, Peru, and Chile. Gold fever ignited the world.

Prospectors pan for gold in 1848.

Wagon trains carry supplies for the miners.

Fire was a major hazard. Half a dozen major conflagrations broke out between 1848 and 1851, every one of them destroying several blocks at a time, but each was followed by sturdier rebuilding.

SAN FRANCISCO'S EMPEROR

San Francisco's first laudable lunatic was "Emperor" Joshua Norton. In 1859, with a sword, plumed hat, and a military uniform, Norton declared himself "Norton I, Emperor of the United States and Protector of Mexico." San Franciscans delighted in his eccentricities, like the "order" to dissolve the United States Congress, and they took the money that bore his name as valid currency. Around the city, he and his two dogs, Lazarus and Bummer, were loved and well fed. On his death in 1880, the front page of the *San Francisco Chronicle* read "Le Roi est Mort." An estimated 30,000 San Franciscans paid their respects, and many donated money for his funeral.

Several of Emperor Norton's "Imperial decrees" had a certain wisdom: he proposed a "League of Nations," and a suspension bridge connecting Oakland to San Francisco. The San Francisco Board of Supervisors attempted to name the Bay Bridge after him. He is also remembered in the writings of Robert Louis Stevenson and Mark Twain.

By 1854, San Francisco had a library, churches, schools, and theaters among the many substantial stone or brick buildings, and horse-drawn streetcars traversed the now-tidy streets. It was becoming clear that the Gold Rush was reaching an end, although immigrants were still arriving, and with them, shiploads of supplies that could no longer be paid for. Stores and businesses were going bankrupt, and the streets became crowded with penniless miners.

Whatever chance California may have had of becoming placid was swept away in 1859 by yet another torrent of riches flowing down the Sierra slope. This time it was silver, not gold, that led to the rush.

Boom town to fancy town

One of the most uncomfortable outposts of the Gold Rush had been centered on Nevada's Sun Mountain on the dry eastern slope of the Sierra near modern-day Lake Tahoe. There was a little gold up in the Virginia Range, but eking a living from the area's bluish clay was unrewarding work. In June 1859 a sample of "that blasted blue stuff" found its way to the office of one Melville Atwood, an assayer in Grass Valley. Atwood found an amount of silver worth an astounding $3,876 in that one sample of ore. The seam of silver was called the Comstock Lode, and was probably the greatest single mineral strike ever made.

At first it appeared that the Silver Rush would mimic the Gold Rush of a decade earlier. "Our towns are near depleted," wrote one spectator. "They look as languid as a consumptive girl.

San Francisco's Market Street in 1865.

What has become of our sinewy and athletic fellow citizens? They are coursing through ravines and over mountaintops," looking for silver.

One of the young men who rushed up to the Virginia Range was Mark Twain. In his book *Roughing It* he describes how he and his fellow almost-millionaires "expected to find masses of silver lying all about the ground." The problem for Twain and the thousands like him was that the silver was in, not on, the steep and rugged mountains. And getting it out was not a matter of simply poking and panning.

The Silver Rush, it turned out, was a game for capitalists, men with money to buy up claims, dig tunnels, and install the expensive machinery and mills that transformed that blue stuff into cash. By 1863, $40 million of silver had been wrestled out of the tunnels in, around, and through Sun Mountain. Two thousand mining companies traded shares in San Francisco's Mining Exchange. Fortunes were made, lost, and made again as rumors of bonanza or *borasca* (profitless rock) swept into town. At one time, more speculative money was wrapped up in Comstock mining shares than existed in real shares on the whole of the Pacific Coast.

Newspaper tycoons

An efficient transportation system was one of San Francisco's earliest achievements, with half a dozen companies operating horse-drawn services by mid-century. But the hills were steep and slippery and watching a horse fall down on one of them, pulling the carriage with it, was the event that inspired British engineer Andrew Hallidie with the idea for a cable car. By 1873, Hallidie's cable cars were operating on a 2.5-mile (4km) route along Clay Street.

> A major hazard in hastily built San Francisco was fire, where most buildings were constructed of wood and cloth, and where ocean winds fanned the flames of wood-burning stoves and oil lamps.

The discoveries of mineral wealth added a new impetus for contact between the East and West coasts. Although regional railroads were running, there were no transcontinental lines. It was not until 1853 that the federal government allocated funds for the survey of feasible routes,

19th-century travel agents encouraged migration to the West by sea.

with California's gold boom making the state a top contender for the terminus over previously favored Oregon.

The main form of transport from the Europe and the East Coast to California was by clipper ship, which took six or eight months to sail from Boston to San Francisco. In the year 1849, after President Polk declared that "the abundance of gold in [California] would scarcely command belief," almost 800 ships set off from the East Coast. Within a dozen years, 50 steamers out of San Francisco carried passengers and freight not only up and down the West Coast, but to and from ports as far away as China and Australia.

Concurrent with this development of clippers – and by 1860 this era was over – was the growth of the overland stage. They were initially financed by regional postmasters, spurred on by a need to deliver the mail.

Pony Express and the railroads

For a brief period, the glamour of the Pony Express captured the public's imagination (see

WILLIAM RANDOLPH HEARST

George Hearst, a successful mine owner, poured some of his millions into a newspaper, the *San Francisco Examiner*, turning it over to his son, William Randolph, in 1887. This was the beginning of what was to become the largest publishing empire the world had known.

By the time of his death in 1951, William Randolph Hearst had extended his empire to more than a score of daily newspapers (including two New York papers and two more in Chicago), 14 magazines in the US as well as two in England, 11 radio stations, and five news services employing a total of 38,000 people.

Hearst served two terms as congressman for Califor-

nia but was defeated in his campaigns to become governor, mayor, and president.

Hearst's personal spending was said to run to $15 million a year, of which at least $1 million was spent on art and antiques; the bulk of this was destined for his extravagant hilltop ranch at San Simeon, to the south of San Francisco.

Hearst, the model for Orson Welles' 1941 movie *Citizen Kane*, also owned an estate in Mexico, St Donat's Castle in Wales, the 67-acre (27-hectare) estate Wyntoon in northern California, and commercial and residential property in various US cities.

Engineer and inventor Andrew Hallidie at the controls of his first cable car in 1873.

page 42), but the intervening Civil War also brought the telegraph system – the first on the West Coast was erected on Telegraph Hill in North Beach – and the sending of letters for $5 each lost its appeal.

Plans for a railroad to link the East and West coasts had been mooted for many years. But when the Civil War broke out, Congress was intent upon securing California's place in the Union and the process was accelerated.

In the winter of 1862, the Pacific Railroad Act granted vast tracts of western land, low-interest financing, and outright subsidies to two companies – the Central Pacific, building from Sacramento, and the Union Pacific, building from Omaha, Nebraska.

Henry George, a journeyman printer and passionate theorist, had warned that the increasing dominance of the railroads would be a mixed blessing. He predicted that western factories would be undersold by the eastern manufacturing colossus, and that the Central Pacific's ownership of vast parcels of land along its right-of-way would drive the price of much-needed agricultural land prohibitively high. George even foresaw the racial tensions that resulted from the railroad's importation of thousands of Chinese laborers, who flooded

the state's job market in the 1870s and became the target of bitter discontent.

> When gold seekers abandoned their vessels in 1850, hundreds of ships were sunk, changing the shape of the coastline. The ships' remains still lie beneath Jackson Square and the old Barbary Coast.

Distrust and dislike

George's pessimism rang true with the coming of the first train. In San Francisco, real-estate dealing of $3.5 million a month fell to less than half that within a year. "California's initial enthusiasm soon gave way to distrust and dislike… an echo of the national conviction that the railroads were responsible for most of the country's economic ills," was how historian John W. Caughey assessed the prospects in his book *California*. The genius of the Central Pacific was a young engineer named Theodore Dehone Judah, builder of the Sacramento Valley line, whose partners were uncommonly cunning and ruthless men. Charles Crocker, Mark Hopkins, Collis Huntington, and Leland Stanford, who

A racist cartoon makes light of the discrimination faced by Chinese immigrants.

The domination of the Central Pacific Railroad by the Big Four was the target of indignant press protests.

became known as "The Big Four," had been lured west by the Gold Rush.

The Big Four were originally Sacramento shopkeepers when they invested in Judah's railroad scheme. Shortly after Congress issued them with vast tracts of land, they forced Judah

PONY EXPRESS

When California gained statehood in 1850, mail from the East took six months to deliver. Overland stagecoaches cut this to less than a month, but in 1860, the sinewy riders of the Pony Express brought San Francisco much closer to the rest of the nation. Mail traveled over hostile territory from the end of the railroad in St Joseph, Missouri, to the young city in only 10 days. Riders had just a revolver, water sack, and a mail pouch, the most famous of them being 15-year-old William "Buffalo Bill" Cody. Just as quickly, though, came the Transcontinental Telegraph, and on October 26, 1861, the Pony Express closed its doors. The Wells Fargo bank continued to use the Pony Express logo until 2001.

out. He died, aged 37, in 1863, still trying to wrest control from his former partners. The Central Pacific made the Big Four insanely rich.

The government's haste to get the railroad built, together with Leland Stanford's smooth political maneuvering, made the Central Pacific the virtual dictator of California politics for years. Between them, the railroad barons raised private investment, earned government subsidies, acquired bargain-priced land, imported cheap labor from China, and by their monopolistic practices became multimillionaires.

San Francisco railroad barons

As the largest landowners and biggest employers, the immensely wealthy railroad barons were able to manipulate freight rates, control water supplies, keep hundreds of thousands of acres of productive land for themselves and subvert politicians and municipal leaders. It was many years before state regulation of the railroads became the norm, although many people were enjoying the riches the railroads brought with them.

Chinese workers toiling on the railroad.

> "The Big Four" railroad tycoons were the most powerful Californians of the 19th century. They built ostentatious mansions on Nob Hill, each trying to outdo the others.

In the mahogany boardrooms of San Francisco's banks, on the editorial pages of its newspapers, and on the floor of the overheated stock exchange, the verdict of public opinion was clear: the railroad would bring firm and fabulous prosperity to the state of California.

In April 1868, five years after construction began on Sacramento's Front Street, the first Central Pacific train breached the Sierra at Donner Pass. On May 12, 1869, the Golden Spike was driven at Promontory Point, Utah, and the East and West coasts were linked. "San Francisco Annexes the Union," read one San Francisco headline.

But the rush of prosperity did not come with the new rail connections. In the winter of 1869–70 a severe drought crippled the state's agriculture. Between 1873 and 1875 more than 250,000 immigrants came to California. Many were factory workers and few could find work: the "Terrible '70s" had arrived. The head of the Bank of California in San Francisco and a Comstock mining tycoon, William Chapman Ralston, had presided over the seemingly endless boom, born of the Gold Rush. By the mid-1870s, the booms gave way to the dark bloom of depression.

April 26, 1875 would become known as Black Friday when a run on the Bank of California forced it to slam shut the oak doors at Sansome and California streets. The bank was driven into debt by the Comstock mining losses and the railroad's failure to deliver on the anticipated prosperity. Sadly, William C. Ralston drowned the next day while taking his customary swim in San Francisco Bay. Ralston's sudden death signaled the end of the Californian boom.

With the massive unemployment that followed the economic crash, unionization took hold amid the laboring populace. For the next 60 years, the state of California suffered from intractable labor strife. And as if that weren't enough, early in the new century, disaster struck the City by the Bay.

THE 1906 EARTHQUAKE

A few terrifying seconds at 5.15am on April 18, 1906, marked the worst natural disaster the United States had suffered to date.

In 1906, San Francisco accounted for 40 percent of California's population, and the effect of a huge earthquake (measured at 8.25 on the Richter scale) was cataclysmic. The greatest destruction came from the fires that raged for three days after; with its hydrant and alarm systems badly damaged, the fire department was unable to cope. The commandant of the Presidio, Brigadier General Frederick Funston, exceeded his authority; his improvisations destroyed beautiful mansions along Van Ness Avenue and spread the fires still farther. Many people were trapped in smoking ruins as city blocks (like the Mission, above) were leveled.

More than 300 deaths were reported, but today's estimate puts the toll at over 3,000; 225,000 became homeless. People were shot or bayoneted by Funston's ill-prepared militia, who poured onto the streets to bring order and prevent looting. Fortunately, aid poured in from all over the world, $8 million worth within the first weeks. Even the much-reviled Southern Pacific Railroad pitched in with goods and free passage out of the city.

Soup kitchens were set up to feed those whose homes were destroyed. Golden Gate Park was covered in tents and blankets; 300,000 people camped out after the quake and fires.

Spectators gathered to watch as flames from the three-day fire, which was much deadlier than the quake itself, overtook the city. Estimates put the total damage at $400 million, which is worth about $6 billion in 2016.

A split on the north end of East Street from the earthquake, East St is now the Embarcadero.

Although the earthquake lasted only 48 seconds, the rubble spread out over the whole city. At least 315 people were killed, six were shot, and another 352 were missing, many never to be found.

AN EYEWITNESS ACCOUNT

Author Jack London, whose San Francisco family homes were destroyed in the fires following the earthquake, filed this first-hand report.

"Within an hour after the earthquake shock, the smoke of San Francisco's burning was a lurid tower visible a hundred miles away. And for three days and nights this lurid tower swayed in the sky, reddening the sun, darkening the day, and filling the land with smoke.

I watched the vast conflagration from out on the bay. It was dead calm. Not a flicker of wind stirred. Yet from every side, wind was pouring in upon the city. East, west, north, and south, strong winds were blowing upon the doomed city. The heated air rising made an enormous suck. Thus did the fire itself build its own colossal chimney through the atmosphere…

Just 24 hours after the earthquake, I sat on the steps of a small residence on Nob Hill… To the east and south at right angles were advancing two mighty walls of flame. I went inside with the owner… He was cool and cheerful and hospitable. 'Yesterday morning,' he said, 'I was worth six hundred thousand dollars. This morning, this house is all I have left. It will go in 15 minutes.'"

San Franciscans have never allowed anything to stand between them and a good meal. In this picture, a group sits down at a linen-covered makeshift table to dine and to watch their city burn.

The Panama Pacific International Exposition was held in San Francisco in 1915.

MODERN TIMES

From the ashes of the 1906 earthquake rose a city that gave a home in the 1950s and '60s to beatniks, hippies, and, later, yuppies. By 2000, their children were at the forefront of the tech revolution.

Before the 20th century, San Francisco was already California's most prosperous center, a city of 27,000 buildings, where 1,700 architects were perfecting the "tall, narrow rowhouse with vertical lines and a false front to make the house look more imposing," as described by the city archivist. These characteristically Victorian-style Edwardian and Queen Anne homes survived the 1906 fire in at least half a dozen neighborhoods and still remain today.

San Andreas Fault

A geologist named Andrew Lawson discovered and named the San Andreas Fault more than 10 years before 1906, yet despite two earthquakes in the 1890s, little attention was given to planning for geological emergencies. When the Big One arrived, there had been the warning of

> The architect of the Palace of Fine Arts, Bernard Maybeck, intended the building to impart a certain "sadness modified by the feeling that beauty has a soothing influence."

strange behavior by domestic animals such as dogs and horses on the previous evening, but no alarm was raised.

A prediction in Zadikiel's Almanac for 1906 also went unheeded. It read: "In San Francisco Mars and Saturn are on the fourth angle, or lower meridian. In the vicinity of that great city underground troubles – probably a serious earthquake – will be destructive about

San Francisco in the Summer of Love, 1967.

Christmas day or the latter half of February. The winter will be stormy and cold."

When the quake did hit (see page 44) despite widespread devastation, San Franciscans responded with a spirit of determination. The Committee of Forty on the Reconstruction of San Francisco was formed. A.P. Giannini's tiny Bank of Italy made loans to small businesses' rebuilding efforts, and was a leader in restoring the city's fortunes. The bank later became the Bank of America.

Successive years were marked by happier events: the first was the opening of the Panama Canal in 1914, which cut many days off the

Steelworkers high above the city constructed the Golden Gate Bridge, which opened in 1937.

ocean route from the East and made the long journey around Cape Horn obsolete. Then, on January 25, 1915, only a month after Thomas Watson received the very first transcontinental phone call from inventor Alexander Graham Bell, the Panama Pacific International Exposition opened in San Francisco. During the year of the exposition, 19 million visitors traveled to the city to marvel at the new fashions and inventions.

The distant war in Europe had few repercussions in the Bay Area other than boosting industry, manufacturing, and mining. A drop in employment followed the end of World War I, and the city languished for the next few years.

Major labor troubles typified the Depression and the following years, all leading to the General Strike of 1934 when the International Longshoremen's Union halted traffic in the port. At one demonstration, two strikers were killed and 100 people were injured.

BUILDING BRIDGES

Although it is the Golden Gate that is San Francisco's enduring image, the Bay Area's other bridges are also spectacles in their own right. The gorgeous and sometimes overlooked San Francisco-Oakland Bay Bridge, completed in 1936, brought about new engineering challenges due to the depth of the water and a bay floor of mud. But the Bay Bridge was so successful it was declared the seventh wonder of the world in 1955 by the American Society of Civil Engineers.

The San Mateo-Hayward Bridge earned the same organization's "outstanding civil engineering achievement" honor when it opened in 1967.

Alcatraz

Opened in 1934, Alcatraz island – just over 1 mile (1.6km) out across tide-ripped San Francisco Bay – was the site for America's most famous prison for 30 years. Blanketed with flowers like lavender lippia, orange nasturtiums, red fuchsias, and purple pelargoniums, the tranquil setting contrasted with the harsh realities of a sentence on the Rock. One of the prisoners described his time on Alcatraz as "like living in a tomb."

The exercise yard of Alcatraz.

The oldest operating lighthouse on the West Coast of the United States guided ships through the perennial fog from among the pelicans, cormorants, and guillemots on top of Alcatraz island.

The prison's administrative code was "Complete Control." At no time did the main building's 450 cells hold more than 250 captives, and the staff ran as high as 100 people.

This did not prevent three inmates – Frank Lee Morris and two brothers, John and Clarence Anglin – from tunneling out with sharpened spoons in 1962. The feat took years, and the prisoners were never found, although speculation as to how they could survive in the frigid waters surrounding the island led most to conclude that they either drowned or froze to death. Nevertheless, the escape of the "Alcatraz three" influenced the Prison Board's decision to close down the institution not long after.

A golden bridge

Around the time that the prison first opened on Alcatraz, ground was broken for the Golden Gate Bridge. It wasn't dedicated until 1937, six months after the even longer Bay Bridge joined San Francisco to Oakland. Unfortunately the opening of the Golden Gate was marred by tragedy; only a few weeks before the opening, 11 workmen died when their scaffold collapsed.

The Golden Gate, more than any other landmark, has been the romantic icon for the city in the national psyche. In 1987, traffic on the bridge came to a standstill for hours as more than half a million people walked across to celebrate its 50th birthday. "To pass through the portals of the Golden Gate," wrote Allan Dunn, "is to cross the threshold of adventure." Author Gene Fowler asserted: "Every man should be allowed to love two cities; his own and San Francisco."

In 1937, work began on the creation of Treasure Island, a joint project of the federally funded Works Progress Administration, the Army Corps of Engineers, and the city's Public Utilities Commission and Public

At least 110,000 people of Japanese descent, most of whom were US citizens, were sent to detention camps after the bombing of Pearl Harbor.

Gay protests in 1979.

Peace and love.

Works Authority. Attached to the new Bay Bridge and constructed of fill dredged from the bay, Treasure Island was completed within 18 months, in time to house the Golden Gate International Exposition, which 17 million people visited. The Expo lasted for two years, and 27 countries took part.

> During World War II, Fort Mason was the major port of embarkation for the Pacific theater, funneling more than 1.5 million American troops to the front.

World War II

Marshall Dill, the Expo's 1940 president, said it would become an enduring memory: "another chapter in San Francisco's prismatic history in which we can all take pride… The fest is over and the lamps expire." World War II had begun by the time the fair closed, and with such architectural marvels, it made a fitting backdrop for the founders of the United Nations, whose first headquarters were here in San Francisco (see page 51).

Even with the thousands of new workers to staff the wartime factories and the bustling port, and the numbers of servicemen who remained behind when the war was over, the city's population in 1945 was still only 825,000, less than half that of Los Angeles, its rival 450 miles (725km) to the south. Nevertheless, World War II had a tremendous impact on the local economy – "as great as any event since the Gold Rush," wrote historian Oscar Lewis. Since long before the war, San Francisco, with its obvious ties to oriental ports, had begun to harbor a large component of Asian immigrants.

At least 110,000 Nisei (second-generation Japanese) had their property seized, and were rounded up and sent to detention camps in the xenophobic days after Pearl Harbor. Accused of no crime, they lived behind barbed wire under military guard. Americans of Japanese heritage were estimated to have lost $365 million in property from having to sell their homes at

A People's Park demonstrator stands his ground against the National Guard, May 19, 1969.

under-market prices at this time. It wasn't until 1988, after a prolonged battle, that $1.6 billion in reparations was set aside by the federal government for surviving internees and their heirs.

The 1950s, 1960s, and early 1970s were a time of unparalled turmoil and creativity, as San Francisco repeatedly hit the headlines of the world's newspapers. By the late 1970s, gay men and women were commonplace and some variances from the currents of mainstream America were accepted.

This part of the state is also a major player in the country's ecology movement, providing a home to such groups as the Sierra Club, Friends of the Earth, and Greenpeace. Towns like Petaluma passed no-growth ordinances, and San Franciscans have fought long and hard to avoid big-city urbanization, resulting in a city with great green spaces and well-organized parks.

The battles have not always been peaceful: in 1978, San Francisco mayor George Moscone and Harvey Milk, an openly homosexual city official, were murdered in City Hall by an outraged homophobe.

Political growth

On May 21, 1979, when Dan White was convicted of manslaughter and given a lenient sentence rather than first-degree murder, 5,000 people took to the streets and rioted, causing more than $1 million in damage to public

UNITED NATIONS

The forerunner to the United Nations in New York City was here in San Francisco. Days after Germany surrendered, delegates from 50 nations came to form an international organization to prevent future global calamities. As early as 1942, Allied leaders wanted to replace the moribund League of Nations, which failed to prevent World War II. The delegates' charter gave the new organization authority to enforce international law, strengthen human rights, and provide a forum for grievances. On June 25, 1945, the United Nations Charter was signed at the War Memorial Opera House, across the street from City Hall. San Francisco is proud of its role in the organization's creation. In 1975, the United Nations Plaza was built at nearby Market Street to commemorate this event.

Beatniks, Hippies, Riots, and a Rebellious Heiress

From the 1950s until the mid-70s, San Francisco underwent immense social and political rebellion that led to the formation of the city it is today.

In the 1950s, San Francisco saw a cultural renaissance, beginning with what local columnist Herb Caen christened "beatniks." Writers Allen Ginsberg *(Howl)* and Jack Kerouac *(The Dharma Bums and On the Road)*, supported by Lawrence Ferlinghetti of North Beach's City Lights Bookstore, led the Beats life of poetry readings,

An FBI-released photo of Patty Hearst as a Symbionese Liberation Army member, 1974.

marijuana, and dropping out of the mainstream – a potent example that held a wide appeal, and soon brought streams of youthful admirers to the North Beach coffee houses and, in the following decade, to the streets of the Haight-Ashbury district.

On the Berkeley campus of the University of California the axis of dissent was the Free Speech Movement, which kept up a steady assault against racism, materialism, the stifling effects of the "multiversity" itself, and the Vietnam war machine. Antiwar protests, which eventually spread around the world, swelled and took root here with the writers and protesters clustered around Max Scherr's *Berkeley Barb*, one of America's five earliest "underground" newspapers. Max Scherr, a bearded radical who operated a bar called Steppenwolf, took to the streets to sell his paper, which, at its peak, reached a circulation of 100,000 – an astonishing figure for a newspaper that was still largely put together by a group of amateurs around a crowded kitchen table.

Thousands of colorfully dressed hippies – successors to the Beats – descended on Golden Gate Park in January 1967 for what was termed a Human Be-In. The 100,000-strong gathering was addressed by Ginsberg, psychedelic drug guru Tim Leary ("Turn On, Tune In, Drop Out"), Mario Savo, and others of the Free Speech Movement, plus a daredevil parachutist who dropped from the clouds straight into the center of the (largely stoned) gathering.

The resultant worldwide publicity made the Haight-Ashbury district irresistible to disaffected young people across the world, substantial numbers of whom clogged San Francisco's streets, with predictable results. The euphoria was short-lived and within a year or two it was all over, with begging, drug dealing, and exploitation by greedy landlords the most obvious side effects. From Haight-Ashbury, the notorious murderer Charles Manson recruited some of his most earnest disciples.

One offshoot of the rebellious era was the kidnapping in 1974 of Patty Hearst, daughter of the newspaper tycoon, by a group who called themselves the Symbionese Liberation Army. Their members died in a shootout with the city police after Hearst was rescued, but not before the heiress turned the tables and took up arms, describing herself as an "urban guerrilla."

The hippie movement, the struggles, the poetry, and the New Left shaped and changed the American psyche, nowhere more so than in San Francisco.

Aftermath of the 1989 earthquake.

property, including City Hall. A plaza in the Castro District was named in honor of Harvey Milk. In 1986, a few blocks away, another significant memorial to gay victims was established, with a gallery specially built to house the Names Project Memorial Quilt – each patch commemorates a victim of Aids. Today there are tens of thousands of these patches, and active communities around the world promote the quilt.

The political tide turned irrevocably in 1978 when local politician Dianne Feinstein was elected mayor, with massive support from the gay population. For 10 years, from 1978 to 1988, San Francisco's reputation for tolerance flourished, as members of the LGBT (lesbian, gay, bisexual, and transgender) community moved into all areas of the political arena, from the police to the fire department and the Board of Supervisors.

Natural disasters have never been far away. In October 1989, a major earthquake estimated at 7.1 on the Richter scale hit the Bay Area, killing 62 people. A freeway collapsed, and caused about $3 billion worth of damage. Within a

year a US Geological Survey report recorded more than 7,000 aftershocks, some as high as 5.4 on the Richter scale.

> *More people were not killed during the 1989 earthquake because the Bay Area's two home teams were competing in the World Series, and most people were either at the baseball stadium or at home glued to the television.*

San Francisco's political climate changed dramatically in the mid-1990s when State Assembly speaker Willie Brown – forced out by term limits after a 15-year tenure – was elected mayor after a divisive campaign.

Willie Brown quickly endeared himself to San Franciscans with a gigantic and celebratory party for the people at Fisherman's Wharf. By 1997 Brown was basking in the acclaim awarded to him for presiding over a booming economy displayed in an $80-million budget surplus.

Same-sex couple celebrate the U.S. Supreme Court's rulings on gay marriage in City Hall, June 2013.

The city and Silicon Valley

The first two years of the 21st century were fertile times for the technology industries in Silicon Valley. Small and large companies made millions from ideas that dominated the internet and became the basis of the new economy. The dot-com bubble burst in October 2002 in one of the steepest nose-dives of the stock market.

DOT-COM BOOM AND BUST

At the start of the millennium, the future looked bright in San Francisco. Nearby Silicon Valley invigorated established industries and spurred thousands of start-up companies. Venture capitalists threw money at shiny ideas, stock prices soared, and the housing market hit new heights. Recent college graduates earned more money than they could count, but much of the prosperity owed more to innovative book-keeping than real business acumen. The bubble burst on October 9, 2002, and many of these new millionaires were forced to return home to their parents.

BART station, Union Square.

On February 12, 2004, Mayor Newsom authorized the city to begin issuing marriage licenses to same-sex couples, inciting a 29-day wedding frenzy in which some 4,000 couples married. A month later licenses were halted by order of the California Supreme Court and the marriages already made were declared invalid. The legal battle raged until June 2013 when the ruling abolishing the notorious Proposition 8 (which defined marriage as a union between men and women only) eventually went into effect. Hours later, plaintiffs Perry and Stier became the first same-sex couple in California to get legally married.

Life and lifestyles

Elsewhere, new building and new projects, some started before the bust, continued apace. The San Francisco Giants made history in 2010 by defeating the Texas Rangers to win the World Series in baseball. The city exploded in Giants pride for their ragtag team of misfits who were considered underdogs going into the series. Over the next four years, the Giants repeated the same feat twice, each time causing elation among the fans. Meanwhile in 2015, Golden State Warriors basketball team defeated the Cleveland Cavaliers in great style to clench the NBA championship title.

The Asian Art Museum moved to the Civic Center; the 1898 Ferry Building became a

The opening of baseball's AT&T Park spearheaded a revival of the South Beach and China Basin area near the Bay Bridge.

thriving farmers' market; and City Hall got a face-lift, while the San Francisco Museum of Modern Art (SFOMA) reopened in May 2016 following a three-year long expansion project.

Being at the forefront of controversial issues is a hallmark of San Francisco, including ecological movements and personal, gender, and other political issues. San Francisco's local legislation is often driven by activists out to make a difference – the lists of propositions put to the electoral vote in this city is sometimes a mile long. Among the most progressive laws recently adopted was the decision in 2016 requiring employers to offer six weeks of fully paid leave for new parents. However, sometimes the states liberal policies backfire as evidenced in 2015 when 32-year old San Franciscan Kathryn Steinle was shot dead by a homeless illegal immigrant from Mexico. The fact that the perpetrator had been previously deported on numerous occasions sparked national debate on San Francisco's status as a sanctuary city.

FASCINATING FIGURES ABOUT SAN FRANCISCO

Here are a few figures about one of the world's most fabulous cities:

4.5 feet (1.4m) in the narrowest city street
5 number of bridges
7.5 miles (12km) of waterfront
8.25 magnitude of the 1906 earthquake
11 historic districts
14 number of islands in the bay
29.5 miles (47km) of shoreline
32 number of fog signals around the bay
43 number of hills in the city

62 museums
85 theaters
118 nightclubs and dancehalls
215 landmark buildings
229 parks, playgrounds, and squares
1,017 acres (412 hectares) in Golden Gate Park
14,000 Victorian houses
320,300 commuters per day
815, 258 population of San Francisco County
1,400,000 number of visitors to Alcatraz annually
9,600,000 yearly cable-car riders

The Zapatista Mural, one of many murals around town.

Claes Oldenburg's safety pin sculpture sits outside the de Young Museum.

BAY CITY ARTS

The light, the hills, the evocative fog, and the exuberant diversity of San Francisco are the lifeblood of a dynamic arts community.

It's nearly impossible to go a single day in San Francisco without rubbing elbows with an artist, poet, actor, or writer – or at the very least, a critic. While traditional artistic expressions such as opera, symphony, and ballet are well respected and hold a firm place in the city's cultural story, the Bay Area has really built its reputation as a breeding ground for experimental work.

Conventionally, artists of all inclinations flock here to work, then travel to Los Angeles and New York to be marketed; this holds true in theater, visual arts, and the music industry. Some historians may trace this appetite for new creative ventures back to the city's Barbary Coast era, but it's more likely due to the national upheaval of the 1960s, when San Francisco became the quintessential counter-culture city.

These days, San Francisco's tolerance seems inexhaustible: African-American, Asian-American, and Latin American artists have made bi-culturalism an integral part of both their work and the Bay Area culture. The influence of the Pacific Rim has contributed too; as a port city, San Francisco has always felt the presence of cultures from far away.

Visual arts

The first group effort to bring visual art to the forefront of the city's culture was in 1871, when 23 visual artists formed the San Francisco Art Association, exhibiting in a loft above a market. By the 1890s, art had become a social concern, and a rich patron donated a Nob Hill palace to the Art Association to display its work.

A captivating performance by the San Francisco Ballet Company.

Neighborhoods like the Western Addition and Hunters Point play an important role in the hyphy movement – the Bay Area's response to commercialized hip-hop.

A flamboyant neo-Egyptian Exhibition Hall, built for 1894's Midwinter International Exposition in Golden Gate Park, evolved into the de Young Museum. The permanent collection includes important works in the California School of Painting, characterized by Thomas

Art, Silicon Valley style.

The Asian Art Museum, Civic Center.

Hill, Alfred Bierstadt, and William Keith. These landscape artists specialized in mountain gorges, Yosemite landscapes, and natural light. The de Young highlights the harmony between modern architecture and the natural landscape.

In 1915, the huge Panama Pacific International Exposition brought a $40-million

MURALS

San Francisco has almost 600 murals that adorn the city's walls. The most vibrant are in the Latino-influenced Mission District, in the care of Precita Eyes, who offer walking tours around the area. The Zapatista Mural on City Lights Bookstore reproduces and commemorates a piece from the Mexican village, Taniperla, destroyed in a massive raid by Mexican troops in 1998. The work's designer, Serio Valdéz, was given a nine-year jail sentence for the political work, called Vida y sueños de la cañada Perla (Life and Dreams of the Pearl River Valley). In keeping with the Zapatista tradition, the City Lights piece was painted voluntarily by local artists and activists.

collection of paintings and sculpture to San Francisco. Local artists discovered and adopted elements of French estheticism when Bernard Maybeck's Palace of the Legion of Honor, devoted primarily to French art, opened in the 1920s.

Money, climate, and the University of California at Berkeley were the lures that brought artists Diego Rivera and Mark Rothko to San Francisco. With them, public murals and abstract expressionism came into the regional culture, traditions followed not only by the muralists of Coit Tower, but also by the contemporary Hispanic artists with their Mission District murals, notably in Balmy Alley.

The spectacular San Francisco Museum of Modern Art, designed by Swiss architect Mario Botta, displays works by Henri Matisse, Georges Braque, Vasily Kandinsky, Joan Miró, Georgia O'Keeffe, Frida Kahlo, Jackson Pollock, Clyfford Still, Jasper Johns, Robert Rauschenberg, and Bay Area artists Richard Diebenkorn, Elmer Bischoff, David Park, and Sam Francis.

The San Francisco Ballet Company at work.

The vast Yerba Buena Center for the Arts holds four rounds of visual arts exhibits each year. The contemporary space features national and international artists with strong ties to popular culture. The center also holds innumerable year-round theater, dance, and cross-disciplinary performances. Other recent additions to the SoMa area are the Museum of Craft and Folk Art, the Museum of the African Diaspora, the Cartoon Art Museum, and the Contemporary Jewish Museum.

Known for his magnificent and extensive pioneering portfolio of American landscape photography, Ansel Adams was raised in his family's home near Golden Gate Bridge and spent most of his life here. His exquisite photos of Yosemite and the Sierra Nevada are his best-known works. Many Ansel Adams pictures are on permanent display at SFMoMA.

Bad-boy rock 'n' roll photographer Jim Marshall, a San Franciscan legend with a salty wit and a fondness for guns and whisky, is famous for his archetypical '60s photography.

His images of musicians such as Jimi Hendrix, Janis Joplin, Jim Morrison, and Johnny Cash earned him worldwide recognition. Portraitist Annie Leibovitz burst into the limelight from *Rolling Stone* magazine (created in San Francisco by publisher Jann Wenner). Her work regularly graces the pages of *Vanity Fair*; she studied at the San Francisco Art Institute.

In 1877 the mother of modern dance, Isadora Duncan, was born in San Francisco. Her bold and revolutionary spirit still inspires the city.

Classical music

When San Francisco was a young city, a passion for opera sprouted alongside the music halls and cabarets. In the 1850s, opera houses appeared. Fire brigades escorted favorite divas through the crowds to performances, and San Francisco became a regular stop for European

The Adicts put on a show at The Fillmore.

1960s poster from the Fillmore Auditorium.

troupes. The Bay Area supports no fewer than seven opera companies. Each fall, Free Opera in the Park is hosted in Golden Gate Park. There are more classical concerts per capita here than in any other city in the country, a phenomenon one critic called an "unreasonable profusion," although others think it's just perfect. Chamber music, too, is well served, with regular concerts in intimate settings.

CAFE SOCIETY

Poetry, spoken word, fiction, and other related arts intersect every September at Litquake, a four-day festival to celebrate the city's literary roots. Local celebs like Michael Chabon (author of *The Amazing Adventures of Kavalier and Clay*), Marin County resident Isabelle Allende, and others join to ensure the city's traditions for decades to come. Film-maker Francis Ford Coppola rejuvenated the local scene with his magazine *Zoetrope: All Story*, headquartered in the copper-clad North Beach Sentinel Building. Coppola also hosts literary events (many at Café Zoetrope on the Sentinel's street level) as well as engaging the public with an online workshop. Go to: www.zoetrope.com.

Rocking the Fillmore

The concerts and the famous light shows staged at Bill Graham's innovative Fillmore and the Avalon ballroom established the gold standard for rock shows all around the world. Locally based artists like the Grateful Dead, Carlos Santana, Jefferson Airplane, and Janis Joplin regularly headlined at these venues, as well as performing high-profile outdoor concerts in Golden Gate Park.

For the biggest names in rock, pop, and alternative music, the venerable Warfield Theater and the Fillmore (both run by Bill Graham Presents for years after the promoter's death) are joined by the Great American Music Hall, the Independent, and Slim's as the city's larger venues.

Regardless of the dance moves, there is no shortage of places to kick up your feet in San Francisco. Although nightclubs are all over the city, there are two main neighborhoods for music. The most vibrant and varied is along Mission and Valencia streets between 16th and 26th streets. One single block of 11th Street between Folsom and Harrison has several clubs.

The San Francisco Symphony Orchestra.

Porgy and Bess performed by the San Francisco Opera.

The best bet to see what's up is the listings of SF Weekly.

Theater

San Francisco has a long, although varied, theater tradition. In the second half of the 19th century, melodeons (theater-bar-music halls) proliferated. The bawdiness and the musicals are still here. Big productions from New York arrive each season, and burlesque remains surprisingly popular. Most theaters are located near Union Square.

More traditional or serious theater dates from the turn of the 20th century, when San Francisco regularly hosted stock companies from England and from other parts of the United States. Fifty years later and across the country, Herbert Blau and Jules Irving founded New York's Actors Workshop in 1959 on the premise that theater belonged to actors and directors – *not* to producers and promoters. Local theaters began to develop new works and talent rather than simply staging Broadway shows.

Most notable was the American Conservatory Theater (ACT) led by Bill Ball, a visionary who helped create the model for regional theaters. From the start, ACT had a penchant for Molière and other classical European works. Other regional theaters were dedicated to developing young writers.

San Francisco has a thriving improv scene. Every year the city is host to SF Sketchfest, a festival that draws big names in the comedy community.

At the Magic Theatre, a young playwright named Sam Shepard began a career that has made him one of the best-known contemporary dramatists, in addition to his parallel career as a movie star. The Eureka Theatre, Asian-American Theatre Company, and Berkeley Repertory Theatre also provide a forum for new playwrights; David Henry Hwang (author of M. *Butterfly*) first produced his plays at AATC.

Just about every theatrical form thrives in San Francisco, from poetry performances to agitprop to Shakespeare.

LITERARY SAN FRANCISCO

From the Beats and Dashiell Hammett to Amy Tan and Armistead Maupin, the City by the Bay inspires its own writers and lures others from all over the world.

bronze plaque in Union Square's Burritt Alley, just off Bush Street, reads: "On approximately this spot, Miles Archer, partner of Sam Spade, was done in by Brigit O'Shaughnessy." The memorial doesn't mention the classic detective story *The Maltese Falcon* or its author, but leaving the alley and walking toward Powell Street, the mystery is solved as you pass "Dashiell Hammett Street" on the right. A plan proposed by the celebrated City Lights Bookstore has been a great success: to rename 12 streets for prominent writers and artists who lived and worked in San Francisco.

Mark Twain

"San Francisco is a truly fascinating city to live in... The climate is pleasanter when read about than personally experienced," wrote Mark Twain in his 1871 memoir, *Roughing It*. Twain,

Ken Kesey, counter culture figure and author of One Flew Over the Cuckoo's Nest.

> While in San Francisco, Mark Twain wrote *The Notorious Jumping Frog of Calaveras County*, based on a tale heard in a saloon in Angels Camp. An annual jumping-frog contest is held there.

born Samuel Clemens, came from Missouri in 1861. His dreams of riches in the gold mines didn't pan out, and he took to writing humor and travel pieces for Virginia City's Territorial Enterprise newspaper. His travels continued westward, and in 1864 and 1865, Twain worked in San Francisco, covering the police, fire, and theater beats for the *Morning Call* newspaper,

later writing lampoons and commentaries for the *Golden Era* and the *San Francisco Chronicle*.

Other Gold Rush literary figures include Bret Harte (who befriended Twain during his stay) and Ambrose Bierce. Like Twain, Harte contributed to the Golden Era. He was also the most popular Western writer of his day, earning $10,000 in 1870 from the *Atlantic Monthly*, and contributing to every issue.

Bierce, author of the flawlessly cynical *Devil's Dictionary*, in addition to acclaimed short stories about the Civil War, was one of the first recognized columnists in American journalism. His

Mural by T. Scott Sayre in Jack London Square, Oakland, California.

unmissable Sunday column, "Prattles," appeared in William Randolph Hearst's *The Examiner*, and skewered pomposity with a fierceness that earned him the nickname "Bitter Bierce."

Robert Louis Stevenson is honored by several monuments in San Francisco, despite spending less than a year in northern California. In 1879, he traveled from his native Scotland in pursuit of Fanny Osbourne, a married woman with whom he had fallen madly in love. Trying unsuccessfully to support himself by writing, he spent several impoverished months living in a room at 608 Bush Street, waiting for Mrs Osbourne's divorce to be finalized. Afterward, Osbourne and Stevenson were married and sojourned in Napa Valley, where Stevenson recuperated from tuberculosis.

Although Stevenson wrote his major works after his return to Scotland in July 1880, a monument dedicated to him in the northwest corner of Chinatown's Portsmouth Square depicts the *Hispaniola*, the galleon featured in the classic pirate novel, *Treasure Island*. The inscription is taken from his "Christmas Sermon." Stevenson often came to Portsmouth Square to write and to watch the ships.

An oyster pirate named Jack

Born in San Francisco in 1876, Jack London kept close ties with the Bay Area through the course of his short, celebrated life. *In Martin Eden* (1909) and *John Barleycorn* (1913), London recalls the Oakland waterfront where he grew up. At the age of 14, he bought a sloop, the *Razzle Dazzle*, and became an oyster pirate along the shoals of the San Francisco Bay.

London traveled across the US and Canada, on a schooner off the Japanese coast and, in 1897, to the Klondike with the Gold Rush. After each adventure, he came back to Oakland. Returning from the Klondike with scurvy, London began to document his experiences on the rough Alaskan frontier. *The Son of the Wolf* (1901), his first collection of short stories, was an immediate success and he worked this seam to produce acclaimed, bestselling novels.

Apart from the plaque at 605 3rd Street to mark his birthplace, there are few Jack London landmarks in San Francisco itself; most of his family's homes were destroyed in the fires following the 1906 earthquake (see page 44). But the city of Oakland has not forgotten him: Oakland renamed its waterfront shopping

The Beats in Mexico; photo by Allen Ginsberg. Clockwise from left: Jack Kerouac, Allen Ginsberg, Peter Orlovsky, Lafcadio Orlovsky, Gregory Corso.

plaza Jack London Square in 1951, where you'll find Heinhold's First and Last Chance Saloon, an actual haunt from London's waterfront days. Supposedly, London sealed the purchase of his first sloop here. A house was brought from Alaska where he lived, and there are others in East Oakland, among them 575 Blair,

where in 1903 he wrote his popular novel, *The Call of the Wild*.

Two years after, London and his wife Charmain moved north to a ranch (dubbed Beauty Ranch) in Glen Ellen, in Sonoma's wine country. At the then-incredible cost of $70,000, London built his dream home, Wolf House, only to see it burn

THE BEATS

In the mid-1950s, the writing emerging from the cafés and bars of North Beach commanded national and international attention as the arbiter of a cultural revolution. The "Beat Generation" had been first defined on the East Coast a decade earlier by Jack Kerouac, Allen Ginsberg *(left)*, and John Clellon Holmes experimenting with spontaneous writing based on the rhythms of jazz and bebop. But it wasn't until Kerouac and Ginsberg came out west in 1954 and 1955, encountering writers Lawrence Ferlinghetti, Gary Snyder, Michael McClure, and others, that the Beats galvanized a literary movement (see page 52). All of this came together in San Francisco on October 7, 1955, at a poetry reading at the Six Gallery, an artists' cooperative. Organized by Kenneth Rexroth, the "Six

Poets at the Six Gallery" reading featured Rexroth, Snyder, McClure, Ginsberg, Philip Whalen, and Philip Lamantia, and introduced the first public reading of Ginsberg's incendiary poem, *Howl*. Kerouac recounts the event in his novel *The Dharma Bums*.

The poem created a sensation when it was published in 1956 and was immediately confiscated by officials who deemed it "obscene" literature. Ferlinghetti's City Lights Bookstore, the first paperback bookstore in America, and the publisher of *Howl & Other Poems*, was brought up on criminal charges. The ensuing trial (which City Lights won) established a legal precedent and brought the Beats to national prominence, as did Kerouac's book *On The Road*, published in 1957.

Francis Ford Coppola's influence is evident in both literature and film.

Latin American novelist Isabel Allende, a Marin County resident since 1987.

down in 1913 – the night before he and his wife were set to move in. Since 1959 the ranch has been open to the public as the Jack London State Historic Park (www.jacklondonpark.com). A short path from the house leads to the ruins of Wolf House and the grave where London's ashes were buried after his death in 1916.

Although writer Gertrude Stein was born in Allegheny, New York, in 1874, the Steins moved

---

DASHIELL HAMMETT

In 1921, Dashiell Hammett moved to San Francisco to marry Josephine Dolan. Though they planned to return East, they stayed on, living in rented apartments. Based on his experience as a private detective, Hammett created an indelible character in Sam Spade, the cynical gumshoe inhabiting foggy San Francisco nights, memorably portrayed by Humphrey Bogart in John Huston's 1941 movie of The Maltese Falcon. Like many others in the 1950s, Hammett fell on the harsh mercies of the House Un-American Activities Committee for reported associations with communists. He was jailed, and his career destroyed.

---

west to Oakland in 1880 where she grew up. She traveled east in 1891 to study at Radcliffe and Harvard, and in 1901, sailed to Europe where she remained an expatriate for years.

In 1934, Stein and her companion Alice B. Toklas revisited the area during a US lecture tour. She is still remembered in Oakland, not always fondly, for having written "There is no there there," about the city, in her 1937 memoir, *Everybody's Autobiography*.

New-style detective

Dashiell Hammett lived in San Francisco from 1921 to 1929, when he produced such books as *Red Harvest* and *The Dain Curse*, a hard-boiled style of novel writing that redefined the American mystery story.

Born in Maryland in 1894, Hammett was raised in Baltimore and Philadelphia. At 14, he dropped out of high school to help support his family, and shortly afterward joined the Pinkerton Detective Agency. Many of the shady characters in his fiction were based on people he encountered in his five years as a Pinkerton man. Aficionados of *The Maltese Falcon* can still stop by John's Grill, at 63 Ellis (between Powell and Stockton streets).

Established in 1908, John's Grill is one of the few restaurants mentioned in the novel that is still open for business. There is Hammett memorabilia on display there, and lots of photos.

The beatniks gave way to the hippies, and the Beats were followed by the Merry Pranksters. Led by Ken Kesey, author of *One Flew Over the Cuckoo's Nest*, the Pranksters were early experimenters with hallucinogens and organized

John's Grill, 63 Ellis Street, opened in 1908, was frequented by Sam Spade in The Maltese Falcon.

massive LSD-tinged gatherings, or Acid Tests, among them the legendary Trips Festival in January 1966. The event reportedly drew 20,000 adventurers to Longshoreman's Hall in Fisherman's Wharf: Tom Wolfe's *The Electric Kool-Aid Acid* Test recounts their exploits.

At the same time, San Francisco was the home for *Rolling Stone* magazine and its incorrigible correspondent, Hunter S. Thompson. Thompson lived in the Haight-Ashbury district in the mid-1960s while he was researching for *Hell's Angels*, his off-kilter views inside the notorious motorcycle gangs.

The great columnist Herb Caen is immortalized with a section of the Embarcadero renamed "Herb Caen Way." The community nurtured poet Adrienne Rich, playwright and poet Cherríe Moraga, as well other feminist writers.

Internationally known authors Amy Tan (*The Joy Luck Club*), Alice Walker (*The Color Purple*), and Anne Rice (*Interview with the Vampire*)all lived and worked in San Francisco, and most have the city as a backdrop to one or more of their highly charged novels.

Daughter of Fortune, set during the California Gold Rush, is by acclaimed Latin American writer Isabel Allende, who has been a Marin County resident since 1987.

Armistead Maupin is a North Carolina native who relocated to San Francisco in 1971. His serial column, "Tales of the City," began to chronicle the complex interweavings of young gay and straight San Franciscans in the *San Francisco Chronicle* in 1976.

> *Armistead Maupin's Tales of the City began as a newspaper serial in the San Francisco Chronicle. Detailing the lives of gay and straight urbanites, the columns were republished and became bestselling books.*

Dave Eggers chronicled life in Berkeley while caring for his younger brother in *A Heartbreaking Work of Staggering Genius*. He now lives in San Francisco and created 826 Valencia, a writing studio for young students that doubles as a pirate store. Meanwhile Khaled Hosseini, an Afghan immigrant and author of bestsellers *The Kite Runner* and *The Mountains Echoed*, settled in San Jose.

THE CITY ON SCREEN

San Francisco's iconic views have played supporting roles in movies from *Vertigo* to *Star Trek*. Francis Ford Coppola has headquarters here, and George Lucas has established a digital arts center in the Presidio.

The memorable chase scene from Bullitt.

San Francisco has always offered high-value locations for movie-makers, with a range of romantically iconic views and backdrops. Barbra Streisand deftly maneuvered her Volkswagen between two cable cars in *What's Up Doc?*; Kim Novak hurled herself from a (nonexistent) tower in *Vertigo* with a backdrop of the Golden Gate Bridge; and Steve McQueen bounced a Mustang over the city's hills in *Bullitt*. More recently, bad mutants inventively used the Golden Gate Bridge against good mutants to win the spectacular battle over a genetic facility located (digitally) on Alcatraz in *X-Men: The Last Stand*. The same bridge also featured heavily in the 2015 hit *Terminator Genisys*.

San Francisco's movie identity dates back to the 1930s with Howard Hawks' Barbary Coast and W.S. Van Dyke's San Francisco, which depicted the city collapsing in the 1906 earthquake. In 1941, John Huston's The Maltese Falcon had Humphrey Bogart, Peter Lorre, and Sydney Greenstreet skulking in the alleys and backways of Nob Hill.

Bedroom to film set

The Fairmont Hotel has featured in movies from *Vertigo* in 1958 to *Petulia* (with Julie Christie and George C. Scott) exactly a decade later, to the Sean Connery drama *The Rock* in 1996.

The North Beach area is regularly jammed with lights, camera cranes, and trailers. The renowned Saints Peter and Paul Church on Washington Square was the site of a shoot-out in 1971's Dirty Harry, and the Bank of America at 555 California Street became "America's tallest skyscraper" in 1974 as 86 fictional stories were added and then torched in Irwin Allen's disaster movie The Towering Inferno. The Transamerica Pyramid, one of the city's iconic buildings, has featured in dozens of films including the 1978 remake of Invasion of the Body Snatchers. In part produced by the Transamerica Corporation, the building occupied a number of iconic shots by the hometown director, Phillip Kaufman. With the aid of time-lapse photography, director David Fincher used it, as well as a number of other buildings that transformed the city's skyline in the 1970s, to dramatic effect by

Jimmy Stewart and Kim Novak.

chronicling its rise to convey the passage of time in his 2007 film, Zodiac.

Four blocks north, City Lights Bookstore was the setting for Flashback, a 1960s film starring a radical played by Dennis Hopper. The bookstore also featured in the 1980 Beat-inspired movie Heart Beat with Nick Nolte, Sissy Spacek, and John Hurt.

The Tosca Café, across the street at 242 Columbus Avenue, featured in Basic Instinct, starring Michael Douglas and Sharon Stone, as did the country-and-western bar Rawhide on 7th Street. Extra guards were needed to be secured due to protests by gay activists on the sets of Basic Instinct – they thought the script was homophobic and should be banned or censored.

Star locations

Alcatraz, of course, has made regular appearances (*The Birdman of Alcatraz*, 1962; *Escape from Alcatraz*, 1979; *The Rock*, 1996), as has City Hall (*The Right Stuff*, 1983; *Class Action*, 1990) and the Golden Gate Bridge (*Superman*, 1978;

A *View to a Kill*, 1985; *Interview with the Vampire*, 1994, and many more). The bridge and Mission Dolores provided backdrops for *Vertigo*, whose Carlotta Valdez (Kim Novak) lived in an apartment at 940 Sutter Street, now the York Hotel.

COPPOLA AND LUCAS

"Just say Francis Coppola is up in San Francisco in an old warehouse making films," announced Coppola in 1971. Two years before, he and fellow upstart George Lucas left Hollywood to start their own studio, American Zoetrope. Lucas now has 1,300 employees at his Skywalker Ranch in nearby Nicasio and other Marin County locations. His $2-billion business included the *Star Wars* movies, and now comprises the *Indiana Jones* franchise, the THX sound system, and Industrial Light & Magic. Lucas's San Francisco home is the Letterman Digital Arts campus in the coveted Presidio near the Golden Gate Bridge. Lucas' film *Indiana Jones and the Kingdom of the Crystal Skull* opened to great acclaim at the Cannes Film Festival in 2008.

Gay Pride parade.

THE GAY COMMUNITY

Since World War II, this creative and sociable community has been a vital and vocal element in San Francisco's rich cultural mix.

After rioting in the streets, refurbishing entire neighborhoods of decaying Victorian homes, wielding a powerful voting bloc in local politics, taking government posts in national politics, and building substantial businesses, the San Francisco gay community has earned the city its reputation as an international gay mecca.

The city's unabashed, and sometimes volatile gay community represents the most significant sociological development in San Francisco's history since the early days of the beatniks and the hippies. There is no definitive record of the number of gays and lesbians living in San Francisco – though officials speculate endlessly – but this city of nearly 800,000 is home to at least 80,000 same-sex snugglers.

Like nearly every aspect of San Francisco's history, the transformation of the Gold Rush town into a homophile Oz grew from the most improbable beginnings.

Boot camp

It started in the waning days of World War II. The US military began systematically purging its ranks, booting out suspected homosexuals at their point of debarkation. For the massive Pacific theater of the war, this was San Francisco.

The purges created an entire class of men who had been officially stigmatized as homosexual. Unable to return home and face inevitable shame, they stayed in the Bay Area, socializing in discreet bars or, more often, at intimate soirées. Another migration of professional gays came during the early 1950s in the gray days of the anti-communist McCarthy era,

A local couple out and about.

With its large picture windows looking out at busy Market and Castro streets, Twin Peaks was the first openly gay bar in the US.

when the federal government drummed thousands of homosexuals out of apparently secure government jobs.

Local authorities, meanwhile, did not like the idea of gays grouped in the bohemian bars of North Beach. They regarded any gathering of more than a few dozen gay people as an insurrection. Bar raids, mass arrests, and harsh prosecutions of men and women accused of frequenting "disorderly houses" became distressingly common.

Candlelight march in 1979 to honor Harvey Milk and George Moscone; the event was estimated to have between 25,000 and 40,000 attendees.

Activist origins

By 1960, gays began moving toward an open campaign for civil rights, a course unthinkable a few years earlier. It started humbly enough in 1955 with the formation of America's first lesbian group, the Daughters of Bilitis. Homosexuals banded together in pressure groups was considered novel, but quickly caught on. Political cadres formed, such as the Society for Individual Rights and the Mattachine Society, whose then-radical publication asked

HARVEY MILK

In 1977, neighborhood voters elected Harvey Milk to the Board of Supervisors. A Castro Street camera shop owner and gay activist, Milk organized the area's merchants' group, and became the first openly gay city official to be elected in American politics. In 1978, former supervisor Dan White, the city's most anti-gay politician, gunned down Milk and Mayor George Moscone in cold blood right in their City Hall offices. The city reeled in shock, and a somber, mixed crowd marched from Castro Street to City Hall, silently bearing candles. Six months later, a jury sentenced double-murderer White to only five years, sparking the massive "White Night" riots. White, paroled in 1985, killed himself in the same year that *The Life and Times of Harvey Milk* won the Oscar for best documentary. In 2009, a movie, *Milk* starring Sean Penn as Harvey Milk was released.

whether homosexuality was a "disease or way of life," and whether gays should be rehabilitated or punished.

In 1961, José Sarria, a prominent female impersonator who was sure he was neither diseased nor in need of rehabilitation, got so irate over police raids on his Black Cat bar that he took off his dress and high heels and donned a three-piece suit to run for the Board of Supervisors, San Francisco's style of city council. Sarria polled an astounding 7,000 votes, and clued the fledgling gay groups in to the power of the ballot box. By 1964, liberal candidates for the Board of Supervisors sought gay endorsements, their careers safe from pious moralists. When the 1969 board election came along, so did 35-year-old political newcomer, Dianne Feinstein. Later to become mayor from 1978 to 1988, and a US Senator in 1992, Feinstein campaigned energetically among gays, later crediting her landslide victory to gay ballots.

Having seen the effectiveness of the political voice, studies suggest that, proportionately, gays vote in larger numbers and give more money to political candidates than do heterosexuals.

Hippie influence

As Feinstein campaigned at the Society for Individual Rights, hippie counterculture was in full bloom in Haight-Ashbury, fertile territory for the Gay Liberation Movement sweeping

Celebrations outside City Hall after the U.S. Supreme Court passes the right to same-sex marriage in San Francisco on June 26, 2015.

On February 12, 2004 at City Hall, 15 same-sex couples were married, and dozens of marriage licenses were issued. A ban was then imposed. In 2008, the state Supreme Court struck down the ban, but the legal battle raged on until 2013 when same-sex marriages were finally resumed.

from New York City on the heels of the anti-war movement. Slowly, a few dozen, then a few hundred gay hippies moved over the hill from Haight Street into Castro Street, a former Irish-American enclave.

Many working-class Catholics were terrified by the "gay invaders," and moved out in panic. They left behind a huge, if dilapidated, stock of quaint 1880s Victorian homes, perfect for gentrification. The city's first Gay Pride Parade (now called simply, Pride) was held in 1972, an event now attended by hundreds of thousands. Castro Street symbolized the drive for acceptance, and in late 1975, gay votes elected George Moscone, the first wholly sympathetic mayor.

The menace of AIDS was cited when, in April 1984, San Francisco's Department of Public Health used emergency powers to close all the city's bathhouses. Two years later, Cleve Jones began the Names Project Memorial Quilt; tens of thousands of patches commemorate victims of the disease. Originally in a gallery/workshop on Market Street, portions of the quilt are now on view all over the world. The San Francisco patches can be seen in the Interfaith Chapel at Grace Cathedral, 1100 California Street.

In 1981 the first openly lesbian judge, Mary Morgan, was appointed to the San Francisco Municipal Court. Three years later, Berkeley became the first city in the world to award the same spousal benefits to lesbian and gay city employees as to other employees. For years now, the city has had openly gay and lesbian elected officials, supervisors, police officers, and congressional aides, as well as judges.

The ravages of AIDS have been a dark catalyst; the illness and deaths of friends and lovers have become part of the way of life, and the once-lusty nightlife has toned down. More conservative dating and courtship practices have become the norm.

Nevertheless, revelers remain on the scene in sufficient numbers, and with wild enough abandon, to give the city some of the liveliest and most colorful gay bars anywhere.

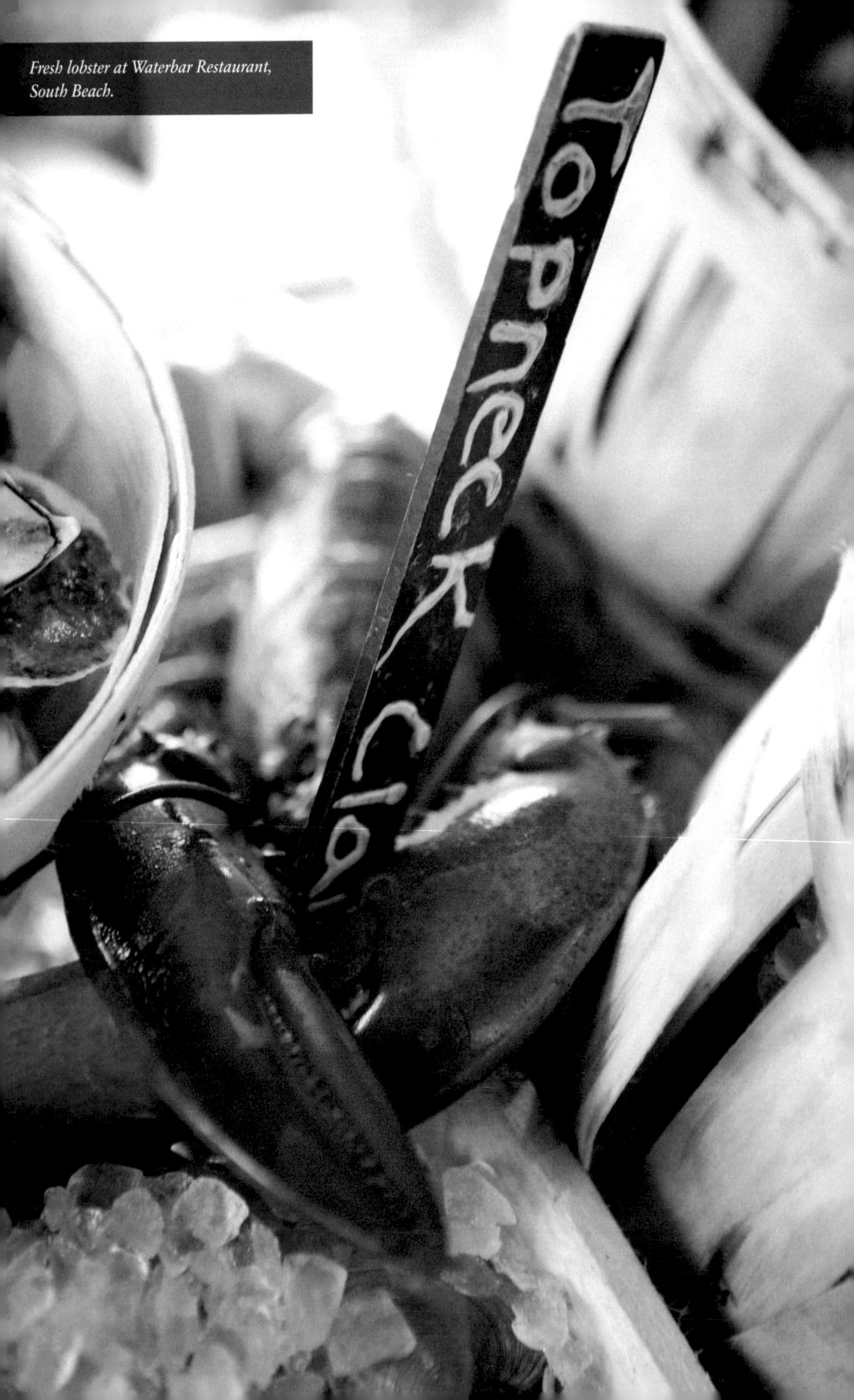

Fresh lobster at Waterbar Restaurant, South Beach.

THE GOURMET'S CITY

California cuisine, cultural diversity, celebrity chefs, and bounty from the sea and the trees – the City by the Bay has a varied and voracious appetite.

When it comes to food, the Bay Area has always been slightly ahead of the competition. Consider this: the city once claimed to have the only restaurant in America serving pizza, it opened the first Chinese and Japanese restaurants in the West, insists it invented the fortune cookie, and also gave rise to that culinary catch-all phrase "California cuisine" which essentially means creative fresh food from local purveyors.

With more than 3,000 eating and drinking establishments in San Francisco – said to be more per capita than anywhere else in the world – and a compact array of ethnic neighborhoods spilling over into one another, it's no surprise that an appetite for fresh and innovative cuisine, combined with a spirit of experimentation, helped to confirm San Francisco's reputation for fine food.

> Chefs fear him and owners schmooze him. Michael Bauer, San Francisco Chronicle food critic, can make or break a restaurant. Go to: www.sfgate.com and search blogs for "bauer."

It has always been this way, or so it seems. At the time of the Gold Rush in 1849, which forever changed the face of the West, San Francisco was little more than a transient shanty town, filled with houses made of paper and men with dreams of gold. Populated by hotel dwellers and apartment renters, none of whom were provided with kitchens, eating out

Eat, drink, and be merry at the Ferry Building.

became a tradition by necessity, rather than as a luxury.

A free lunch

Perhaps the noblest practice in the city's memory is the "free lunch" saloon. In even the simplest corner grocery or "bit" saloon, hard-working clerks and brokers could, for the meager price of a mug of beer, feed on an impressive array of cheeses, bologna, and pickles. Author Jack London wrote of one, south of Market Street: "Especially I liked the San Francisco saloons. They had the most delicious dainties for the taking – strange breads

Nice and cozy in a North Beach eatery.

The Garden Court at the Palace Hotel.

and crackers, cheeses, sausages, sardines – wonderful foods that I never saw on our meagre home-table."

By the turn of the 20th century, the city had come to be known as the "American Paris." When the 1906 earthquake leveled San Francisco, some muttered that the city was getting its just desserts and prophesied that this would teach it to appreciate the value of a more modest appetite.

They were wrong, of course. Amid the rubble, restaurateurs set up trestle tables and

---

COFFEE

San Francisco is serious about coffee, and offers plenty of alternatives to the worldwide chains. In fact, you can't walk a block in the Financial District without passing people scurrying along clutching a to-go cup filled with latte or cappuccino.

Coffee has evolved into an art form here. In North Beach you'll find popular family-run establishments like Caffé Trieste, which currently owns three locations in the city and others around the Bay Area, and sells its own beans and ground coffee.

Peet's Coffee & Tea originated across the bay in Berkeley and there are many devotees of their rich, intense brew. (Some people know Peet's as the place where the founders of Starbucks used to go to buy their beans.)

Newer kids on the block include Blue Bottle Coffee Co. and Ritual Coffee Roasters, who both approach coffee brewing in much the same way that wine makers approach wine. Blue Bottle calls their process "artisan microroasting" and uses organic, shade-grown beans.

Greens, in the Marina District.

San Franciscans have a long-standing love affair with chocolate, starting with the Ghirardellis in 1852.

served meals. Dinner over, they set about the business of rebuilding. The rest of the country soon learned that it took more than an earthquake to dull the appetites of San Franciscans.

If the earthquake failed to turn the city sober, Prohibition made another attempt. With one bar for every 100 inhabitants, San Francisco may have been the most bibulous city in the States. When alcohol was outlawed by the government, the locals merely shrugged their shoulders and said, "We might as well eat."

The early ethnic diversity of the city always offered plenty of fare for San Franciscans to choose from. Mexican missionaries were joined by scores of Chinese, French, and Germans who arrived in the city in 1849 – enticed by the Gold Rush, but who remained to cook. Vietnamese, Thai, and Cambodian immigrants have since added Asian options to the city's international and endless variety of dishes.

Historical appetite

Word of the culinary riches soon whetted the appetites of food connoisseurs the world over, who were drawn to the intrigue of the American Paris. Once in San Francisco, visitors could sample and purchase – as they still can today – Crab Louis salad and fresh petrale sole from the dockside stands of Fisherman's Wharf; Italian gnocchi and oven-fresh focaccia bread from the tiny storefronts of North Beach; armfuls of French bread;

Fisherman's Grotto - Italian and seafood dishes since 1935.

Kenwood Vineyards & Winery, Sonoma Valley.

California rolls.

warm tortillas and chili-laden salsas from the Mexican-influenced Mission; Thai fish cakes and Chinese pot stickers from Clement Street, deep in the heart of the Richmond area.

In 1935, after a trip to San Francisco with her companion Gertrude Stein, Alice B. Toklas recalled her adventures in her cookbook: "In San Francisco we indulged in gastronomic orgies. Sand dabs meuniere, rainbow trout in aspic, grilled soft-shell crabs, paupiettes of roast fillets of pork, eggs Rossini, and tarte Chambourde. The tarte Chambourde had been a specialty of one of the three great French bakeries before the San Francisco fire.

CALIFORNIA CUISINE

Alice Waters opened Chez Panisse (see page 213) in 1971. Waters set out with no formal training, just a year spent abroad experiencing European food. To Waters, freshness was the cardinal virtue and foods were cooked simply so as to bring out their natural flavors. Chez Panisse opened as a typical French bistro. Frustrated by an inability to get the quality goods that she found in France, Waters began encouraging local purveyors to bring produce to her door. Farmers grew special vegetables to complement a specific dish and hand-reared livestock and poultry according to meticulous specifications. Small-time fishermen sold her their catch and, for the first time in years, local oysters were farmed.

Armed with local ingredients, the Chez Panisse kitchen went to work. The result? The strictly French food became less French, and the menu suddenly offered dishes such as ravioli made like gnocchi from potato starch and garlic, and the very English jugged hare.

Waters-trained chefs began to branch out on their own, and the Chez Panisse philosophy spread to other restaurants. The fervor for freshness chimed with the Californian ethos, and in a few short years, chefs had been elevated to celebrity status.

Zona Rose restaurant Haight Ashbury.

Mexican tacos to go.

It's easy to get a good Mexican meal in San Fran.

To my surprise, no one in Paris had ever heard of it."

While the unique French tart may have been news to Parisians, it could not have surprised many long-time San Franciscans, raised as they were on such a cross-cultural stew. They began to feel that they ate so much sushi, pasta, dim sum, and pâté that they began to reinvent these favorites as courses in their own new, native cuisine.

Fueled by the culinary riches of the world, local chefs rebelled against the convention that French food belonged in French restaurants, Chinese in Chinese restaurants, and so on. Experimentation became the notion du jour, and over the years, the mixing and melding of international ingredients – along with a decidedly Western touch – gave rise to the culinary revolution known as "California cuisine."

Gourmet revolution

The gourmet revolution was happening all over San Francisco, but nowhere with more of

> The Richmond District is perfect if you're hungry for ethnic food. On Clement Street alone you can choose between Burmese, Thai, French, Italian, Russian, and many different styles of Chinese cooking.

a passion than across the Bay Bridge in nearby Berkeley, where eclectic cuisine was introduced most dramatically.

A welcome addition to the cuisine scene is the revamped Ferry Building at the foot of San Francisco's Market Street. The old premises have been transformed into a hugely popular farmers' market and eating and shopping destination, where all the ingredients are locally grown and produced. An afternoon spent in the Ferry Building is a gourmet's dream, and presents all the hungry visitors with an opportunity to taste for themselves some of the real California culinary dream (see page 82).

FERRY BUILDING

Once a thriving terminal, the Ferry Building is now a classy emporium designed to satisfy the local passion for food.

Before the rise of the automobile and the construction of bridges over San Francisco Bay, the Ferry Building was one of the world's most active transit terminals. Built in 1898 on the site of the original wooden ferry house at the foot of Market Street, the long and graceful building with its distinctive clock tower received thousands of ferry commuters, who arrived daily from Marin County and the East Bay.

When speedier alternatives came on the scene in the 1930s, passengers abandoned the ferries. By the mid-1950s, the once-airy Grand Nave was clogged with offices, sealing out the natural light. Next, the building was walled off by the Embarcadero freeway. Although dimmed and obscured, the treasured San Francisco landmark refused to be buried.

The earthquake-damaged freeway was demolished in 1991 and the neglected Ferry Building, now in full view, inspired plans for the structure's regeneration. Meticulously restored, it now has a food hall that is open daily with artisan shops, restaurants, and cafés, and a Farmers' Market twice a week. The ferries with their cross-bay commuters have returned, too.

There are several restaurants in the Ferry Building, including Taylor's Automatic Refresher that originated on Highway 29 near St Helena in Wine Country.

The Essentials

Address: Market Street;
www.ferrybuildingmarketplace.com
Telephone: 415-983-8030
Opening Hours: Mon–Fri 10am–6pm, Sat 9am–6pm, Sun 11am–5pm
Entrance Fee: free
Transport: bus: 2, 6, 9, 14, 14X, 21, 31; metro: J, K, L, M, T, N; streetcar: E, F; BART: all; ferries: all

Fresh, organic, Bay Area produce and artisan food items are the highlights of the Farmers' Market, held every Tuesday and Saturday until 2pm.

Free walking tours are conducted at noon on Saturdays and Tuesdays. The dramatic focus of the Ferry Building is the three-story, skylit Grand Nave that spans the length of the former terminus. Two open market halls run underneath the Nave on the bay side of the building.

Classic Italian ice cream on sale in the Ferry Building.

Market mushrooms.

Local Californian wines by the bottle.

Ferries operate from the Ferry Building to the Bay Area towns of Alameda/Oakland, Sausalito, Larkspur, Harbor Bay Isle, and Tiburon/Vallejo.

SHOPPING

From high-end haberdashers to live chickens in Chinatown to trendy boutiques and vintage fashions – start buying now.

San Francisco is a mix of cultures, each with its neighborhood filled with specialty import items. Chinatown is awash with souvenirs, Asian-inspired porcelain, and live produce – don't miss the Saturday market. Japantown's mall is the place to go for teapots, books, and lanterns. Mission Street between 16th and 24th streets has a distinctly Mexican feel – most of the trinkets are inexpensive, and the people-watching is superb.

The city has its high-end emporia, too – mainly concentrated around Union Square. Some are imports, like Armani and Chanel; others began in the years following the Gold Rush of 1849.

Another local brand is the cosmetics outfit, Benefit, started by twin sisters in the 1970s. Now international, Benefit's locations and packaging have a cute, retro feel about them, perfect for pairing with clothes from a San Fran thrift store. If you buy from Out of the Closet, you'll not only look good, but you'll do good, too – proceeds go towards Aids care and awareness.

Peking Bazaar, Grant Avenue.

The stained-glass ceiling at Neiman Marcus, at 150 Stockton Street in Union Square, is said to contain 2,600 pieces of glass and was modeled after a department store in Paris.

Vintage stores are popular.

THRIFT SHOPPING

The city's quirky microclimate – chilly mornings and evenings, with warm afternoons sandwiched between – lends itself to dressing in layers and accessorizing with scarves, gloves, leggings, and hats to stay comfortable. San Franciscans have turned function into fashion, making this layered, accessorized look an imprint of San Francisco style.

Boots and leather jackets are worn year-round, bohemian looks never go out of fashion, and many stylish San Franciscans like to blend old with new to create their own signature styles. San Franciscans are also dedicated recyclers of all things, including accessories.

To this end, vintage shops, thrift stores, consignment stores, and second-hand clothiers thrive here and can be found in almost every neighborhood.

The largest troves of these shops are in the upper Haight from Masonic to Shrader streets and in the inner Mission district. There are also pockets on Polk Street, Sacramento Street, in Bernal Heights, and on Grant Avenue in North Beach.

Shops range from upscale, vintage-specific boutiques to larger department-style emporia overflowing with racks of clothing and other gently used items. There are also a few vintage jewelers in the city that sell lovely estate pieces.

Comb through the vintage shops for one-of-a-kind items to add flair to your wardrobe, or scope out offbeat tchotchkes and accessories as cool souvenirs, and take a little San Francisco style home.

You can always find treasures at the local thrift stores.

Hippy fashions in Haight Ashbury.

Saks Fifth Avenue, San Francisco store.

A foggy morning over The Golden Gate Bridge.

The Painted Ladies on Alamo Square.

Fisherman's Wharf at twilight.

The Transamerica Pyramid, Financial District.

INTRODUCTION

A detailed guide to the city with the principal sites
clearly cross-referenced by number to the maps.

For a city just seven miles (18km) square, San Francisco covers a huge variety of terrain, both natural and social. At least a dozen distinct neighborhoods are tucked inside the narrow city limits, with an array of fascinatingly different styles, all set in a sea-fringed frame of stunning natural beauty. Social, cultural, and ethnic diversity is an easy backdrop, with class boundaries softly blurred. The most visible extremes are the wealthy elite on Nob Hill and the homeless of the Tenderloin District, but San Francisco is a collage of cultures – ad hoc, yet hanging together with a comfortable sense of permanence.

Castro district.

The many and varied hills – more than 40 named ones – offer visitors to the city a variety of panoramas and vistas. On foot these can be a challenge (albeit worthwhile), but by bus, auto, or cable car, every trip is an adventure. Whether walking or riding, the views make it all worthwhile, unfolding glimpses of the bay, the bridges, and the streets that so often retain a Victorian or Edwardian character, but with an individual, urban West Coast style.

A visit is happily unpredictable, although a healthy attitude to surprise, and a good pair of walking shoes, are useful. There are also wonderful treats, especially if you venture away from the beaten path.

Golden Gate Park.

Neighborhoods and beyond

The following sections are mapped out as a series of city neighborhoods full of attractions, experiences, and activities. After these essential sites, we travel farther afield, around the bay from the Bay Bridge to the Golden Gate, and to Oakland, Berkeley, and the Bay Area. Finally, for those with more time for spectacular northern California, there is a series of excursions: wild coastlines, pleasing wineries, and hot-tub heavenly spas just waiting for you to savor before heading back to San Francisco.

Oh, and if you do leave your heart, as so many often do, you can always come back for it next time.

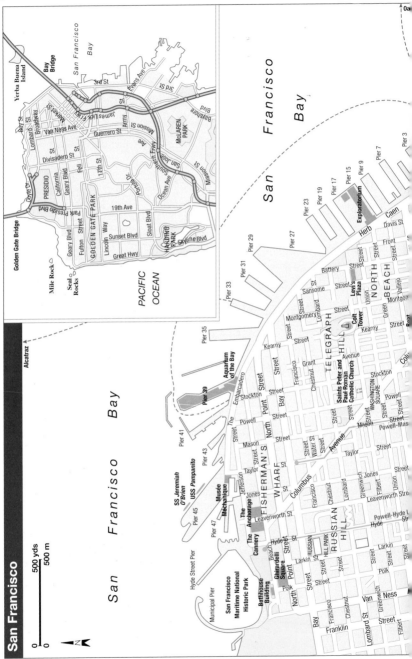

San Francisco

0   500 yds
0   500 m

N

San Francisco Bay

San Francisco Bay

San Francisco Bay

PACIFIC OCEAN

Bay Bridge

Yerba Buena Island

Golden Gate Bridge

Mile Rock

Seal Rocks

PRESIDIO

GOLDEN GATE PARK

McLAREN PARK

Sutro Park

3rd St
Evans Ave
Army St
James Lick Fwy
Market St
Broadway
Lombard St
Pine St
Van Ness Ave
Guerrero St
Mission St
San Jose Ave
Southern Fwy
Bayshore Blvd
Ocean Ave
Portola Dr
17th St
Fell St
Divisadero St
California St
Doyle Dr
Park Presidio Blvd
Geary Blvd
Fulton St
Geary Blvd
Street
Lincoln Way
19th Ave
Sunset Blvd
Sloat Blvd
Skyline Blvd
Great Hwy

Alcatraz

Exploratorium

Pier 3
Pier 7
Pier 9
Pier 15
Pier 17
Pier 19
Pier 23
Pier 27
Pier 29
Pier 31
Pier 33
Pier 35
Pier 39
Pier 41
Pier 43
Pier 45
Pier 47

Aquarium of the Bay

SS *Jeremiah O'Brien*
USS *Pampanito*
Musée Mécanique
The Anchorage
The Cannery
Ghirardelli Square
Bathhouse Building
San Francisco Maritime National Historic Park

Hyde Street Pier
Municipal Pier

Colt Tower

Saints Peter and Paul Roman Catholic Church

Levi's Plaza

TELEGRAPH HILL

NORTH BEACH

WASHINGTON SQUARE

RUSSIAN HILL PARK

RUSSIAN HILL

FISHERMAN'S WHARF

Caen
Herb
Davis St
Front Street
Battery Street
Sansome Street
Montgomery Street
Kearny Street
Grant Avenue
Stockton Street
Powell Street
Mason Street
Taylor Street
Jones Street
Leavenworth Street
Hyde Street
Larkin Street
Polk Street
Van Ness
Franklin
Columbus Avenue
The Embarcadero

Union Street
Green Street
Vallejo Street
Filbert Street
Greenwich Street
Lombard Street
Chestnut Street
Francisco Street
Bay Street
North Point Street
Beach Street
Jefferson Street
Water St
North Point
Bay Street
Chestnut Street
Lombard Street

Powell-Mason
Powell-Hyde Line

Montgom
Green St

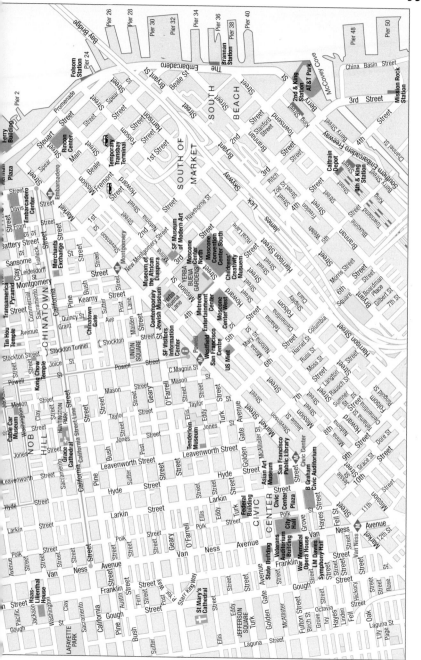

Fisherman's Wharf is always a hub of activity.

FISHERMAN'S WHARF

San Francisco's waterside is famous for its seafood, family attractions, and sea lions; you can also learn a lot about the city's history at the Maritime Museum and the Aquatic Park.

The city's 45-acre (18-hectare) **Fisherman's Wharf** is one of the most visited places in San Francisco. A bright, family-oriented carnival of attractions, despite the crowds and occasional tackiness, the Wharf also has tons of seafood restaurants, good little stores tucked between the souvenir stands, two garden parks with open space for picnicking, and mouthwatering places to buy food.

In summer months, the narrow boardwalks are jammed with people and it's easy to forget that this is one of the city's more important historic spots. Alongside hundreds of sailboats and yachts and the ferries packed with visitors and commuters, much of San Francisco's maritime past is moored here.

HYDE STREET PIER ❶

Address: Jefferson Street at Hyde Street; www.nps.gov/safr
Telephone: 415-561-7000
Opening Hours: daily 9.30am–5pm
Entrance Fee: pier free, charge for vessels
Transport: bus: 10, 20, 30, 47; cable car: Powell-Hyde; streetcar: F

The waterfront retrospective starts here, where the Maritime Museum (see page 98) operates a fleet of

vintage vessels open to the public. Built in 1890, the steam-driven *Eureka* is the last of 50 paddle-wheel ferries that transported people and cars over the bay between San Francisco and Tiburon, until the eye-catching Golden Gate and Bay bridges stretched across to become part of the scenery. The *Alma*, a scow-schooner, hauled hay, produce, and lumber around the bay, while the *Eppleton Hall*, built in England in 1914, traveled as far as Panama. The wooden-hulled C.A. *Thayer* was a hard-working lumber

Main Attractions
Hyde Street Pier
Maritime Museum
Ghirardelli Square
Pier 45
SS Jeremiah O'Brien
USS Pampanito
Pier 39
Aquarium of the Bay

Map
Page 98

A sea lion catches the sun on Pier 39.

The Aquatic Park Bathhouse Building is the place to marvel at WPA murals and historic dioramas in the lobby or Bufano sculptures on the veranda.

ship that hauled coal from Europe as well as wool from Australia and New Zealand. Built in 1886, the *Balclutha* made 17 trips around Cape Horn, was shipwrecked, and served a brief stint in the movies before her final sail in 1930.

San Francisco Maritime National Historic Park Visitor Center ❷

Address: 499 Jefferson Street (at Hyde Street); www.nps.gov/safr
Telephone: 415-447-5000
Opening Hours: daily 9.30am–5pm
Entrance Fee: free
Transport: bus: 10, 20, 30, 47; cable car: Powell-Hyde; streetcar: F

Headquartered in the premises of the former Del Monte cannery, the visitor center has brochures, maps, and other information on the city's nautical past.

The Maritime Museum is located in the **Bathhouse Building** ❸ (900 Beach Street; www.nps.gov/safr; tel:

415-561-7100; daily 10am–4pm; free) and displays intricate models of boats and muralist Hilaire Hiler's surrealist vision of Atlantis. The somewhat whimsical, shipshaped building was commissioned by the federal government as one of the Works Progress Administration projects in the 1930s, a major relief measure that was established to create jobs for the many unemployed people in the city at the time. Much of this watery area west of the Hyde Street Pier has been designated by the National Historic Register as an historic district, and operates under the banner of **Aquatic Park** ❹.

Ghirardelli Square ❺

Address: 900 North Point Street (at Larkin); www.ghirardellisq.com
Telephone: 415-775-5500
Transport: bus: 10, 30, 47; cable car: Powell-Hyde; streetcar: F

South of the Maritime Museum and occupying the entire block bounded

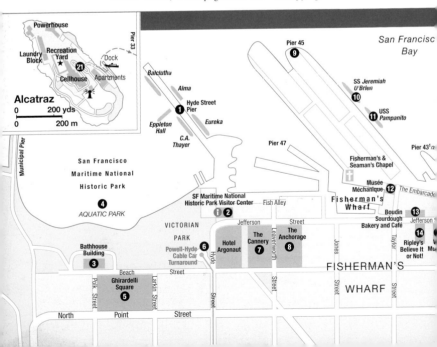

by North Point, Polk, Beach, and Larkin streets, Ghirardelli Square is a shopping center geared toward visitors, with its own interesting past.

Chocolate kings

Domingo Ghirardelli opened his first chocolate factory in San Francisco in 1852, after he failed to strike it rich in the Gold Rush. The hugely successful family business moved to these premises in 1893. So much chocolate was made here that (it is said) when it rains, chocolate still oozes from the old walls. Although the working factory has moved, there is still a retail outlet and candy store. (Be sure to try a hot fudge ice-cream sundae.)

Even if you don't have a sweet tooth, Ghirardelli Square has other

The Ghirardelli Chocolate Company has been in SF since 1852.

Learn about vintage vessels.

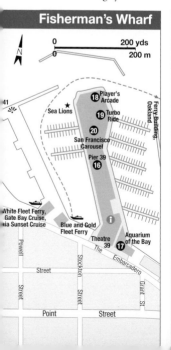

Fisherman's Wharf

0   200 yds
0   200 m

41

Sea Lions ★

18 Player's Arcade

19 Turbo Ride

20

San Francisco Carousel

Pier 39

16

Ferry Building, Oakland

White Fleet Ferry, Gate Bay Cruise, via Sunset Cruise

Blue and Gold Fleet Ferry

Theatre 39
The

17 Aquarium of the Bay

Embarcadero

Powell

Stockton

Grant St.

Street

Street

Street

Point   Street

San Francisco Maritime
National Historical Park

Visitor Center

TIP

For on-site maps and information, stop by the California Welcome Center on Pier 39. For discounts on cruises, attractions, museums, parking, shopping, and dining, log on to www.fishermanswharf.org.

Family-friendly Bubba Gump shrimp emporium.

Beach Blanket Babylon.

stores and restaurants, many with wonderful views of the bay. The courtyard shelters 120-year-old olive trees that provide the perfect spot for rest and people-watching.

The corner of Hyde and Beach is a good place to stop for a hot drink if San Francisco's "summer days" have given you a chill. At the **Buena Vista Café** (www.thebuenavista.com) you can enjoy an Irish coffee served to perfection, as it has been for more than 50 years. At the same time, watch the busy cable-car activity at the **Powell-Hyde Cable Car Turnaround** .

A short walk east leads to **The Cannery** ❼ (2801 Leavenworth Street; tel: 415-771-3112), once the largest fruit and vegetable cannery in the world. Converted to a three-story shopping complex in the late 1960s, it is a maze of stores, cafés, restaurants, and bars. The open brick patio between the Cannery and the Argonaut Hotel (formerly the Haslett Warehouse; www.argonauthotel.com) was originally a railroad siding and platform. It now serves as a beer garden and is a perfect place to spend an afternoon listening to live music. Next door to The Cannery is **The Anchorage Square** ❽ (www.anchorage square.com), another shopping and dining complex.

Fisherman's Wharf is one of the best places in the US for seafood. The corrugated metal sheds lining the docks are known as **Fish Alley**, where the catch of the day is packed, ready to be sold.

The USS Pampanito saw active service in World War II.

Musée Méchanique is an exercise in nostalgia.

DRINK

A popular annual event at the Wharf is *Uncorked!*, a wine and food festival (http://uncorkedwinefestivals.com), held each May in association with COPIA, the American Center for Wine, Food & Arts, located in Napa Valley.

PIER 45 ❾

An appetite for fruits of the sea can be satisfied in a more relaxed fashion by strolling down **Jefferson Street**, the wharf's main drag. Sidewalk vendors boil and steam shellfish all day long. Walk east and back along the waterfront to **Pier 45**, which remains as much of a working site as Fisherman's Wharf can offer. Fishermen depart before dawn and return with sand dabs, scallops, Dungeness crabs, and sea bass.

SS Jeremiah O'Brien ❿

Address: Pier 45 (Embarcadero and Taylor Street); www.ssjeremiahobrien.org
Telephone: 415-544-0100
Opening Hours: daily 9am–4pm
Entrance Fee: charge
Transport: bus: 10, 30, 47; streetcar: F
The *SS Jeremiah O'Brien* is moored at Pier 45. It was one of a great fleet that sailed during World War II, and is America's last unaltered Liberty ship still in operating condition.

USS Pampanito ⓫

Address: Pier 45 (Embarcadero and Taylor Street); www.maritime.org
Telephone: 415-775-1943
Opening Hours: May–daily from 9am, closing times change seasonally
Entrance Fee: charge
Transport: bus: 10, 30, 47; streetcar: F

BOUDIN BAKERY

The Boudin Bakery (www.boudinbakery.com) harks all the way back to the Gold Rush. It was established in 1849 in a small shop in Dupont Street by Isidore Boudin, the son of a family of master bakers from Burgundy in France. Isidore blended the sourdough popular with Gold Rush miners with French baking traditions.

The bakery was bought in 1941 by an artisan baker from Italy, Steven Giraudo, and changed hands a number of times before two of Giraudo's sons bought it back. It now has a claim to be San Francisco's oldest continuously run business.

As well as the bistro, store, demonstration bakery, and museum at 160 Jefferson in Fisherman's Wharf, there are outlets at Disney's California Adventure Park, and other cafés scattered throughout California. The main San Francisco bakery is in the Richmond District on the corner of Tenth Avenue and Geary Boulevard. The bakery still uses the "starter" yeast culture that it developed during the Gold Rush.

Futuristic arcades offer fun 3D experiences.

Go underwater and stay cool at the Aquarium of the Bay.

The USS *Pampanito*, a 300ft (90 meter) submarine, played an active role in World War II and is berthed at Pier 45. Audio tours are available.

On Pier 45 at the end of Taylor Street is the **Musée Méchanique** ⑫

Try fresh crab at one of the many seafood eateries.

(http://museemecaniquesf.com), an exercise in nostalgia with its coin-operated pianos, antique slot machines, and a 1910 steam-driven motorcycle. Nearby is the **Boudin Bakery and Café** ⑬ where you can watch the bakers work the dough. Things can get pretty bizarre at **Ripley's Believe It or Not!** ⑭ (175 Jefferson Street; tel: 415- 202 9850; www.ripleys.com/san francisco), a museum based on the collection of illustrator Robert Ripley. Almost as creepy (and as silly) is the **Wax Museum** ⑮ (tel: 866 223 4240; www.waxmuseum.com).

You can charter a fishing trip at the wharf (www.sportfishingsf.com; tel: 510-478-3111) or take fishing day trips for salmon, halibut, or whatever is in season (the height of fishing season is Mar–June). **Pier 41** is the place for trips around the bay, Tiburon, and Angel Island (see page 220). Check where the boats depart from, as this can vary.

For a change of pace from the souvenir stores, **Frank's Fisherman Supply** (366 Jefferson Street; tel: 415-775-1165; www.franksfisherman.com) has nautical antiques among marine supplies, nautically themed gifts, and

WHALE WATCHING

Just 27 miles (43km) from Fisherman's Wharf lie the Farallon Islands, once called the "Devil's Teeth." These jagged outcroppings provide a rich sanctuary for 23 species of marine mammals, including 18 types of whales and dolphins, plus seals, seabirds, and great white sharks that migrate here to breed in summer and fall.

A whale-watching excursion allows for the ultimate vantage point to observe these magnificent creatures as they frolic and cavort in their temporary environment. **SF Bay Whale Watching** (tel: 415-331-6267; www.sfbaywhalewatching.com) runs expeditions from Fort Mason to the Gulf of the Farallones. You can get up close to gray, blue, and humpback whales, dolphins, seals, and sea lions as you sail from Fisherman's Wharf beneath the Golden Gate Bridge, past the Point Bonita lighthouse and the majestic hills and cliffs of the Northern California coast, and into the roiling waters of the Pacific Ocean. A naturalist expert is on board the motor-catamaran *Outer Limits* (www.sfbayadventures.com) to narrate throughout the trip, point out areas of special interest, and answer questions about local wildlife. Be sure to dress warmly and be advised that water outside the Golden Gate can be quite choppy.

Iconic attractions of Fisherman's Wharf.

seaworthy garb. You might glimpse local San Franciscan rivals on the wharf at one of the city's clubs, the **South End Rowing Club** (http://serc. com) or the adjacent **Dolphin Club** (www.dolphinclub.org).

PIER 39 16

Fisherman's Wharf's major tourist area is home to its most photographed inhabitants, the boisterous **sea lions**. The pier has more than 110 stores, restaurants, and attractions.

Aquarium of the Bay 17

Address: Pier 39 (Embarcadero at Beach Street); www.aquariumof thebay.com
Entrance Fee: charge; tickets can be bought on-line
Opening Hours: daily Jul–15 Sep 9am–8pm, fall and spring 10am–7pm, winter 10am–6pm
Transport: bus: 10, 39, 47; streetcar: F

The Aquarium of the Bay allows visitors to travel through the ocean as if they were diving themselves.

Flashing light and thumb-twitching fun is found in the **Player's Arcade & Sports Grill** 18 (www.playerssf.com), the largest in the city. A more nostalgic ride is the **San Francisco Carousel** 20. Handcrafted in Italy, the two-tier structure depicts local landmarks.

Among good-natured tackiness, San Francisco and the bay meet with crowd-pleasing exuberance.

Buy puppets, pretty trinkets, and all things fishy on the harbor's popular piers.

Iconic attractions of Fisherman's Wharf.

ALCATRAZ

A windswept island and former fort in the frigid waters of the bay was once home to some of America's most notorious criminals.

TIP

Be sure to dress in layers as the ferry crossing can be windy. Also, don't miss the audio tour, narrated by former inmates and prison guards.

Map
Page 98

Set in one of the world's most beautiful harbors, accessible only by ferry, this hump of rock with tales of legendary inmates has fascinated visitors since the days of Prohibition and American gangsters.

Alcatraz ㉑

Address: www.nps.gov/alcatraz
Telephone: 415-981-7625
Opening Hours: daily tours 9am–3.50pm

The Rock as seen from the air.

Entrance Fee: charge to get to the ferry
Transport: take: bus: 10, 8X, 82X; streetcar: F; metro: all; BART: all ferries depart from Pier 33 (Embarcadero at Bay Street)

Escape from Alcatraz required a treacherous, 1.5 mile (2.5km) swim to San Francisco. Triathletes now swim the course in about 25 minutes, but without having to tunnel through solid rock or slip past armed guards under cover of darkness. Nor do the more than 1 million tourists who visit each year.

Surrounded by the frigid waters and swift currents of San Francisco Bay, 22.5 acre (9 hectare) Alcatraz island was once residence for the most notorious criminals of the 20th century, including Chicago mob boss Al Capone and "Machine Gun" Kelly. It is (surprisingly) a very beautiful spot, with rare plants and wildlife on its outer fringes that many visitors miss. The island is so close to the city, it's said the inmates could hear chattering and laughing from mainland cocktail parties that caught the breeze and floated across the bay.

Solitary confinement

Prison cells were designed for maximum security. Just 5ft by 9ft (1.5 meters by 3 meters), inmates had to spend 16 to 23 hours a day in them. All privileges were earned by good behavior, and infractions of the rules were punished by confinement in the Segregation Unit, otherwise known as solitary confinement, where even light could be denied to an inmate deemed "unworthy."

The solitary life of a prison inmate was conveyed to a wide audience in *The Birdman of Alcatraz*, starring former circus acrobat Burt Lancaster. The movie is based on the life of Bob Stroud, who spent his 53 years of incarceration studying the science of birds, and eventually became a world authority (although, contrary to Hollywood lore, Stroud didn't keep any birds during his stay on Alcatraz).

Perhaps the most surprising chapter of The Rock's history began on November 20, 1969, six years after the prison facility closed. A large band of Native Americans under the banner "Indians of All Tribes," led by Mohawk Richard Oakes, broke into the disused penitentiary. The occupation was mounted as a protest against the US Government's broken promises to the tribes, and lasted 18 months, until June 11, 1971. While the protest ended with no demands being met, it jump-started the Pan-Indian Movement and prompted a new policy of Indian self-determination from the federal government.

Daily tours depart from Pier 33, operated by Hornblower Cruises (http://alcatrazcruises.com). Tickets can be bought online at www.alcatrazcruises.com, by phone (tel: 415-981-7625), or at the ticket office at Pier 33.

Chicago mobster Al Capone (1898–1947) was one of Alcatraz island's better-known residents.

Guards and their families lived on the island, and considered it to be so safe they rarely locked their doors.

HISTORY OF THE ROCK

Alcatraz was christened *La Isla de los Alcatraces* (the island of the pelicans) by Spanish explorers in 1775. Its position in the bay made it ideal for use as a defensive and disciplinary facility, and by the mid-1800s, US Army soldiers stood guard. The island became used as a prison in 1895, when Moqui Hopi tribe leaders were held. The first military prisoners to serve time in the concrete cell blocks were among those who built it in 1912. Approximately two decades later, the Federal Bureau of Prisons decided Alcatraz was the ideal facility to house its most hardened criminals. Just three privileges were available to the best-behaved inmates of Alcatraz: the recreation yard, the library, or a job in one of the on-site factories.

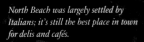
North Beach was largely settled by Italians; it's still the best place in town for delis and cafés.

NORTH BEACH TO TELEGRAPH HILL

Beatniks, Sicilian sailors, history-lovers, gourmets and club-goers are all drawn to this Italian neighborhood beneath the Coit Tower.

Italian immigrants called **North Beach** ❶ "the Little City" when they settled here more than 100 years ago. Situated below Telegraph Hill's Coit Tower, North Beach is – loosely speaking – the bohemian, low-lying neighborhood that occupies the area bordered by Broadway and Washington Square.

Cultural shifts

Although more recent trends and events have overlaid the culture, the Italians – and Italian roots – are still much in evidence in the North Beach of the public's imagination. In the past, a number of *prominenti* distinguished themselves from the crowds of faces in the neighborhood and succeeded in winning the respect of the city as a whole. A.P. Giannini brought financial power to the common folk with his Banco d'Italia, an enterprise which some people at the time disparaged as being small and inconsequential. The name of the establishment was later changed to the Bank of America, and Giannini's bank became one of the largest financial institutions in the world.

A fascinating history of literary figures, comedic celebrities, and strip joints has added immeasurably to the neighborhood's great color.

The Beat poets once gathered here for java and inspiration; a young Woody Allen and Bill Cosby had their taste of the limelight at the Hungry i; and Barbra Streisand, Johnny Mathis, and Lenny Bruce plied their trades in the area's nightclubs, like the Purple Onion, sadly closed in 2012 after almost 60 years in business.

In recent years the Italians and other long-standing communities of Irish, Basque, and Mexican families have been joined by a significant

Café Puccini on Columbus Avenue.

Broadway, where Carol Doda performed the Condor Club's first topless dance in 1964.

Asian population (mainly Chinese), adding diversity to the ethnic mix.

On Broadway

The two blocks of **Broadway ❷**, north of Montgomery toward Columbus Avenue, were once San Francisco's "Great White Way," a run of sex shops and strip joints offering the standard variety of commercial vice. Sleazy bars, watered-down liquor, and live sex acts were the norm. Carol Doda made history at Broadway's Condor Club (http://condorsf.com): sitting topless on a piano, she was lowered onto the stage, to the delight of the audience (who got to see what implants were all about).

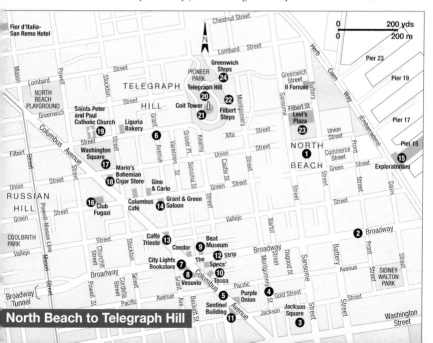

North Beach to Telegraph Hill

As the strip clubs are closing down, new nightspots are springing up in their place. North Beach has always been a late nightspot, and intends to stay that way.

AROUND JACKSON SQUARE

A good place to start a tour is just south of Broadway in a part of town known as **Jackson Square** ❸. The name is deceptive: you'll find no square here, just as you'll find no beach in North Beach, and no telegraph on Telegraph Hill. What can be found, however, are a few vestiges of the Barbary Coast (see page 112) and a handful of beautifully restored buildings from the Gold-Rush era. It's a pleasant place for a stroll.

North Beach

Before the Gold Rush, North Beach was the home of Juana Briones and her family, who built their adobe house in 1836 near the intersection of Powell and Filbert streets. Señora Briones operated a small rancho on the outskirts of the village, where she supplied fresh meat and produce to passing ships, and occasionally gave shelter to a deserting sailor.

When gold was discovered in the Sierra foothills in 1848, thousands of immigrants poured into Yerba Buena Cove in the wildest boom to hit the west. Settlers began squeezing into the valley between Russian and Telegraph hills toward the northern shore, from which North Beach takes its name.

Where's the beach?

In the early days, the bay reached as far inland as Francisco Street to the north and Montgomery Street to the south, before landfill extended the area to accommodate boatloads of new San Franciscans, many of whom had just deserted ship. Now, entire city blocks stand on land that was once a harbor in which sailors left ships to rot while they abandoned uniforms and official orders in order to make their fortune from golden nuggets.

When fires swept through the area after the earthquake of 1906

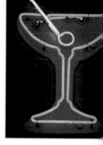

Cocktails at North Beach.

Both Woody Allen and Bill Cosby performed at the Hungry i before its name was taken over by a strip club.

and devastated most of the city (see page 44), the Italians on Telegraph Hill who were trapped without water reportedly fought the blaze with buckets of the neighborhood's local wine. For many months, the homeless occupied Washington Square as survivors set about the arduous task of reconstruction, but within little more than a year North Beach was almost completely rebuilt, and it was one of the first of San Francisco's districts to recover from the earthquake.

Edwardian facades

Most of the buildings without the benefit of architects were variations of a simple Edwardian style. Many have been renovated, some with an Art Deco stucco from the 1930s, but much of North Beach remains as unadorned two- or three-story wooden frames with bay windows and back alleys. Both the buildings and their layout give North Beach the feel of a European *quartier*, an intimate enclave of simple homes sheltered from the modern architecture towering nearby. Fans of urban restoration

Jack Kerouac Alley runs between two local landmarks, City Lights Bookstore and Vesuvio Bar, both popular among members of the Beat Generation of the 1950s.

might like to check out the 700 block of **Montgomery Street ❹**. Notable among the renovations are the fine **California Steam and Navigation Building**, and the **Ship Building**, all from the late 1850s or 1860s.

COLUMBUS AVENUE

Columbus Avenue ❺ cuts diagonally across Broadway, leading directly into the heart of North Beach. This is the district's main thoroughfare, and every year on Columbus Day hordes of revelers fill the street in a celebration.

Restaurants, delis, pastry shops, and cafés line the avenue. For the most part, the cuisine here is northern Italian with a few Chinese, Mexican, and sushi places mixed in for good measure. The ambiance ranges from no-frills pizza joints to first-class dining rooms.

The intersection of Broadway, Columbus, and Grant marks the meeting place of four neighborhoods. **Grant Avenue ❻** is the center of North Beach's social world, and every day here seems to be a celebration of

The Beat goes on.

North Beach's unique character. There are still a number of family-run businesses on Grant, while in between them galleries, boutiques, bars, clubs, antiques shops, restaurants, cafés, and Chinese markets are nestled.

City Lights Bookstore ❼

Address: 261 Columbus Avenue; www.citylights.com
Telephone: 415-362-8193
Opening Hours: daily 10am–midnight
Transport: bus: 8X, 30, 45

Columbus's most famous location is a National Literary Landmark. Owned by Lawrence Ferlinghetti, who founded it in 1953, this was the first bookstore in the country to sell only paperbacks. The cornerstone of "beatnikdom" in San Francisco, City Lights Bookstore gained national notoriety three years later for its publication of Allen Ginsberg's incendiary poem *Howl*, which became the subject of an obscenity trial.

To this day, City Lights remains one of San Francisco's most important literary centers. The shop is known for leftist leanings, and accordingly has a good selection of books on social change.

Poetry, of course, is also well served, with a whole room dedicated to the bards. City Lights also sponsors a schedule of readings from new and established writers; check the bulletin

FACT

Dashiell Hammett Street is just one of the thoroughfares named after writers who lived or worked in San Francisco. Among the many authors commemorated in such a way are Ambrose Bierce and Mark Twain.

The area is full of boho cafes.

This low-key watering hole has been cool for decades. Be sure to sample the Martinis.

boards in the shop or ask one of the clerks for details about upcoming events; alternatively, check the website.

Vesuvio Café

Address: 255 Columbus Avenue
Telephone: 415-362-3370
Opening Hours: Mon–Fri 8am–2am, Sat–Sun from 6am
Transport: bus: 8X, 30, 45

Next door to City Lights is another beatnik haunt, a bar adorned with colorful stained-glass windows that became known for the words, "We are itching to get away from Portland, Oregon," painted over the entranceway. In its heyday, Vesuvio was owned by Henri Lenoir, whose collections of exotic bar-room paraphernalia still adorn the delightful but cramped bar. Near the front door a list of names is drawn in cement, commemorating a handful of North Beach's outstanding "mad ones."

Before taking over Vesuvio Café, Lenoir managed **Specs'** Twelve Adler Museum Cafe (12 Saroyan; tel: 415-421-4112), across Columbus in a tiny alleyway. Specs' was a bohemian hotspot in the 1940s, a famed lesbian bar called 12 Adler Place, a nightclub featuring jazz, belly dancers, and Middle Eastern music. Tucked away in the corner of this blind alley, Specs' has

Coppola's Sentinel Building.

somehow maintained its low profile as a watering hole for San Francisco's underground. The offbeat bar is decorated with an exotic hodgepodge of sailor and dock-worker memorabilia, fine Inuit carvings, posters, scrimshaw, wartime propaganda – even a dried whale penis. The large round tables encourage everyone to talk to the strangers sitting next to them.

Beat Museum

Address: 540 Broadway;
www.kerouac.com

Caffé Trieste, the first espresso coffee bar on the West Coast.

TALES OF THE BARBARY COAST

Modern-day Jackson Square is a pleasant place to stroll around, but it is ironic that one of the city's quieter neighborhoods was, during the Gold Rush, a place of unparalled vice. The Barbary Coast (as it was then named) was a vast marketplace of flesh and liquor. Sailors and miners found fleeting pleasures, fast money, and, just as likely, a violent end. Second to gambling, shoot-outs were the favored sport, and fortunes rode on the wink of an eye. Most businessmen in the Barbary Coast trafficked in human bodies; either selling sex to '49ers or selling kidnapped sailors to the captains of hell ships.

Both enterprises returned high profits, and local politicians turned a blind eye for a piece of the action. Red lights burned on almost every block, from both high-class "parlors" and squalid "cribs," where prostitutes worked in rooms barely big enough to hold a bed. In the worst cases, Chinese girls were bought as slaves and made to work until they became sick or died.

Telephone: 415-399-9626
Opening Hours: daily 10am–7pm
Entrance Fee: charge
Transport: bus: 8, 10, 12, 30, 30X, 8AX, 88X

The life and times of Jack Kerouac and his literary compatriots are celebrated at this groovy little museum of all things Beat. The collection includes a rare edition of Allen Ginsberg's *Howl*, letters from Kerouac to Carolyn Cassady and a clever invitation to a poetry reading by Charles Bukowski. Pick up some souvenirs, T-shirts, pulp-fiction paperbacks, glossy coffee-table books, even a Keroauc bobble-head doll. Visit the website for info on the many events.

A few years ago, North Beach alleys took on the names of famous writers. The tiny street that divides City Lights from Vesuvio became Jack Kerouac Alley, and Specs' insisted that its end of the alley be named **Saroyan Place**, to honor the late Armenian-American novelist William Saroyan.

Tosca ⑩

Address: 242 Columbus Avenue; http://toscacafesf.com
Telephone: 415-986-9651
Opening Hours: Tue–Sun 5pm–2am
Transport: bus: 10, 12, 30, 8AX, 88X

A famous stomping ground on Columbus Avenue with the original red Naugahyde booths, operatic selections on the jukebox, and a signature coffee drink, Tosca maintains a regular clientele of locals, bohemians, socialites, and politicos.

Stepping out of Tosca, turn left and walk south on Columbus to the intersection of Kearny Street. The fabulous flatiron structure on the southwest corner is the **Sentinel Building** ⑪ (Columbus Tower), housing the headquarters of Francis Ford Coppola's production company, American Zoetrope. A small bistro serves Coppola's wines, and Francis himself is often seen in the nearby cafés. Note that local etiquette prevents one

Record Music Store.

approaching Mr Coppola with lines from *The Godfather*.

Head north on Columbus, cross Broadway, and turn right. This is the heart of **The Strip** ⑫, a hangover from North Beach's bawdier days, with adult bookstores, strip clubs, and peepshows. Bars and clubs still abound, but in recent years this area has become overrun by the bridge

Pub life in North Beach.

Beach Blanket Babylon at Club Fugazi.

is the **Grant & Green Saloon** (www.grantandgreensaloon.com; tel: 415-693-9565). Open from 2pm to 2am, this down-and-dirty North Beach institution has dark corners, Anchor Steam beer on tap, and live music every night.

Half a block away, around the corner on Green Street, is Gino & Carlo (www.ginoandcarlo.com), a neighborhood watering hole with all the qualifications of the quintessential North Beach bar: strong drinks, pool tables, and much Sinatra on the jukebox. A few doors down are other atmospheric places, like the **Columbus Café** (http://columbuscafesf.com), with a mural depicting the mighty nautical journey of its namesake, Christopher Columbus.

Farther up Green is **Club Fugazi** (tel: 415-421-4222; https://beachblanket babylon.com), home to the fantastically camp and perpetually sold-out *Beach Blanket Babylon*, the longest-running musical review in San Francisco's theatrical history. Since 1974, it has told the tongue-in-cheek story of Snow White and the quest for her prince, while meeting such updated characters along the way as Arnold Schwarzenegger, Hillary Clinton, and Elvis. This is a fantastic way to cap an evening in North Beach, but don't wait until you're here to buy a ticket, and be sure to get in line at least 45 minutes prior to show time.

and tunnel crowd and there is a strong police presence on weekend nights.

Caffé Trieste

Address: 601 Vallejo Street; www.caffetrieste.com
Telephone: 415-392 6739
Opening Hours: Sun–Thu 6.30am–10pm, Fri–Sat 6.30am–11pm
Transport: bus: 12, 30, 41; cable car: Powell/Mason

At the intersection of Grant and Vallejo is this favored haunt of musicians where you can enjoy a real treat – live opera on Saturdays. Farther up Grant

North Beach restaurant owners.

WASHINGTON SQUARE

East down Green Street, turn left on Stockton and head north one block to cross Union Street to **Washington Square** . Many Chinese people practice tai chi here, and a flock of brilliantly colored wild parrots roosts in the park's lush treetops. At the park's southwestern corner is **Mario's Bohemian Cigar Store** (tel: 415-362 0536). On nearby Stockton Street, the quaint little **Liguria Bakery** has been on this corner for more than 50 years, producing melt-in-the-mouth

North Beach buildings with Saints Peter and Paul Church peeking above.

focaccia bread. They close when they sell out – usually by 3pm, so get here early to buy provisions for a picnic in Washington Square.

Typical of North Beach, the statue located in the center of Washington Square is not of anyone named Washington but of Ben Franklin. The statue was a gift to the city from H.D. Cogswell, an eccentric dentist who amassed a fortune by putting gold into miners' teeth – a sign of status in a town that worshiped the glistering metal.

Cogswell, an avid teetotaler, swore to build a public fountain for every saloon in San Francisco. Famous for his offbeat humor, he labeled the three water spouts at the base of the statue *Cal Seltzer*, *Vichy*, and *Congress*. On the west side of the square is a statue dedicated to the city's volunteer firemen, bequeathed to the city by Lillie Hitchcock Coit, the heiress who also raised the Coit Tower (see page 120).

Saints Peter and Paul Catholic Church ⑲

Address: 666 Filbert Street; http://salesianssspp.org
Telephone: 415-421-0809
Opening Hours: Masses said daily
Transport: bus: 8, 30, 39, 41, 45; cable car: Powell/Mason

This picturesque, 80-year-old cathedral has a Romanesque facade, and

TIP

North Beach is a very challenging place to park a car. It's much easier to walk, take the bus, or hail a cab, Uber or Lyft to its many bars, clubs, and restaurants.

Tableside at a local trattoria.

A local cafe.

Saints Peter and Paul Church.

moves all things shines throughout the universe).

A broad church

A sign in the vestibule promises the rights to special religious services here for all San Franciscans of Italian descent; another sign lists the schedules for English, Italian, and Chinese Masses. Soon after it was consecrated, the newly opened church was the target of anarchistic bombings, and a close look reveals the scarring on its white facade left by the explosions.

On the first Sunday in October, Sicilian parishioners conduct a procession honoring *Maria Santissima del Lume* (Mary, Most Holy Mother of Light) along Columbus Avenue and down to Fisherman's Wharf, where the traditional Blessing of the Fleet is given.

Fior d'Italia (www.fior.com), established in 1886, claims to be the oldest Italian restaurant in America. Its previous location was directly across Washington Square with a view of Saints Peter and Paul's spires, but after a devastating fire in 2005, Fior d'Italia reopened in new spacious digs at the historic **San Remo Hotel** at 2237 Mason Street (www.sanremohotel.com).

TELEGRAPH HILL

From Washington Square, the easiest route to **Telegraph Hill** ⓴ is directly up Union Street, where the sidewalk gives way to flights of stairs that make the climbing a little easier. It still makes for an energetic climb, though. From the top of Union, visitors can take one of the several footpaths that wind around the uppermost peak to eventually arrive at **Pioneer Park**.

Telegraph Hill has always been a part of, and apart from, North Beach. It was largely ignored by early settlers, who preferred to fill in the shallows of the bay below rather than build on the hill's steep shoulders. Irish stevedores were among the earliest inhabitants, although the Italians

strong historic roots in the Italian community. It remains the favorite setting for traditional Italian weddings. Above the entrance is an inscription from the first canto of Dante's *Paradiso*: "*La Gloria Di Colui Che Tutto Muove Per L'Universo Penetra E Risplende*" (The glory of Him who

soon displaced them. San Francisco's bohemian crowd were often seen partying on the hill in clapboard shacks, until the well-to-do figured out what all the fuss was about, and they claimed the slopes of the hill for their own. Today, real estate around Telegraph Hill is among the most sought-after in all of San Francisco.

Signal Hill

Originally named *Loma Alta* (high hill) by the Spaniards, the hill has had a number of names over the years, including Goat Hill, Windmill Hill, Tin Can Hill, and Signal Hill. The last name refers to the efforts of two enterprising merchants who constructed a signaling station at the top of the hill to notify townspeople of ships approaching the harbor. Some years later, in 1849, the semaphore was replaced by the first telegraph on the West Coast, later by an observatory, and, most recently, by Coit Tower.

During the Gold Rush, Chilean prostitutes put up tents in a shanty town of South American immigrants on the hill's western slope, called Little Chile. Around the same time,

A statue of Benjamin Franklin in Washington Square.

TIP

The North Beach Festival takes place in June. If you're not in town that month, you may like to know that the SF Museum and Historical Society sponsors a self-guided walk called the Barbary Coast Trail – bronze medallions set in the sidewalk linking 20 historic sites. For more information, go to: www.sfhistory.org.

on the eastern side of the hill, a similar ramshackle cluster was known as Sydneytown, for the Australian convicts called Sydney Ducks. In February 1849, the Ducks clashed with members of a gang that called itself the Hounds, later renamed the Regulators, men who made a career of extorting local shopkeepers

The Savoy Tivoli has been in North Beach since 1906.

The park by Levi's Plaza is a tranquil spot near the Embarcadero and other very busy streets, but is tucked away and secluded.

Telegraph Hill.

An old-fashioned barber shop.

and harassing the Chileans. When a Chilean shopkeeper, in fear and frustation, eventually shot one of their members, the gang stormed Little Chile, killed and wounded several people, and raped a number of women.

The attack outraged many of the upstanding citizens, and a group of 250 vigilantes banded together to round up the worst offenders. They arrested 19 people, but only two of them were sent to prison; the others escaped with warnings. Although largely ineffective, this early display of public action set the pattern for the later Vigilance Committees of 1851 and 1856, both of which were considerably more aggressive than the earlier 250-member committee.

AROUND COIT TOWER

At the top of Telegraph Hill is **Coit Tower ㉑**. It is an elegantly simple, fluted monument, with fantastic 1930s murals inside, which were a Public Works of Art Project, the first of the New Deal federal employment programs for artists. The tower itself was constructed with funds bequeathed expressly for the purpose by the eccentric heiress Lillie Hitchcock Coit (see page 121).

Filbert steps

When you're ready to head down the hill, the **Filbert Steps ㉒** might seem a little precarious, but it is certainly worth making the effort for the sight of some of San Francisco's oldest buildings. The rambling staircase begins at the top of the hill on the southeastern side of Coit Tower at Telegraph Hill Boulevard and winds past lovely gardens, bursting with wild roses, poppies, bougainvillea, lilies, and fruit trees.

Breathtaking views break suddenly through the gaps in the foliage.

Along the Filbert Steps, narcissus and fuchsia grow among palm trees and ferns. Some of the gardens are meticulously tended and manicured, while others are unkempt and over-run with wild irises.

Levi's Plaza

The steps end on Sansome Street, directly across from **Levi's Plaza** ㉓, the corporate headquarters of Levi Strauss & Co., which opens onto a large, sunny, brick-and-granite court-yard. A small but interesting visitor's center in the main building's lobby chronicles the company's story, the development of the riveted blue denim jeans, and exhibits some of Levi's many ground-breaking adver-tising campaigns. Stores, restaurants, and cafés are nearby, while the small but perfectly manicured **Levi's Plaza** Park definitely has its devotees.

One block north of Sansome, you can climb the hillside parallel to the Filbert Steps. These lesser-traveled **Greenwich Steps** ㉔, made of steel and concrete, are nearly enveloped by the dense, lush landscape – so much so that you may forget that you're actually within the limits of a big, international city.

South of the Levi'S Plaza at the Pier 15 is the new **Exploratorium** (www.exploratorium.edu; Sat–Thu 10am–5pm, Thu also 6–10pm for adults only, Fri 10am–10pm), an inspiring interactive and educational museum with hands-on exhibits. The glass and steel obser-vatory offers amazing views of the bay. Exploratorium was founded by Frank Oppenheimer, the brother of Robert Oppenheimer, known as "the father of the atomic bomb."

Learn about Levi Strauss (1829–1902) and the history of blue jeans by visiting the company's headquarters in Levi's Plaza.

Levi's Plaza.

COIT TOWER AND TELEGRAPH HILL

Eccentric heiress Lillie Hitchcock Coit bequeathed this landmark to reflect one of her grandest passions.

The Coit Memorial Tower rises 212ft (55 meters), including its base, above 284ft (87 meter) Telegraph Hill, the site of an early telegraph station. The architect was Arthur Brown Jr, a protégé of Bernard Maybeck, creator of SF's Palace of Fine Arts. Inspiration for the tower's controversial Art Deco Modernism came from the current European vogue in power stations, most notably Sir Giles Gilbert Scott's Battersea Power Station in London. The monument, whose windows have been covered with Plexiglass, was built in 1933 with a bequest of $125,000 left by heiress Lillie Hitchcock Coit.

Murals and marvelous views

Inside Coit Tower, spectacular murals depict images and themes from American labor in the 1930s. After seeing them, visitors can take advantage of the elevator to ride to the top of the tower. On a clear day, a splendid panoramic view awaits: the bridges and hills of the city, the bay islands, farther out to Marin County, and all the way north to the forested summit of Mount Tamalpais.

The Essentials

Address: 1 Telegraph Hill; www.coittowertours.com
Telephone: 415- 249 0995
Opening Hours: daily 10am–5pm (Apr–Oct till 6pm)
Entrance Fee: charge for elevator; exterior murals and vista points are free
Transport: bus: 39; parking extremely limited

Coit Tower.

Mural detail of the San Francisco public library system; it features the names of classic and contemporary authors.

Mural artists painted for 30 hours a week and were paid up to a dollar an hour. The Public Works of Art Project was part of President Franklin D. Roosevelt's New Deal initiative, and was much reviled at the time for producing "pinko art."

This mural is a pastiche of downtown locations, including City Hall, the Main Library, and the Stock Exchange.

View across to Alcatraz from Coit Tower.

LILLIE HITCHCOCK COIT

Lillie Coit.

Lillie Coit was born at West Point Military Academy on August 23 in 1843, the daughter of an army surgeon. She came with her family to San Francisco in 1851. As a teenager – before the family moved to France for many years – she was an avid firebuff, hitching rides on outgoing fire engines and spending long hours playing cards and parading around in the uniform of Knickerbocker Engine Company No. 5, who adopted her as their mascot. Returning to the Bay Area in 1925, she spent her last four years speechless after a stroke, and left one-third of her fortune to the city in her will. The Coit Advisory Committee had the area around Telegraph Hill re-zoned after the tower was completed in 1933, so that future buildings would not exceed four stories. The tower is built on the site of the first West Coast telegraph, a semaphore completed in 1849, later replaced by an observatory that burned down in 1903.

A team of 26 artists started work on the Coit Tower murals in 1934. Together they depicted the ideals of the national New Deal program to lift the economy out of the Great Depression.

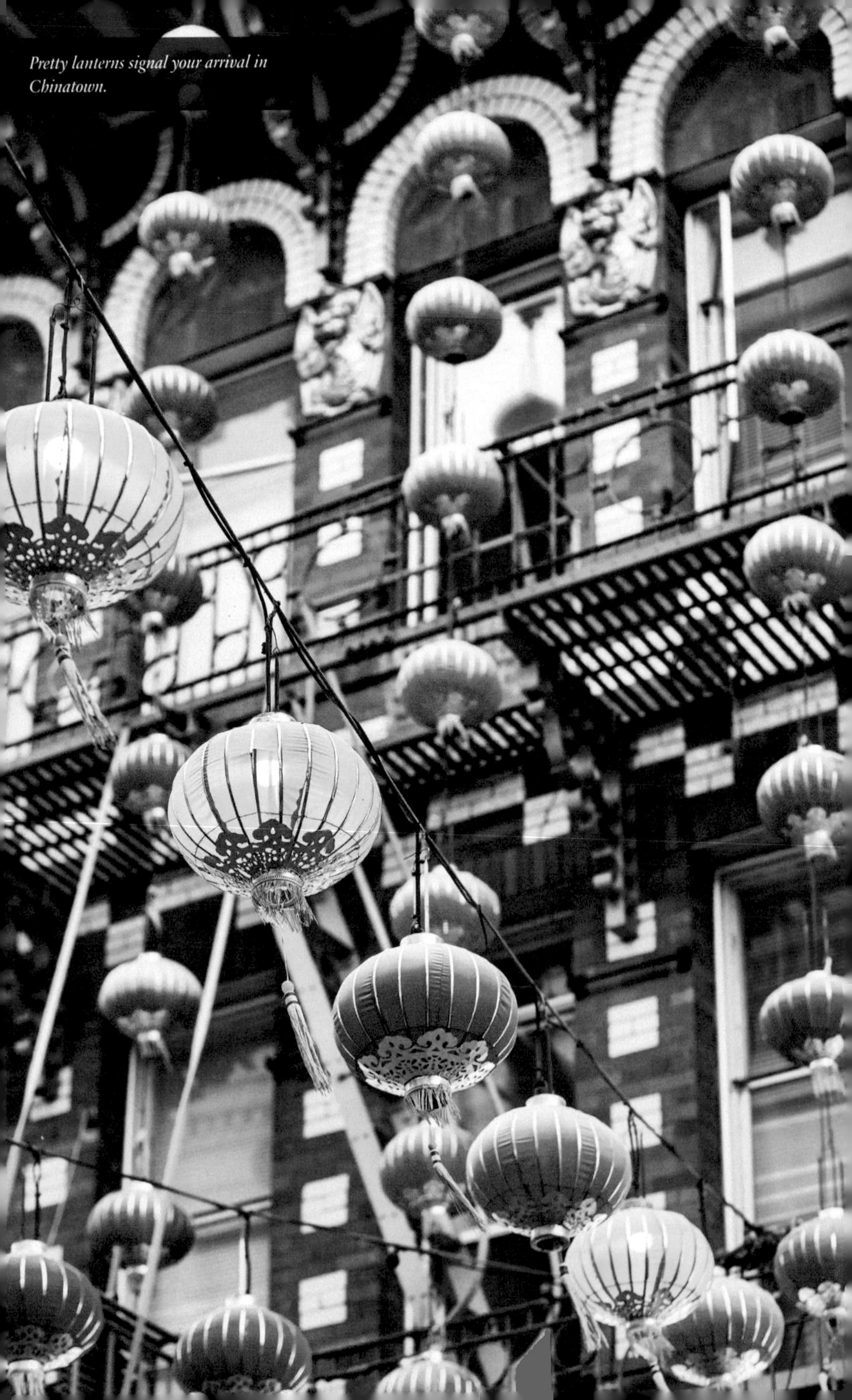

Pretty lanterns signal your arrival in Chinatown.

CHINATOWN

This city within a city is one of the largest Chinese communities outside Asia. It has temples, peaceful squares, and a lot of great dim sum.

San Francisco's **Chinatown** is the quintessential city within a city. Shop windows beckon with crowded displays of silk, porcelain, teak-wood furniture, and hand-wrought jewelry, in addition to the more usual and mainstream bric-a-brac. The entrance to this exoticism is at the corner of Bush Street and Grant Avenue, the **Chinatown Gate** ❶, a monument of jade-green tiles, crouching stone lions, dolphins, and dragons. At the top of the gate, four gilded Chinese characters in raised relief translate as: "Everything in the World is in Just Proportion." Walk a little deeper into the area and you'll find aromatic open-air markets, glitzy emporia, busy alleyways, and herbalists' stores packed with jars of roots and spices.

Fortune hunters

At the time that gold was discovered in 1848, China was undergoing a period of upheaval. The Manchu Dynasty was corrupt and weakening, floods and droughts resulted in widespread famine, and peasant rebellions were becoming commonplace. The decade-long T'ai-p'ing Rebellion in the 1850s severely reduced the population of southern China. Many Chinese people took the opportunity to leave and come to California's new mining towns in order to seek their fortunes. Of the estimated 30,000 Chinese immigrants in the state during the 1850s, half of these people made their homes in San Francisco.

Little Canton

Chinatown grew up around what was then the heart of San Francisco – Portsmouth Square – with merchants setting up shop near the major hotels and rooming houses. This area became known as Little

Main Attractions
Chinatown Gate
Grant Avenue
St Mary's Church
Stockton Street
Portsmouth Square
Chinese Culture Center
Chinese Historical Society
Tin Hou Temple
Golden Gate Fortune
  Cookie Factory

Map
Page 132

Chinese New Year.

Almost one-third of San Francisco's population is Asian.

Canton in 1850 and had 33 retail stores, 15 pharmacies (Chinese herbal cures were much in demand in a city with few doctors), and at least six restaurants serving both Chinese and non-Chinese food. The term "Chinatown" first appeared in the local press in 1853.

ALONG GRANT AVENUE

Grant Avenue ❷, named in honor of Ulysses S. Grant, extends seven blocks from Bush Street to Pacific Avenue, and is considered Chinatown's main strip, with most stores open daily until 10pm. The Sam Wo restaurant has been an institution for years but recently moved to another nearby location (www.samworestaurant.com; tel: 415-989- 8898; open until midnight, Sat–Fri till 3am, closed Tue; no credit cards) on Washington Street, just off Grant, but it is better known for its charm, cheap fare and hustling staff than top-flight cuisine.

What you save on food you could spend on drinks at the **LiPo Bar** (www.lipolounge.com) at 916 Grant, named for the famous 1st-century Chinese poet, Li Po, known for his verse celebrating the joys of drunken revelry. There is a Buddhist shrine in the corner, Chinese men playing dice for shots of Remy, and unbeatable drinks prices over the counter.

The Sun Yat-Sen statue in front of Old St Mary's Church.

This bank used to be the Chinese Telephone Company.

Old St Mary's Roman Catholic Church ❸

Address: 660 California Street (at Grant Avenue); www.oldsaintmarys.org
Telephone: 415-288-3800
Transport: bus: 1, 8, 8AX, 30, 45, 88X; cable car: California

Situated two blocks north along Grant Avenue from Chinatown Gate, this was the city's main Catholic church from 1853 to 1891. Its sturdy

KEEPING CLEAN IN EARLY CHINATOWN

According to the US census of 1890, there were 20 Chinese men in San Francisco for every woman. This was primarily because these early immigrants, or "sojourners," didn't intend to settle in the United States; their goal was to make money and return home as soon as possible – hence their remarkable entrepreneurial zeal.

In 1850, Washerwoman's Lagoon, a large watering hole at the base of Russian Hill, was the city's largest laundry. Much of the work was done by Native American and Spanish women but, because the lagoon was not large enough to serve the city, some laundry was sent by sea to Honolulu or Canton to be washed, and then returned by steamer months later. Obviously there was a need for laundries closer to hand. Little capital was required to start up such small neighborhood businesses and the Chinese entered the market with determination. Soon the price for laundering shirts plummeted from $8 a dozen to $2.

Intense concentration.

granite foundation, imported from China, and its outer walls made from New England bricks carried round Cape Horn as ship ballast, survived the devastation of the 1906 and 1989 earthquakes. Given the danger of such quakes, early plans for a steeple were rejected in favor of a bell tower, engraved with the famous biblical motto from Ecclesiastes: "Son, Observe the time and fly from evil."

In the past this area of Chinatown was known for its somewhat seedy array of brothels and gambling and opium dens, and often became the setting for violent outbursts between Chinese and other residents of San Francisco. In the late 1800s, a number of attempts were made to clean up the area. All failed, until the fire that came in the wake of the 1906 earthquake destroyed most of the commercial establishments.

Squares and statues

The area surrounding the church, **St Mary's Square ❹**, rests on top of a large underground parking garage and, in the morning, is often filled

with people moving in balletic slow motion as they practice t'ai chi.

An impressive 14ft (4 meter) granite structure, the **Sun Yat-Sen statue**, named for the first president of modern China, stands at the square's northeast corner. Dr Sun lived in Chinatown briefly in 1910 and published a newspaper. The 1938 sculpture was by Beniamino Bufano, who also created the statue of St Francis at Taylor and Beach streets, and several other sculptures around the city (often of whimsical animals).

Day-to-day life in Chinatown is mainly conducted on **Stockton Street ❺**, where most of the produce and fish markets, herbal pharmacies, butchers, shops, and bakeries are found. Spices are also sold here, in large import-export shops.

Another important meeting place is **Portsmouth Square ❻** just to the east, the center of San Francisco in the Gold Rush era and the site in the past of rallies, riots, and hangings, as well as today's romantic trysts and countless family picnics. The square is popular with the older Chinese men who play mah jong at small

Chinatown Gate.

Many Chinese temples are located at the top of buildings. This is said to put them closer to heaven and the gods.

Grant Avenue.

tables dotted around the square. Many of these men grew up in the shadow of the 1924 Immigration Act: unable to find wives, they grew accustomed to bachelorhood.

East of the square, at 750 Kearny Street, is a hotel with a difference: on the third floor is the **Chinese Culture Center** (www.c-c-c.org; tel: 415-986-1822; guided tours available), a valuable research facility for the study of Chinese life in the Western world. Shows are held in its art galleries and entertainment is provided in its own theater.

North of Portsmouth Square is **Buddha's Universal Church** ❽ (720 Washington Street; tel: 415-982-6116; www.bucsf.com), which was built entirely by volunteers. Once the site of a nightclub, the building was bought by church members in 1951 for just $500, only to have the city condemn it as structurally unsound. Volunteers rebuilt it, and the temple was dedicated in 1963. Free tours of the church's altar, library, and rooftop garden are available (2nd and 4th Sun of the month); call for details.

Farther along, at **743 Washington Street** is where the *California Star*, the city's first newspaper, was printed

Shopping in Chinatown.

in 1846. Currently, this attractive, pagoda-like building is a bank.

Chinese Historical Society ❾

Address: 965 Clay Street (at Powell Street); www.chsa.org
Telephone: 415-391-1188
Opening Hours: Tue–Fri noon–5pm, Sat 11am–4pm
Entrance Fee: donations
Transport: bus: 1, 8, 8AX, 30, 45, 88X

The society has a library and a small museum for people wanting general information about Chinese-American history. Its collection includes Gold Rush artifacts, a papier-mâché dragon's head, and an altar from a Napa Valley Taoist temple.

Immigration problems

In 1882, Congress passed the Chinese Exclusion Act, suspending Chinese immigration for 10 years. The act insured that foreign-born wives and children of Chinese-American citizens would be the only Chinese allowed to enter the country. The Exclusion Act was reinforced by the Scott Act of 1888 and, later, by the Immigration Act of 1924. As a result of these measures, the Chinese population in the United States dropped from 132,000

in 1882 to 62,000 by 1920. (Today, the Chinese population in the US is approximately 3.8 million).

Still, from the 1880s to the 1920s, Chinatown expanded from its six-block length and two-block width until it covered eight city blocks, from Bush to Broadway, and three blocks from Kearny to Powell. The area was rebuilt after the 1906 earthquake and became a thriving community, its streets overflowing with traffic and tourists.

After the United States and China became allies during World War II, President Franklin D. Roosevelt signed a measure in 1943 repealing the Exclusion acts, allowing Chinese people to become American citizens and setting a modest yearly quota for Chinese immigration. San Francisco's Chinatown began to flourish.

Settling disputes

An important part of Chinatown's commerce and community is made up of The Six Companies, also known as the **Chinese Consolidated Benevolent Association** (www.ccbausa. org). This far-reaching organization, formed around the turn of the 20th century, became the central government of Chinatown, and acted under a coordinating board of control made up of representatives from disparate organizations, community groups, and clubs. The Six Companies act as a sort of embassy to Chinese visitors, arbitrate disputes within the community, and operate one of the country's largest Chinese language schools, as well as playing a major role in organizing the massive and colorful Chinese New Year's Parade.

The Chinese New Year is celebrated, usually in February, with a noisy three-hour parade downtown and into the very heart of Chinatown. It is tailed by a huge 60ft (18 meter) dragon, often imported from Hong

Grant Avenue and Bush Street is the heart of Chinatown.

Even street lamps are decorated.

Fortune cookies are not part of Chinese food culture. In 1993, a US-based company began producing them in China for the first time, marketing them as "Genuine American Fortune Cookies."

Golden Gate Fortune Cookie Factory.

Kong and carried by at least a dozen men. The dragon is on display every year after the parade, usually at 383 Grant Avenue. Firecrackers explode everywhere during New Year's week.

Temple tour

Temples in Chinatown representing Taoism, Buddhism, and other Asian religions function not only as places of worship but also as providers of community services such as schools, meeting rooms, dormitories, and eating places for the elderly and poor. Most of these temples are located at the tops of buildings – this is in order to place them closer to heaven and the gods. The temples tend to be lavishly decorated with hanging lanterns and other ornaments, and are heavy with the scent of the exotic incense burned in ceremonial offerings.

An alley that runs parallel to Grant Avenue between Clay and Washington streets, **Waverly Place** ⑩ is what might be called the "real" Chinatown – the Chinatown that most visitors don't see. Here, stores sell lychee wine, pickled ginger, rice

threads, dried lotus, and powdered antler horns, reputed to restore male virility. Traditional Chinese jade and terracotta tiles mark the edges of apartment roofs. Waverly is often called the "Street of Painted Balconies."

Tin Hou Temple ⑪

Address: 125 Waverly Place, Fourth Floor (at Clay Street)
Entrance Fee: donations welcome
Transport: bus: 1, 8, 8AX, 30, 45, 88X
Tin Hou, Queen of the Heavens and Goddess of the Seven Seas, is said to protect travelers, sailors, artists, and prostitutes; this is believed to be the country's oldest Chinese temple. The most popular deity is Kuan Yin, a goddess of mercy, or "one who hears prayers." There's a temple dedicated to her in **Spofford Alley**.

From the Tin Hou temple, walk south on Waverly to Clay, turn right and walk west one block to 855 Stockton to see another temple (this one with fine woodcarvings) called the **Kong Chow Temple** ⑫ (daily).

Going north on Stockton will lead you toward tiny **Ross Alley**, where the fortune cookie is said to have been invented (although another claimant to fortune-cookie fame is the Japanese Tea Garden in Golden Gate Park).

Golden Gate Fortune Cookie Factory ⑬

Address: 56 Ross Alley (at Jackson Street)
Telephone: 415-781-3956
Opening Hours: daily 8am–6pm
Entrance Fee: charge
Transport: bus: 8, 10, 12, 30, 30X
These tiny treats are still made here. In the blink of an eye, a worker pulls a hot cookie off a rotating press and folds a fortune inside. You can buy samples hot off the press to eat as you walk around. Today's fortune cookies include adult versions with naughty, X-rated messages inside, as well as cookies containing lottery numbers or quotations from the Bible.

Tin Hou Temple on Waverly Place.

UNION SQUARE TO THE FINANCIAL DISTRICT

The highest concentration of shopping in the city is found near Union Square and the Theater District. Both are conveniently close to the high-earning brokers and bankers of the Financial District.

Though San Francisco is anything but an old-fashioned village, **Union Square** ⓮ still fulfills to some extent the role that plazas and public squares once played in small towns. All walks of life gather in and around here: socialites find their gowns for debutante balls, the business-minded plot their corporate moves, residents come to see plays and to shop, and tourists board a cable car for a ride over Nob Hill or to visit the city's main Visitor Information Center.

San Francisco Visitor Information Center

Address: 900 Market Street; www.sanfrancisco.travel
Telephone: 415-391-2000
Opening Hours: Mon–Fri 9am–5pm, Sat–Sun 9am–3pm, Nov–Apr closed Sun
Transport: bus: 6, 7, 7X, 8, 8AX, 88X, 27, 31, 45; metro: J, K, L, M, N; BART: Powell

Below Market Street in the Hallidie Plaza, the center provides useful information, in 14 languages. In addition to free Muni maps, there are brochures on dining, accommodations, tours, and transportation for the city and nearby destinations.

Bordered by Geary, Post, Powell, and Stockton streets, the square

anchors an active commercial area with a colorful history. First deeded for public use in 1850, Union Square acquired its name during the Civil War years, when pro-Union sympathizers rallied here. At the center of the square is a 90ft (27 meter) Corinthian column, topped with a bronze Victory commemorating Commodore George Dewey's successful Manila Bay campaign during 1898's Spanish-American War. Neither the 1906 earthquake nor the 1942 installation of the world's first

Main Attractions
Visitor Information Center
Maiden Lane
Westfield San Francisco Center
Embarcadero
Ferry Building
Embarcadero Center
Transamerica Pyramid
Federal Reserve Bank

Map
Page 132

Union Square.

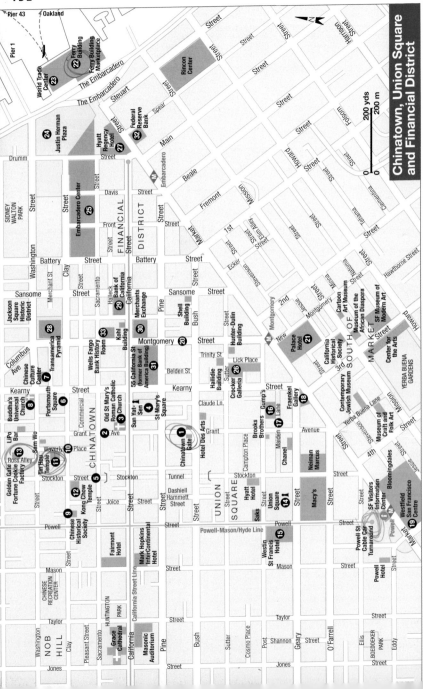

Chinatown, Union Square
and Financial District

0   200 yds
0   200 m

N

Pier 43 — Oakland
Pier 1

World Trade Center **23**
Ferry Building **22**
Ferry Building Marketplace

The Embarcadero

Justin Herman Plaza **24**

Rincon Center

Hyatt Regency Hotel **27**
Federal Reserve Bank **32**

Steuart Street
Spear Street
Main Street
Beale Street
Mission Street
Fremont Street

SIDNEY WALTON PARK

Embarcadero Center **25**

Davis Street
Front Street
Battery Street
Sansome Street

FINANCIAL DISTRICT

Market Street
1st Street
Elm Alley
Ecker Street

Jackson Square Historic District

Merchant St

Bank of California **29**
Halleck
Merchants Exchange **30**
Shell Building

Montgomery Street
New Montgomery Street
2nd Street
Minna Street

Columbus Ave
Chinese Culture Center **7**
Transamerica Pyramid **28**
Wells Fargo Bank History Room **33**
Kohl Building
Montgomery **20**

Pine Street
Bush Street

Hunter-Dulin Building

Palace Hotel **21**
California Historical Society

Cartoon Art Museum
Museum of the African Diaspora
SF Museum of Modern Art

SOUTH OF MARKET

Kearny
Buddha's Universal Church
Portsmouth Square **6**
Old St Mary's Roman Catholic Church **3**
Sun Yat-Sen **4**
St Mary's Square
55 California St (former Bank of America Building) **31**

Trinity St
Belden St
Lick Place **26**
Crocker Galleria
Hallidie Building
Claude Ln.

Center for the Arts
YERBA BUENA GARDENS

Contemporary Jewish Museum
3rd Street

LiPo Bar
Sam Wo
Tin Hou Temple **11**
Waverly Place **10**
Sun Wo
Chinatown Gate **1**
Hotel Des Arts **2**

Gump's **16**
Maiden Lane **17**
Frankel Gallery **18**

Museum of Craft and Folk Art
Yerba Buena Lane
Stevenson Street

Golden Gate Fortune Cookie Factory **13**
Ross Alley
Stockton

CHINATOWN

Brooks Brothers
Campton Place
Chanel
Neiman Marcus

4th Street

Chinese Historical Society **9**
Kong Chow Temple **12**

Tunnel
Dashiell Hammett Street

UNION SQUARE

Hyatt Hotel
Union Square **10 1**
Saks

Macy's

SF Visitors Information Center **i**
Westfield San Francisco Centre **19**
Bloomingdales
Powell M

Fairmont Hotel
Mark Hopkins InterContinental Hotel

Powell-Mason/Hyde Line

Westin St Francis Hotel **15**

Powell St Cable Car Turnaround

Powell Hotel

CHINESE RECREATION CENTER

California Street Line

HUNTINGTON PARK

NOB HILL

Grace Cathedral
Masonic Auditorium

Washington
Clay
Sacramento
California
Pine
Bush
Sutter
Post
Geary
O'Farrell
Ellis
Eddy

Jones Street
Taylor Street
Mason Street
Powell Street
Stockton Street
Grant Ave
Kearny Street

Cosmo Place
Shannon Street

BOEDDEKER PARK

Union Square has a large number of hotels.

Take the historic F line for a ride through history. The cars have all been restored by volunteers, and are often called a museum on wheels.

underground parking lot-cum-bomb shelter rattled the venerable column.

A renovation changed Union Square from a hangout for the homeless to a sleek spot for visitors to take a break or sip lattes in between shopping excursions.

Shop and snooze

A good place to watch the passing street parade is from the oversized steps. From this vantage point, you'll notice the bronze nude atop the memorial to President William McKinley, by sculptor Robert Aitken. As his model, Aitken used a teenager, Alma de Bretteville, who became famous at 22 for marrying Adolph Spreckels, the much older and well-to-do president of the San Francisco Parks Commission. But Union Square is best known for the stores and hotels that have grown up around it.

Fronting the west side is the **Westin St Francis Hotel** ⓯ (http://westinstfrancis.com), which since 1904 has provided lodgings for countless dignitaries and celebrities. The plaza of the more modern **Hyatt on Union Square** (http://sanfrancisco.grand.hyatt.com) is adorned with a Ruth Asawa fountain that really does embody San Francisco. The bronze friezes of typical city scenes were cast in molds made from bread dough by some 250 schoolchildren and other local residents.

An important element here is three of the big department stores: **Macy's** (www1.macys.com), **Saks Fifth Avenue** (www.saksfifthavenue.com), and **Neiman Marcus** (www.neimanmarcus.com). The latter is crowned by an exquisite stained-glass rotunda

Putting a shine on the neighborhood.

salvaged from the City of Paris, San Francisco's first department store and the site's original occupant.

Around the corner from Union Square at 135 Post Street is **Gump's**  (www.gumps.com). It started years ago by selling frames and mirrors to bars and bordellos during the Gold-Rush era, then moved upscale to the present-day store, which is more akin to a museum selling the best in jade, glassware, oriental rugs, silks, and antiques. Also on Post Street are haute couture designer shops like Prada and Chanel.

MAIDEN LANE ⑰

Running east to west parallel to Post Street is **Maiden Lane**, a narrow pedestrian-only alleyway lined with interesting stores and cafés – many with outdoor seating – that are perfect for a quiet lunchtime snack.

As well as theater, the Union Square area is known for its visual arts. The **Fraenkel Gallery** ⑱ (49 Geary Street; https://fraenkelgallery.com; tel: 415-981-2661; free) is among the best of the many galleries on the surrounding streets.

Maiden Lane is perfect for drinks and alfresco dining.

The San Francisco Center – shopping heaven.

Westfield San Francisco Centre ⑲

Address: 865 Market Street; www.westfield.com/sanfrancisco
Telephone: 415-512-6776
Opening Hours: Mon–Sat 10am–8.30pm, Sun 11am–7pm
Transport: bus: 5, 6, 7, 9, 21, 31, 66; streetcar: F; metro: J, K, L, M, N, T

This beautiful, newly renovated shopping center at Market and 5th streets is a nine-story vertical mall that spans most of the block on 5th

The shops along Maiden Lane.

Street between Market and Mission streets and has hundreds of stores. These include the luxury department stores Nordstrom and Bloomingdale's, an array of dining options, and a nine-screen movie theater. It inhabits the old Emporium space, a San Francisco retail legend. Steps were taken to ensure that the Emporium's stunning 102ft (31 meter) -wide skylit dome and the original Art Deco escalators were saved and faithfully restored.

Despite its commercial bias, the flavor of old San Francisco can still be found. **Montgomery Street** ⑳, east of Post Street, is hallowed in city lore. Sam Brannan ran the length of Montgomery Street when he announced the discovery of gold in 1848, and soon the boulevard was overrun with '49ers. Mark Twain found inspiration in a local fireman called Tom Sawyer. Black Bart, Lotta Crabtree, Jack London, and Jack Kerouac have all paced the avenue.

THE FINANCIAL DISTRICT

The original '49ers sailed into San Francisco Bay, dropped anchor, and set off north to pursue their dream of striking gold. It wasn't long before the city's original shoreline began to burgeon, contributing to the birth of today's soaring **Financial District**. Brokers, bankers, and insurance agents now pursue wealth on several acres of landfill on and around Montgomery Street. The interiors of many of these buildings are just as interesting as their facades, and some are open for public viewing.

The American Conservatory Theater on Geary Street was the first theater to win a Tony award for the quality of its training.

The Embarcadero rings the bayside edge of the city.

Old-world opulence

The **Garden Court** of the lovely **Palace Hotel** ㉑ (www.sfpalace.com; 2 New Montgomery; tel: 415-512-1111) is replete with old-world opulence. Its magnificent dining room, opened in 1909, is surrounded by 16 marble Ionic columns and an intricate iron framework that supports a leaded glass skylight 48ft (15 meters) above the floor, in addition to 10 crystal chandeliers.

Art Deco, Romanesque, and Modern are just a few of the styles that contribute to the architectural kaleidoscope of the Financial District, but the city's older facades also provide countless surprises (see margin).

THE EMBARCADERO

An important component of the Financial District is the **Embarcadero**, an area built on land mostly reclaimed from the sea. Condominiums, restaurants, and stores close by give the area its economic vitality.

The heart is the **Ferry Building** ㉒ at Market and Embarcadero. Opening in 1898, it also survived the earthquake of 1906, with no more consequence than a stopped clock – the first time it had ceased to tick. The 230ft (70 meter) tower is a near copy of the campanile of Seville's cathedral. Before the construction of the bay bridges, the Ferry Building was the second-busiest passenger terminal in the world, and even now ferries from here carry commuters to the Bay Area.

Ferry Building Marketplace

Address: One Ferry Building; www.ferrybuildingmarketplace.com
Telephone: 415-983-8030
Opening Hours: Mon–Fri 10am–6pm, Sat 9am–6pm, Sun 11am–5pm; tours and tastings Tue and Sat noon
Entrance Fee: free
Transport: bus: 6, 7X, 9, 14, 14X, 21, 31; streetcar: F ferries to Bay Area towns

This rapturously received marketplace of food merchants and eateries is a popular dining destination (see page 82).

The Embarcadero is more than just the Ferry Building Marketplace, however. Covarrubias's mural colorfully lights the ramp to the **World Trade Center** (www.wtc-sf.com); the mural was preserved from the 1939 Golden Gate International Exposition. Walking south on **Justin Herman Plaza** ㉔, leads to Steuart Street and the emerging **City Front District**.

Looming above is the **Embarcadero Center** (http://embarcaderocenter.com), a massive retail and office complex. Its only rival for such variety in the Financial District is the **Crocker Galleria** shopping arcade, between Post and Sutter streets, which straddles the divide between Union Square and the Financial District.

The Garden Court's modern architectural counterpart is the Embarcadero's immense **Hyatt Regency Hotel** ㉗ (Embarcadero 5; tel: 415-788-1234; http://sanfrancisco.regency.hyatt.com), a microcosm where guests don't even need to leave the building to enjoy nature: the indoor atrium is

The Ferry Building clock tower.

20 stories high and houses more than 100 trees and 15,000 hanging plants.

Birds flit about the overhead skylight, while 170ft (52 meters) below, visitors sink into the plush conversation pits that line the lobby. Even Charles Perry's geometric sculpture – rising only four stories above the pool of water that reflects it – is huge.

City within a city

John Portman envisioned a "city within a city" when he designed the Embarcadero Center – and it is both well planned and uniform, and is also very much self-contained. The aforementioned plaza is an interwoven complex of restaurants and retail stores and a comedy club, all linked by pedestrian bridges and outdoor courtyards filled with displays of sculpture.

Exiting the plaza at the northwest corner, walk five blocks up Clay to the corner of Montgomery where the **Transamerica Pyramid** ❷ (the observation deck not open to the public; www.transamerica.com) commands attention because of its size and unusual shape. Its appeal was debated when it was first constructed in 1972, but now

Running around The Embarcadero Center.

almost everyone seems to agree that its singular shape is welcome on the San Franciscan skyline. At ground level, flanking the building, may be one of its more surprising features – a grove of redwood trees, something rarely seen in urban developments.

Wall Street West

Turning left on Clay Street and three blocks down Sansome is the **Bank of California** ❷ (400 California Street), the district's oldest bank. Check out its magnificent entrance hall.

Crossing California Street and heading west leads to another notable

The exterior of the Embarcadero Center.

The attractive façade of the Pacific Gas and Electric Company.

marker of San Francisco's history, the **Merchants Exchange** ③⓪ (465 California Street; www.merchantsexchange building.com). Its heyday was early in the 20th century, when excited traders awaited news of arriving merchant ships – relayed from towers along the coast. Inside are fine paintings by the Irish artist William Coulter (1849–1936). The two men's clubs within the building, the Julia Morgan Ballroom (http://juliamorganballroom. com) and the Merchants Exchange Club (http://mxclubsf.com) have been revamped and they host lavish events, weddings and parties.

The smell of money

One block west, between Montgomery and Kearney, is **55 California Street** ③① , the former Bank of America headquarters. On the way out, take a second look at the building's exterior and notice the red carnelian granite facade and the outdoor plaza's centerpiece sculpture *Banker's Heart*, a huge stone of polished granite.

The Embarcadero extends from the Financial District to the Bay Bridge and beyond.

A few blocks east is the **Federal Reserve Bank** ③② (101 Market Street; www.frbsf.org; tel: 415-227 4133). *The Fed Center: Exploring our Nation's Central Bank* is a permanent installation at the San Francisco Fed, designed to teach the public about the functions of the US Central Bank through a series of guided hands-on and visually engaging experiences. Whimsical and thought-provoking elements in the exhibit include giant iconic representations of financial concepts, such as a free-floating sphere, a suspended safe, and a 14ft (4 meter) tilting chair. Also featured is a newly designed Currency Collection. Group tours, by appointment only, can be scheduled Mon–Thur at 9.30am or 1pm (90 min).

Leaving the building at the California exit, head west back toward Montgomery Street. Turn left to cross California Street and go north one block to the **Wells Fargo Bank History Room** ③③ (www.wellsfargo. com or www.wellsfargohistory.com; tel: 415-396-2619; Mon–Fri 9am–5pm; free), which offers a look at some hefty gold nuggets as well as insights into San Francisco's financial and Gold Rush history. There are banking articles, miners' equipment, and dioramas. A fine **Wells Fargo Overland Stage**, once used on the coaching trails of the Old West and for many years the bank's logo, forms the centerpiece of the museum.

The Transamerica Pyramid was a controversial design when built in 1972.

CIVIC CENTER TO SOMA

Dignified architecture and the Opera House define Civic Center on one side of Market Street, while innovative galleries, specialist museums, and good restaurants characterize SoMa on the other.

San Francisco's collection of historic public buildings is the **Civic Center**, a downtown complex bisected by Van Ness Avenue, the city's widest street. Arthur Brown, Jr (1874–1957), the most celebrated architect of his era, was responsible for many of the Bay Area's outstanding buildings, including Sproul Hall on the University of California's Berkeley campus.

Architectural ensemble

Brown's City Hall, and the adjoining San Francisco War Memorial and Performing Arts Center (SFWMPAC), have been acclaimed by one historian as the greatest architectural ensemble in America.

City Hall ❶

Address: 1 Dr Carlton B. Goodlett Place (Polk Street at McAllister Street); http://sfgov.org/cityhall/
Telephone: 415-554-6068
Opening Hours: Mon–Fri 8am–8pm free tours
Transport: bus: 5, 5R, 6, 7, 19, 21, 47, 49, 7X; streetcar: F; metro: all lines; BART: all trains

Built in 1914, City Hall is a magnificent Beaux Arts structure, honeycombed with municipal offices running from a central rotunda. The

building sits where Van Ness crosses McAllister Street, and was where gay rights activist Harvey Milk and Mayor George Moscone were shot by former city supervisor Dan White in 1978.

City Hall was again the scene of controversy when same-sex marriages were performed here in 2004.

The **Veterans Auditorium Building ❷** (which houses the **Herbst Theater**; tel: 415-392-4400) and The **War Memorial Opera House ❸** (tel: 415-864-3330 for box office), which sit opposite City Hall, make up the

Main Attractions
City Hall
War Memorial Opera House
Asian Art Museum
Museum of Modern Art
Yerba Buena Gardens
Museum of the African Diaspora
Contemporary Jewish Museum
Tenderloin Museum

Map
Pages 142, 144

The atrium of the Public Library.

TIP

The Public Library at Civic Center has unlimited wireless access, but so do nearly all cafés in the city. For more information see: http://sfgov.org/sfc/sanfranciscowifi.

Farmer's Market at the United Nations Plaza.

largest performing art center in the United States – the **San Francisco War Memorial and Performing Arts Center** (http://sfwmpac.org; tours Mon 10am–2pm; tel: 415-552-8338). The opera house was the birthplace of the United Nations and has a drama or two of a different sort. For many years a group of about 50 flower throwers – mostly men – known as the Opera Standees Association was tolerated by, but not formally associated with, the San Francisco Opera. "Opera-throwers" are fans who hurl bouquets at beloved divas during encores. It requires a certain skill to send flowers 35ft (10 meters) over the heads of the orchestra to land perfectly at the desired singer's feet. One successful "member" hurled some 300 bouquets in a single season, each hitting its mark.

Flanking Arthur Brown's Opera House and the Veterans Auditorium is the **State Building** ❹ and, mirroring its curving exterior, the lavish **Louise**

M. Davies Symphony Hall ❺, home of the San Francisco Symphony (and a part of the SFWMPAC). The architects Skidmore, Owings & Merrill also designed the State Building. Just north of here on Turk Street is St. John Coltrane Church (www.coltranechurch.org) – possibly the only church in the world dedicated to a jazz musician (even though John Coltrane had no connection with the church). Located for many years at 1286 Fillmore Street in the Central Neighborhoods, in 2016 it moved to 2097 Turk Street. Note that the Western Addition is still an area where you should stay alert when walking around.

Asian Art Museum ❻

Address: 200 Larkin Street (at McAllister Street); www.asianart.org
Telephone: 415-581-3500
Opening Hours: Tue–Sun 10am–5pm, Thur until 9pm
Entrance Fee: charge

Civic Center

Artefact on display at the Museum of Asian Art.

Transport: bus: 5, 5R, 6, 7, 7X, 16, 19, 21, 47, 49; streetcar: F; metro: all lines; BART: all trains

At the northeastern corner of the Civic Center buildings is the old Public Library, built in 1916, which now houses this museum. It began as a wing of the de Young Memorial Museum in Golden Gate Park in 1966. Thirty years later it moved to a fine Beaux Arts building as part of a Civic Center revitalization project. The acclaimed Italian architect Gae Aulenti converted the building into a museum.

The museum houses one of the world's largest collections of Asian art, and contains not only Chinese art, but Indian, Persian, Southeast Asian, Korean, and Japanese objects. There are over 15,000 pieces in the collection (with about 3,000 showing at any one time), spanning 6,000 years. Highlights of the permanent collection include the oldest dated Chinese Buddha in the world, from AD 336.

The **Public Library** ❼ is next door at Larkin and Grove streets; to the east are the **Federal Building** ❽ and **United Nations Plaza** ❾. This triangular space, in the area between Fulton, Hyde, and Market streets, commemorates the birth of the United Nations in 1945 when the charter was signed.

The last structure in the Civic Center complex is the **Bill Graham Civic Auditorium** ❿ at 99 Grove Street (www.billgrahamcivicauditorium.com; tel: 415-624-8900), named for an irascible impresario responsible for many of the city's rock concerts in the 1960s.

THE TENDERLOIN

East of Civic Center toward Union Square and bordered by Market and Sutter streets is **The Tenderloin** ⓫, or the "loin" as some locals call it. Known in the past as a den for drugs, crime, grime, and the shadier sides of life, the neighborhood also has unique architecture, wonderful and inexpensive ethnic restaurants, and clean, affordable hotels just a hair off the beaten path. But don't be fooled

The German opera Die tote Stadt, performed at the War Memorial Opera House in Civic Center.

TIP

For an uplifting and unforgettable experience, check out a Sunday service (9am and 11am) at the Glide Memorial Church and worship with the Glide Ensemble, a 140-member choir that sings and sways to blues, jazz, gospel, and spirituals every week.

by the hip hotels and bars, as this neighborhood can still be dangerous: during the day keep your eyes open, and at night be extra alert.

The Tenderloin is not without its gems, however. Crowds line up most nights to hear live music in the historic **Great American Music Hall** (tel: 415-885-0750; www.slimspresents.com), once a Barbary Coast bordello with a voluptuous rococo interior, now a venue hosting musicians from all over the world.

The former brothel is by the Mitchell Brothers O'Farrell Theater (http://ofarrell.com) – the city's most notorious strip club. It was created on the lot of a former car dealership and has been open since 1969, minus a few hiccups for trafficking obscenity and the shooting of Artie by his brother Jim – a story made into a 1996 TV movie, *Blood Brothers*.

The new addition is the **Tenderloin Museum** (www.tenderloinmuseum.org; Tue–Sun 10am–5pm; walking tours Tue–Sat at 11am and 2pm, Sun

Art at Yerba Buena Gardens.

at 2pm, night tours at 6.30pm) at 398 Eddy Street, presenting the history of the neighborhood and the role of the LGBT activism and countercultural movements in this area.

On the corner of Taylor and Ellis streets at **Glide Memorial Methodist**

Kid playing on Chestnut Street, the heart of the Marina's commercial district.

Heart of SoMa

New Montgomery Street
Jessie Street
Howard Street
Hawthorne Street
Folsom Street
Annie St
Natoma St
Kaplan Ln
Museum of the African Diaspora **17**
Museum of California Historical Society **18**
SF Museum of Modern Art **13**
3rd Street
Market
Center for the Arts **15**
Contemporary Jewish Museum **19**
YERBA BUENA GARDENS **14**
Moscone Center North
Moscone Convention Center South **12**
Lapu Lapu St
Bonifacio Street
Rizal Lane
South Beach
Mission Street
Yerba Buena Lane
ESPLANADE **16**
Dr Martin Luther King Jr Memorial
Metreon Sony Entertainment Center
Childrens' Creativity Museum
Carousel
Harrison Street
4th Street
Clementina
Folsom Street
Shipley
Clara Street
Stevenson Street
Jessie Street
Minna Street
Moscone Center West
SOUTH OF
Tehama Street
SF Visitors Information Center
Westfield San Francisco Centre
Powell
MARKET
5th Street
Market
Stevenson Street
Jessie St
US Mint **20**
Mint St
Mary Street
Minna St
Natoma St
Howard Street
Folsom Street
Street
0 200 yds
0 200 m

Ukulele exhibit at the San Francisco Museum of Craft and Folk Art.

Church (http://glide.org/church) the charismatic Reverend Cecil Williams and his devoted staff and volunteers have been feeding and caring for the poor and homeless for more than 40 years. They have been featured in the moving film *The Pursuit of Happiness* featuring Will Smith.

Also, don't miss the **Shooting Gallery** (886 Greary Street; www.shooting galleryf.com; tel: 415-931-1500), a noteworthy place that showcases offbeat art exhibits, and **Shalimar** (www. shalimarsf.com), one of the city's best Indian/Pakistani restaurants. There are lots of Vietnamese, Cambodian, and Indian eateries, many great diners, and tons of neighborhood gay bars and colorful dives.

SOMA

On the other side of Market Street from Civic Center is a very different kind of neighborhood. Whereas Civic Center is stately, dignified, and elegant, **SoMa** is one of the city's most forward-looking districts. Before San Francisco handed over its working waterfront to neighboring Oakland, the wide blocks stretching south of Market Street to the bay were filled with factories and warehouses.

TIP

The largest city-owned solar installation in the US sits on top of SoMa's Moscone Convention Center. San Francisco was named one of the Top 10 greenest cities in America, in a survey conducted by The Green Guide.

Zeum is a visual arts facility with an animation studio.

The Yerba Buena Gardens often host free concerts during the summer months.

The Contemporary Jewish Museum incorporates part of the Jessie Street Power Substation into its design.

In the evenings another aspect of the area came to life, as the city's original gay neighborhood. Unlike the waterfront activity, the happening gay nightlife still thrives, particularly near Folsom and 11th streets, which the "leather community" calls home. The dot-comers of the 1990s took advantage of the departed docks, turning the empty warehouses into fashionable live-work lofts. They rechristened the dreary South of Market area "SoMa," a chic neighborhood of museums, clubs, and restaurants, all fueled by artistic and entrepreneurial energy.

After the millennium, the gentrification extended east, with the opening of baseball's AT&T Park, and new, cool neighborhoods like South Beach and Dogpatch (see page 196) enjoying the subsequent prosperity

The largest structure in the heart of SoMa is the **Moscone Convention Center** ⓬ (www.moscone.com), home to most of the major conventions held in the city each month. Above Moscone Center South is a well-funded **Children's Creativity Museum**, (http://creativity.org; Tue–Sun 10am–4pm, carousel until 5pm) is a great place for those travelling with kids. It has its own animation and production studios where young ones can make and star in their own music videos.

San Francisco Museum of Modern Art ⓭

Address: 151 3rd Street; www.sfmoma.org
Telephone: 415-357-4000
Opening Hours: galleries daily 10am–5pm, Thu till 9pm; public spaces daily till 9pm
Entrance Fee: charge
Transport: bus: 2, 5, 7, 8, 8AX, 8BX, 88X, 14, 14R, 30, 45; streetcar: F; metro: all lines; bart: all trains

SoMa's biggest attraction is the fantastic San Francisco Museum of Modern Art with its collection of 15,000 works, ranging from paintings and sculpture to media arts (see page 148).

West of the Moscone Center is **Yerba Buena Gardens** ⓮ (http://yerbabuenagardens.com), a 22-acre (9-hectare) site occupying the entire block between 3rd and 4th streets. Yerba Buena is an arts and entertainment complex interspersed with tranquil patches of greenery.

International touring companies give performances at Yerba Buena's theater, in the **Center for the Arts** ⓯ (www.ybca.org; tel: 415-978-2700; Tue–Sun 11am–6pm), where exhibitions, movie showings, dance, and other events are staged.

The arts complex overlooks the **Esplanade**, a pretty downtown park that includes terrace cafés, an outdoor performance area with lawn seating for 5,000, and a walk-through waterfall leading to the **Dr Martin Luther King, Jr. Memorial**.

Next to the Esplanade is an entertainment complex called the **Metreon** ⓰, (www.amctheatres.com and www.shoppingmetreon.com) with a 15-screen movie theater, an imax theater, an decent food court, and interactive exhibits of all things bright and shiny. It is at 4th and Mission.

San Francisco Museum of Modern Art.

Mission Street, might, in fact, be the city's most cultural thoroughfare, with five museums around its periphery. At No. 685, near the Center for the Arts, is the **Museum of the African Diaspora** ⑰ (www.moadsf.org; tel: 415-358-7200; Sun noon–5pm, Wed–Sat 11am–6pm), which explores the idea of Africa as the birthplace of humanity. On the other side of the street is the downtown branch of the **California Historical Society** ⑱ (www.californiahistoricalsociety.org; 678 Mission Street; tel: 415-357-1848; Tue–Sun 11am–5pm).

Another signature building is the new home of the **Contemporary Jewish Museum** ⑲ (415 655 7800; www.thecjm.org; Thu–Tue 11am–5pm; until 8pm on Thu - half-price on Thu after 5pm; free first Tue of the month). Located in an old power substation, the museum explores Jewish culture and history through a variety of ever-changing expositions. The dark-blue stainless steel cube-like building changes color depending on the time of day, weather and vantage point. It has three program spaces, designed by internationally renowned architect Daniel Liebeskind, awarded the winning design of the Freedom Tower at the site of the World Trade Center in New York.

A pedestrian alley of attractions, stores, and cafés that links Mission and Market streets, is called **Yerba Buena Lane**.

At the western end of SoMa is the imposing facade of the former **US Mint**. It is surrounded by the revamped **Mint Plaza**, and has a few restaurant and cafés, including the popular Blue Bottle coffee shop.

The Museum of the African Diaspora.

SAN FRANCISCO MUSEUM OF MODERN ART

The art gallery, a beacon in the SoMa landscape, is almost as much of an attraction as its collections and temporary exhibitions.

SFMoMA reopened in May of 2016 after a huge expansion that includes 4,000 new works from the esteemed Fisher collection. It now houses seven floors of artwork.

The original building was designed by Mario Botta and completed at a cost of $60 million in 1995. The huge roof garden is one of the highlights, and officials call it a "gallery without a ceiling." Inside the museum, space is illuminated by a huge central skylight. This breathes light and air into the exhibits, and conveys a vibrancy and a fresh, vivid quality to the collections and the interior space.

For the vast new expansion, the museum purchased a firehouse next door and hired the international firm of Snohetta to design a sleek horizontal shape with an angular roof and a distinctive wavy exterior.

The collection covers most of the major movements in modern art. Top masters represented include Marcel Duchamp, Georges Braque, Louise Bourgeois, Robert Rauschenberg, Georgia O'Keeffe, Jackson Pollock, Andy Warhol, and Constantin Brancusi.

The Essentials

Address: 151 3rd St; www.sfmoma.org
Telephone: 415-357-4000
Opening Hours: Thur 10am–9pm, Fri–Tue 10am–5pm, the public space till 9pm
Entrance Fee: charge
Transport: bus: 8, 8AX, 81X, 88X, 9, 12, 14, 14X, 35, 45; streetcar: F; metro: all lines; BART: all trains

Opened in 1995, Mario Botta designed the building to show works in maximum daylight. In 2016 MoMA reopened after an extension project by the Norwegian architecture firm Snøhetta which almost doubled the size of the exhibition galleries.

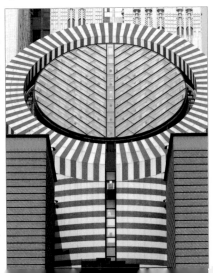

The exterior of SFMoma.

FRIDA AND DIEGO IN SAN FRANCISCO

Painting by Frida Kahlo.

Mexican painter Frida Kahlo and muralist Diego Rivera have powerful associations with San Francisco, visiting and working here several times. The banner at the top of Frida's painting says that this is "*for our friend Mr Albert Bender, and it was in the month of April of the year 1931.*" Kahlo gave the work to Bender in gratitude for his help with an entry visa for Diego, when difficulties arose because of Diego's Communist associations. The painting featured in Frida's first public show of work, held in San Francisco in 1931.

The paintings and sculpture collection has more than 7,000 works to challenge and engage.

Jasper Johns is one of the many American modern masters in the museum's paintings and sculpture collection.

Detail of Femme au Chapeau (Woman with a Hat), by Henri Matisse.

Cable car along Powell Street.

NOB HILL

The robber barons of the Gold-Rush era vied to build the most beautiful mansions possible, creating a lavish and luxurious "hill of palaces".

Nob Hill is a tiny but exclusive neighborhood dominated by a few grand hotels, Grace Cathedral, and Huntington Park. Three blocks in any direction will find you in a different neighborhood – Chinatown to the north, the Financial District to the east, Union Square to the south, and Russian Hill to the west.

Hill of palaces

From a historic perspective there is no better place to start a relationship with San Francisco's gracious homes than at **Nob Hill**. The cable-car lines cross at **California** and **Powell** streets, and from here there is a magnificent view of the bay, crossed by the Bay Bridge and framed by the pagodas of Chinatown and the distinctive spire of the Transamerica Pyramid. The climb up California Street ends atop what the author Robert Louis Stevenson called the "hill of palaces."

In a fevered rush to outdo each other in opulence, the railroad robber barons of the 19th century built palatial homes on this fine hill. Although many of the houses that remain have been converted into condos or multi-dwelling apartment buildings, there

has been little diminishing effect on the overall allure.

The highest of the city's seven major mounds, Nob Hill was not a desirable residential area until the invention of the cable car in 1873 by an immigrant from England, Andrew Hallidie, whose father pioneered wire-rope technology. Only then did the influential railroad barons agree to locate their colossal mansions here, after running cable-car tracks down California Street to the Central Pacific (later Southern

Main Attractions
Cable Car Barn and Powerhouse
Mark Hopkins InterContinental Hotel
Stanford Court
Fairmont Hotel
Pacific Union Club
Scarlet Huntington Hotel
Grace Cathedral
Masonic Auditorium

Map
Page 152

Doorman at the Ritz Carlton – one of the areas many fine hotels.

View from the restaurant in the Mark Hopkins.

Pacific) headquarters on Market Street. The **Cable Car Museum ❶** (see page 158), nerve center and powerhouse of the present cable-car system, can be inspected in a handsome 1910 structure at the corner of Mason and Washington streets on the flank of the hill. The first cable car, from 1873, is exhibited here.

Architectural exuberance

San Francisco's architectural style has always been exuberant. Two years after gold was discovered in 1848, the population exploded from a humble community to nearly 25,000 people. In a short time, San Francisco became a sprawling, teeming mass of speculators bent on striking it rich.

At first, there wasn't time to build proper accommodations. Each day, more tents appeared and shacks were flung up with whatever materials happened to be at hand. Even the schooners that hauled the precious supplies of food and tools around the Cape were pressed into service. Dragged ashore, doors were cut in the hulls, and the ships were transformed into houses, stores, and even hotels.

But the new-found wealth pouring in from the gold fields created a community that wouldn't be satisfied with "tent-city" status. Real houses were built, spreading westward from the bay, at a rate unprecedented for the 19th century – from 15 to 30 a day in 1852. The favored material for construction was wood, cut and shipped in vast quantities from the pine forests of Northern California the Oregon Territory farther up the West Coast. But even with the modern advances of framing and manufactured nails, little could keep pace with the housing demand, and some homes and hotels were shipped as prefabricated kits from the East and assembled on-site.

James Ben Ali Haggin was one of the first to build a mansion, a home of around 60 rooms. The "Big

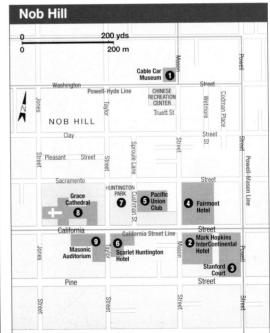

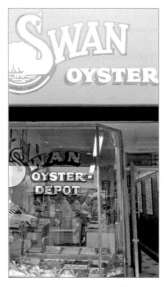

The place to go for oysters and seafood on Polk Street.

quickly followed suit. The real Gold Rush fortunes were made not from mining, but by those who supplied the tools, goods, and services for the hard-earned dollars of the miners.

Techniques that allowed for the mass production of wooden ornamental shapes gave even common houses a splendid aspect. Every architectural fashion of the day was fair game, from Victorian Gothic to Queen Anne, from French Renaissance to Turkish towers. Throughout the city, the result is a dazzling architectural eclecticism.

In San Francisco, Moorish cupolas can be found on an Italianate facade, perhaps accompanied by an Egyptian column or two. For the very rich, no expense was too great, no splendor too excessive. And this reached its zenith on Nob Hill.

Four" (banker William C. Ralston, grocer Leland Stanford, hardware merchant Mark Hopkins, and dry goods purveyor Charles Crocker)

EAT

The Swan Oyster Depot has been lining them up and packing them in since 1912 (www.sfswan oysterdepot.com; tel: 415-673 1101, Mon–Sat 10.30am–5.30pm).

Mark Hopkins InterContinental Hotel ❷

Address: One Nob Hill; www.intercontinentalmarkhopkins.com
Telephone: 888-424-6835
Transport: bus: 1; cable car: California

View from the Top of the Mark.

The Nob Hill Spa may be the most luxurious, but the city has an entire menu of healing and beauty arts on tap.

Close-up of the fountain in Nob Hill's Huntington Park.

This occupies the site of the former Mark Hopkins mansion, which had lavish stables with rosewood stalls, silver trimmings, and mosaic floors covered with Belgian carpets. Hopkins saw much of this luxury destroyed in the fire that raged for three days and nights following the earthquake of 1906, but the house was soon rebuilt. Today, enjoying a cocktail or a meal at the **Top of the Mark** (tel: 415-616-6916), the Art Deco-style restaurant in the sky, is a romantic, time-honored custom for visitors to the city.

The **Stanford Court Hotel ❸** (905 California Street; www.stanford court.com; tel: 415-989-3500) is also a beautiful testament to San Francisco's history. The illuminated glass-domed ceiling and extensive marbling are features of the lobby, and many of the rooms offer stunning vistas of the city.

Fairmont Hotel ❹

Address: 950 Mason Street; www.fairmont.com
Telephone: 415-772-5000
Transport: bus: 1; cable car: California
Here, with a gilded lobby and faux-marble pillars, is even more opulence. The Fairmont Hotel was built on the ashes of a great mansion, and retains an aura of original splendor. It's the perfect place for afternoon tea.

The Mark Hopkins, the Stanford Court, and the Fairmont hotels are, for many people, the essence of San Francisco glamour.

Snob Hill

San Francisco lore has it that the contraction of the word nabob – meaning Mogul prince – gave rise to the name Nob Hill. Less affluent citizens preferred "Snob" Hill. But the nabobs of the late 19th century no longer wield unlimited power in the neighborhood, and while the Pacific Union Club may not be opening its doors to the masses, the general public can be seen everywhere. And there is much to see.

Even at the height of their influence, the nabobs were – occasionally – kept in check. Charles Crocker owned a sprawling mansion that occupied most of the block on California between Taylor and Jones streets.

Crocker's desire to own the entire block was thwarted by a Chinese undertaker named Nicholas Yung who declined to sell his corner lot to Crocker. Infuriated, Crocker erected a 40ft (12 meter) "spite fence" around three sides of the property. An outraged mob marched onto Nob Hill in protest, demanding that the fence be torn down.

Yung never did surrender his property and, when Crocker's mansion

CABLE-CAR TIPS

Nob Hill, known for its magnificent views, is just one of the neighborhoods serviced by the city's famous cable cars. To enjoy the best from these mobile historic landmarks, here are a few tips:
Never refer to cable cars as "trolleys."
The Powell and Market Street turnaround is both the most popular and the worst place to board. It's the point of origin for more than one line, so it can take a long time to get on. The area is also the haunt of panhandlers and scam artists who see out-of-towners as good targets. It's better to board at a less frequented stop along the route.
Riding the cars at night is romantic. They run as late as 10pm, when the nocturnal view is wonderful and the cars are uncrowded.
Never attempt to board a moving cable car, and be ready to squash in tight. Hold packages on your lap.
It's not cool to hang off the sides – it's extremely dangerous.

Huntingdon Park.

was destroyed in the 1906 earthquake, the property was taken over by the Episcopal Diocese and is now the site of Grace Cathedral.

The **Pacific Union Club** ❺ (1000 California Street), directly opposite the Fairmont Hotel, is one of the few surviving buildings from the 1906 earthquake and fire. Built for silver magnate James Flood in 1855, the sturdy brownstone structure, with its pine-framed entrance, is now a private club.

Living in luxury

More welcoming is the 12-story **Scarlet Huntington Hotel** ❻ (1075 California Street; tel: 415-474-5400; www.thescarlethotels.com), refreshingly not owned by a hotel mega chain, which began life in the 1920s as the 140-room Huntington Apartments. The enormous rooms have been retained and embellished with fine antiques, imported silks, and original artwork.

The Huntington's Big 4 restaurant celebrates Crocker, Hopkins, Huntington, and Stanford and evokes the robber baron era with its woody, masculine interior, while it's easy to feel like one of the hill's pampered

residents in the Huntington's **Nob Hill Spa** (tel: 415-345-2888; www.nobhillspa.com). The spa's indoor Jacuzzi and infinity pool have a spectacular views in the city.

During the Christmas season, the Nob Hill hotels host free choral concerts in their festively decorated

The Fairmont Hotel is the perfect place for afternoon tea.

The Masonic Auditorium.

Grace Cathedral.

preening, guys groaning, beggars supplicating from their positions on the icy sidewalks… [but] the really rich carry no cash."

Huntington Park ❼ is a small but well-maintained and pleasant public space with a play area.

Grace Cathedral ❽

Address: 1100 California Street; www.gracecathedral.org
Telephone: 415-749-6300
Opening Hours: Mon–Sat 8am–6pm, Thu till 7am, Sun 8am–4pm
Transport: bus 1; cable car: California

The cathedral, started in 1928 but not consecrated until 1964, is a beautiful replica of Paris's Notre Dame in the French Gothic style. Make sure to take a look at the doors and windows. The doors are cast from Lorenzo Ghiberti's original *Doors of Paradise* in Florence, while the rose window was inspired by the blue glass of Chartres Cathedral. Other windows depict modern heroes like Albert Einstein and astronaut John Glenn. Visitors come to walk Grace Cathedral's two labyrinths – one made of terrazzo in front of the church, and another made of limestone, inside. Walking the intricate and winding paths is a form of meditation and is open to all.

Located diagonally from Huntington Park at Taylor and California streets is the **Masonic Auditorium ❾** (tel: 415-776-7457 for a schedule of concerts and events; http://sfmasonic.com), a multi-functional performance and event space with perhaps the city's best acoustics outside the Symphony Hall or the Opera House. With performances ranging from Tom Jones and Jane's Addiction to Common and comedian Lewis Black, plus a slew of dates for the San Francisco Jazz Festival, the auditorium is a wonderful, comfortable sit-down venue. The lobby has a two-story mosaic laced with Masonic imagery, but no secret handshakes are needed for admittance.

lobbies. And, of course, as in bygone days, the nabobs still descend from the heights to patronize the opera.

The late columnist Herb Caen's description of a particular opening night at the Civic Center's Opera House highlighted the persistent and still-present gap between the city's haves and have-nots. "All the well-worn contradictions of capitalism were very much in evidence," Caen observed. "Limos purring, ladies

The impressive nave of Grace Cathedral.

SAN FRANCISCO'S CABLE CARS

They're more than just a means of transportation; cable cars are officially a National Landmark.

Operating three routes – the Mason-Taylor, Powell-Hyde, and California lines – San Francisco's cable cars are among the last in the United States, at least 100 cities having abandoned them for buses. Underestimating the draw of this tourist attraction, San Francisco tried to get rid of the cars in 1947, but a vigorous local campaign saved them by a City Charter.

Today the cable cars take more than nine million passengers a year, more than half of them local commuters. It is the visitors, of course, who buy the engraved knives, belt buckles, posters, and T-shirts emblazoned with pictures of the beloved cars, or dig into their wallets for genuine cable-car bells.

After a $65 million, 21-month refurbishment took the cars out of service, a city-wide party celebrated their return in 1981. Colored balloons bore the message, "They're Back," and customers waited from dawn to be among the first passengers. In their absence, visitors to Fisherman's Wharf fell by 15 percent. Rudyard Kipling visited in 1889 on his way to India, and wrote, "They turn corners almost at right angles, cross over other lines and for aught I know run up the sides of houses."

The Essentials

Address: Cable Car Museum, 1201 Mason Street; www.cablecar museum.org
Tel: 415-474-1887
Opening Hours: Apr–Oct 10am–6pm, Nov–Mar 10am–5pm, closed holidays
Entrance Fee: free.

Operator Leonard Oats won first prize in the Bell Ringing Competition in 2010 for the third year in a row and then again in 2016.

The cars are pulled by a wire cable that runs beneath the street. The gripman uses a clamp located beneath the carriage to hold or release the cable, which pulls the cable car along the street. The cables pass through the machinery in the cable-car barn at Mason and Washington streets, which is also a working museum that explains the system and displays memorabilia.

The Cable Car Museum is also the wheel house for all the operating lines. The cables are turned on several sets of giant wheels, and maintain a constant speed of 10 miles per hour (16kph).

ANDREW SMITH HALLIDIE

Andrew Hallidie.

The cable-car system was created in 1873 by Andrew Hallidie, a British-born engineer with a reputation for building suspension bridges and experience in mining engineering. Seven years before, it is said, he saw a horse slip, causing the chain to break on an overloaded streetcar it had been pulling uphill. Hallidie set about devising a system that would eliminate such accidents. Although Hallidie and his friends put up the $20,000 to get the cable cars operating, he was anticipated in 1870 by Benjamin Brooks, son of a local lawyer, who was awarded a franchise to operate a similar system, but failed to raise the necessary financing.

When the Hallidie plan came to fruition, skepticism was the order of the day. "I'd like to see it happen," said realtor L.C. Carlson, "but I don't know who is going to want to ride the dang thing."

Critics of the system abide to this day. Some say that the cars, which are on a fixed track and have no ability to duck potential collisions, are inherently unsafe. Columnist Dick Nolan called the braking system "unimprovable" or "blacksmith shop crudity at its worst." And one family living at Hyde and Chestnut streets initiated an (unsuccessful) lawsuit against the loud noise, which measures 85 decibels at street level.

The Clay Street railroad was the first successful cable car in the city.

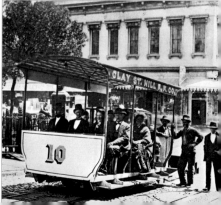

The gripmen who drive the cable cars stay fit on the job. At the start and end of some routes, the cars are rotated by the manually operated turntables. The corner of Powell and Market is the best spot to watch the cars rotate.

San Francisco, city of hills.

CENTRAL NEIGHBORHOODS

The Marina hugs the waterfront, Pacific Heights scales the hills. Japantown has pagodas and parades while Hayes Valley has chic shopping.

Stretching from the bay in the Marina to the heart of the Western Addition, these central neighborhoods each have their own flavor and flair. Whether you seek the boutique shopping of Union Street, soul food on Divisadero, or a walking tour of the mansions of Pacific Heights, these areas offer a few different glimpses into the heart of San Francisco.

FORT MASON ❶

In 1860, **Fort Mason** was one of the earliest residential districts in San Francisco. The US Army took over the area at the start of the Civil War, and retained it throughout World War II, when the fort served as an embarkation point for more than one million soldiers. Decommissioned in the 1970s, this seafront area is now one of the city's premier arts centers. Every day there is a program of shows, lectures, meetings, readings, and other events.

The **Fort Mason Center** (https://fortmason.org) houses a number of museums and galleries. The **Museo ItaloAmericano** (www.museoitaloamericano.org; tel: 415-673-2200; Tue–Sun noon–4pm; free) is the only museum in all of the United States devoted exclusively to the art and culture of

Italy and Italian-Americans. There is a small, permanent collection of paintings, sculptures, and photographs.

The **SFMoMA Artists Gallery** (www.sfmoma.org; tel: 415-441-4777; Tue–Sat 10.30am–5pm; free) is a lofty, light-filled space, and home to an innovative program that offers rentals of artwork (sculpture, paintings, photography, mixed media, etc.) with an option to buy. The scheme is to allow art aficionados the opportunity to experience art in their own space. The gallery also stages 11

Main Attractions

Fort Mason
Marina District
Russian Hill
Lombard Street
San Francisco Art Institute
Union Street
Pacific Heights
Fillmore Auditorium
Japantown
Alamo Square

Map

Page 162

Fort Mason has several museums.

Fort Mason Center for Arts & Culture.

Fort Mason's Magic Theatre.

non-profit arts and environmental organizations, in addition to Greens (http://greensrestaurant.com; tel: 415-771-6222), a waterfront eatery with a fantastic view and delicious vegetarian food. A favorite walk in a city of walkers is the pathway that joins Fort Mason to Aquatic Park, which abuts Fisherman's Wharf.

Heading in the opposite direction is another waterside walk, one that winds all the way to the Presidio.

annual, well-attended exhibitions that showcase Californian artists. The **Magic Theatre** (http://magictheatre.org; tel: 415-441-8822), a long-established resident of Fort Mason, has earned itself recognition and prominence as one of the few theaters in the US dedicated exclusively to developing and producing new plays. The roster of playwrights who have debuted their work here includes Sam Shepard, David Mamet, Michael McClure, Nilo Cruz, and Rebecca Gilman.

The Fort Mason Center also includes a number of offices for

THE MARINA DISTRICT ❷

The waterfront **Marina District** is popular with young urban dwellers, and encompasses the area all the way west over to the edge of the Presidio, passing the grassy space known as **Marina Green**, where people gather on the Fourth of July to watch fireworks, and kite flyers and joggers gather all year round.

There is a trendy, busy shopping district on **Chestnut Street** in the Marina. Though you might have to

Central Neighborhoods

Golden Gate Yacht Club — ★ Wave Organ — Museo ItaloAmericano — Magic Theatre — FISHERMAN'S WHARF — AQUATIC PARK — Bathhouse Building

Marina Blvd — ❶ Fort Mason — North Point Street — SF Art Institute

Jefferson St — Fillmore — Bay — Van Ness — Polk — Hyde — Crooked St ❹

Palace of Fine Arts — Beach St — Nth Pt St — Pierce — ❷ — Francisco St — Chestnut — Lombard St — RUSSIAN HILL ❸

Golden Gate Bridge — Richardson Ave — Bay St — Francisco St — MARINA — Chestnut — Street — Greenwich — Octavia — Franklin — Larkin — Leavenworth

PRESIDIO — Lombard — Scott — Former Vedanta Temple — Buchanan St — Filbert St — Green — Street

Greenwich — Filbert St — Divisadero — Union — ❺ — Octagon House — Vallejo — Avenue

Presidio Ave — Vallejo St — Casebolt House ❻ — PACIFIC — Flood Mansion — Broadway — Pacific Ave

Broadway — HEIGHTS — Bourn Mansion — Street — Street

Jackson — Pacific Avenue — Smith House — James Irvine Home — Whittier Mansion — Haas-Lilienthal House ❽ — Jackson Street — Clay Street

Washington — Street — ❼ ALTA PLAZA PARK — LAFAYETTE PARK — Washington — Clay Street

Clay — Street — FILLMORE — Sacramento — California — Street

Sacramento — Street — California — Pine — Street

California — Pine Street — Bush — JAPANTOWN — Sutter St — Geary — Larkin Street

Pine — Bush — Street — Japan Center ❿ — Konko Kyo Temple — O'Farrell St

Sutter — Street — ⓫ — Fillmore Auditorium — Geary — Ellis — Turk — Van Ness

Post — Street — Webster — Laguna — Gough St

Geary — Expressway — Street — ⓬ — Gate — Ave — McAllister — ⓭ — Van Ness — Market

O'Farrell — Divisadero — WESTERN ADDITION — Fulton St — Golden — HAYES VALLEY

0 — 800 yds — ALAMO SQUARE — ⓮ — Van Ness

0 — 800 m — Ⓜ

Meander to the end of the jetty near the Golden Gate Yacht Club to inspect the unique **Wave Organ** (www.exploratorium.edu/visit/wave-organ), where the unearthly "music" is the product of waves gurgling through an undersea sculpture consisting of 25 pipes jutting into the ocean. As waves crash against them, each pipe produces a different sound.

Continue walking the Golden Gate Promenade for an invigorating route that skirts the Presidio and leads along **Crissy Field** – a shoreline park popular with picnickers, sunbathers, and nature-lovers – to the Golden Gate Bridge (see page 200).

RUSSIAN HILL ❸

The first neighborhood is **Russian Hill**, serviced by the Powell-Hyde cable-car line. Russian Hill is known for magnificent views, stately homes, hidden bistros, and a labyrinth of secret streets, stairways, and alleys like Macondray Lane, which connects

The Marina District's Crissy Field is good for kite flying.

dodge overpriced baby strollers to get into some of the city's well-regarded restaurants, shops, and cafés here, you'll find terrific, independent stores.

TIP

The whole Marina Boulevard is now immersed in free WiFi.

The twists and turns of Lombard Street.

The San Francisco Art Institute Café is perched on top of the school at 800 Chestnut Street, with spectacular views of the Golden Gate Bridge, Alcatraz, Angel Island, and the East Bay. Mon–Thu 8.30am–8pm, Fri 8.30am–3pm.

The whimsical facade of the former Vedanta Temple.

Taylor and Jones streets. Macondray Lane was the inspiration for much of the action in Armistead *Maupin's Tales of the City* books and TV series.

Russian Hill is home to **Lombard Street ❹**, known as "the crookedest street in the world." Between Hyde and Leavenworth streets, this one-block stretch of Lombard takes cars on eight hairpin turns along a cobblestone roadway. As if lining up for some urban roller-coaster ride, tourists drive up to the top on sunny afternoons and wait their turn to traverse this unique slalom course.

Although tales vary, one theory for the curves is that they were carved in the 1920s in order to allow horses to negotiate the hill. To each side are beautifully landscaped homes tucked precariously into the slopes of Russian Hill. Anyone on foot might have an easier time strolling down Lombard's less famous footpath, admiring the architecture, the views, and the gardens along the way.

View from the Alta Plaza Park.

San Francisco Art Institute

Address: 800 Chestnut Street; www.sfai.edu
Telephone: 415-771-7020

The **San Francisco Art Institute**, located in a gorgeous 1920s Spanish Revival building, was responsible for the education of American talents like Annie Leibovitz, Mark Rothko, Ansel Adams, and Dorothea Lange. It's worth stopping by to see the **Diego Rivera murals**, and to admire the view of the bay from the court-yard adjacent to the school's café.

UNION STREET ❺

Four streets south of Lombard is the **Union Street** area, the first neighborhood in the city to convert many of its gingerbread Victorian houses into boutiques, art galleries, and restaurants. Appreciating Union Street's charm is a delightful way to spend an afternoon, but be sure to take some money along – the coffee shops and stores in **Cow Hollow** are pretty upscale. Lovely mansions are a feature of this area, although many are not open to the public. Be sure to note the **Octagon House** (2645 Gough; tel: 415-441-7512; open second Sun, second and fourth Thu of

the month, noon–3pm, closed in Jan and holidays; free), an eight-sided oddity, built in 1861. Furnished with Colonial and Federal period antiques, the house is open to the public about three times a month; call for details.

Turning left on Green Street leads to the former **Vedanta Temple**. The Vedanta Society of Northern California relocated to 2323 Fillmore Street, but the former temple at 2963 Webster is worth seeing to check out the odd yet beautiful amalgam of styles: joined in architectural harmony are Queen Anne turrets, Moorish arches, medieval turrets, parapets, and a Russian onion dome.

At 2727 Pierce is the **Casebolt House**. This massive Italianate edifice dates from 1865 – near the end of California's silver era – and forms a link with the days when San Francisco was a young city with a glittering future.

PACIFIC HEIGHTS ⑥

Southwest of Russian Hill is the neighborhood of **Pacific Heights**, which, for the most part, escaped the 1906 earthquake and fire. Having an address here usually denotes wealth. **Alta Plaza Park ⑦** is a good starting point for an architectural stroll, for the view is magnificent: to the south,

Twin Peaks, Buena Vista, and Potrero Hill are visible in one commanding sweep, while, in the other direction, turning toward the bay, the ships appear dwarfed by the unfolding panorama below. Most houses here are not open to the public.

At 2600 Jackson, across the street from the park, is the **Smith House**, a Jacobean-style brick structure built by shipyard tycoon Irving Murray in 1895 for his daughter. That the house is built of brick is noteworthy: not indigenous to this part of California, bricks had to be brought in, making them a rare and costly material. The mansion was also the first fully electrified house in the city.

Architectural trickery

At 2421 and 2415 Pierce Street is the **James Irvine Home**, designed by Edgar Matthews. Notice the windows with the gracefully designed panes. Inside, the house is beautifully executed – a piece of architectural

TIP

Most mansions in Pacific Heights are privately owned; nevertheless, enjoying the architecture from outside, and the views of the bay, is a pleasant way to spend an afternoon.

The Art Institute has Diego Rivera murals and a good café.

The Haas-Lilienthal House in Pacific Heights is open to the public for tours.

trickery makes the building seem to be much larger than it is by reducing the interior scale. In fact, much of San Francisco was built in this manner, to overcome spatial restrictions.

To the left along Pacific Street is the **Monteagle House**, designed by Lewis Hobart, architect of Grace Cathedral. It is French-Gothic in style, and was built in 1923. The oldest house in Pacific Heights is **Leale House**, at No. 2475. It was built in 1860 as a farmhouse, part of a 25-acre (10-hectare) dairy farm. In time, it became the home of a retired sea captain who wrote a book called *Tule Sailor*.

On the corner of Pacific and Webster is a gorgeous view of San Francisco Bay, one that takes in Alcatraz and Angel islands. At 2550 Webster is the **Bourn Mansion**. This was the town house and office of the richest man in San Francisco during the 1920s and 1930s. William B. Bourn was the president of the Spring Valley Water Company, and he inherited one of California's mines.

THE HEART OF THE HEIGHTS

The two blocks of Broadway and Webster are the heart of Pacific Heights. At 2120 Broadway is the **Hamlin School**, a "palace" commissioned by

A poster for the Fillmore Auditorium.

Comstock mine owner James Flood. The mansion is a magnificent neoclassical revival building, its interior rich with red lacquer, bamboo, a maple library, a walnut and mahogany staircase, and Tiffany skylights. After the earthquake, Mrs Flood expressed fears about the largely wooden-built house. Her husband told her not to fret, because "I'll build you a marble house on a granite hill."

There is no granite in San Francisco, let alone a granite hill. So Mr Flood had a granite slab brought in from outside the city, on which he built the house at **2222 Broadway**. This is a copy of a three-story Italian Renaissance villa and was completed in 1912, six years after Mrs Flood expressed her fears. The building now belongs to the schools of the Sacred Heart.

After continuing down Broadway for two blocks to Laguna, turn left on Jackson. At 2090 Jackson you'll find the **Whittier Mansion**, which was commissioned in 1894 and

THE FILLMORE AUDITORIUM

At the corner of Geary and Fillmore streets, The Fillmore has showcased some of the greatest acts in American pop music, and is largely responsible for disseminating the soundtrack of 1960s San Francisco. Opening its doors in 1912, the auditorium operated as a dance hall, party space, and roller rink, until it began booking up-and-coming R&B acts like James Brown and Ike and Tina Turner. It gained greater notoriety when rock promoter Bill Graham used it to launch home-grown hippie bands like the Grateful Dead, Jefferson Airplane, and Janis Joplin's Big Brother and the Holding Company. The poster art, replete with colorful psychedelic images, helped to define the era and became famous in its own right. In 1968, Graham moved the club to Van Ness and Market, dubbing it the Fillmore West, while the old location became the Elite Club. After suffering severe damage in the 1989 earthquake, the Fillmore moved back to its original location, and remains to this day one of the city's favorite music venues.

completed in 1896. From the outside, the house presents an odd conglomerate of styles, but the Roman temple entranceway abuts the Queen Anne tower with a harmony that attests to the skill of the well-known architect, Edward Swain.

Architecture and romance

At Jackson and Octavia Street, the back of the **Spreckels Mansion** can just be seen. This is one of San Francisco's most elegant mansions, originally commissioned by the wealthy sugar magnate Adolph Spreckels. The gate on the Jackson Street side was the old delivery entrance, and behind the window in the wall was where the gatekeeper lived. The low-rise building behind the mansion houses a covered pool. The Spreckels Mansion is the current residence of romance novelist Danielle Steele (though she lives most of the time in her Paris residence).

At 1925 Jackson is the massive, Baroque **Grenlee Terrace** apartment building. The Haas-Lilienthal House is straight ahead and to the right.

Haas-Lilienthal House ⑧

Address: 2007 Franklin Street; www.sfheritage.org/haas-lilienthal-house
Telephone: 415-441-3000
Opening Hours: one-hour docent tours Wed, Sat noon–3pm, and Sun 11am–4pm
Admission Fee: charge
Transport: bus: 1, 12, 19, 27, 47, 49

This huge, furnished Victorian house, built in 1886 in Queen Anne style, is one of the few homes in Pacific Heights that is open to the public. If, after all this, your feet are tired from climbing, you can turn back here to rest in **Lafayette Park**

THE FILLMORE DISTRICT ⑨

Fillmore Street cuts across Union Street through the **Fillmore District**, which came to fame in the mid-1960s as the location for world-famous rock concerts.

Fillmore Auditorium

Address: 1805 Geary Boulevard; www.thefillmore.com
Telephone: 415-346-3000
Transport: bus: 22, 38

The free summertime jazz festival attracts up to 90,000 people.

The Tragically Hip perform at the Fillmore.

Japanese doll for sale in a Japantown store.

The place to go for authentic Japanese cuisine and stores.

Enjoy some udon soup and good sushi in Japantown.

From here, promoter Bill Graham helped launch the careers of Jefferson Airplane, Janis Joplin, and the Grateful Dead (see box).

Today, the area is also known for an arthouse movie theater, good restaurants, and stores selling both new and vintage clothes. Smaller than the Fillmore, but jumping most nights, the **Boom Boom Room** at 1601 Fillmore Street, tel: 415-673-8000, has live blues, boogie, soul, and funk, in addition to dance grooves from DJs most nights.

Authentic sushi.

JAPANTOWN AND BEYOND

Adjacent to the Fillmore District between Octavia and Fillmore streets is **Japantown** ❿, known to locals as J-Town and home to many of the 12,000 Japanese San Franciscans. Japantown has been undergoing a renovation that includes the updating of the **Sundance Cinema Kabuki** (1881 Post Street; tel: 415-346-3243; www.sundancecinemas.com); and the newly refurbished **Hotel Kabuki**

(1625 Post Street; tel: 800-533-4567), formerly the Miyako Hotel.

The neighborhood is dominated by the **Japan Center** ⓫, an enormous complex of stores, theaters, sushi bars, and restaurants, distinguished by a **Peace Pagoda** 100ft (30 meters) high, with five tiers (odd numbers bring good luck) donated by Japan. The Webster Bridge midway in the Japan Center and links the two indoor malls.

New People (746 Post Street, Mon–Sat noon–7pm; Sun until 6pm; tel: 415-525-8630; www.newpeople world.com), is an interesting stop, housing an anime cinema, art gallery, café, and edgy J-Pop retailers of harajuku fashions and manga inside an ultra-modern glass building.

On Bush Street is the **Konko Kyo Church**. Founded in 1859, Konko-Kyo (faith; www.konkofaith.org) developed as a sect of Shinto, a form of Japanese ancestral worship. The interior is beautiful.

At the intersection on the north side of Sutter is **Super Mira Market**. Specializing in fresh, prepared fish, it sells *sashimi*, *gobo*, and *daikon*, too.

The Saint John Coltrane African Orthodox Church takes music very seriously.

The Peace Pagoda has five tiers, a sign of good luck.

The bar at the Cliff Hotel.

The famous painted ladies light up Alamo Square.

during the past decade. Bordering the Western Addition and Civic Center, today you'll find rows of swanky boutiques and shoe stores, hip restaurants and cafés, as well as artsy design stores, in this area where prostitutes and drug dealers once plied their trade. The changes coincided with the removal of a freeway on-ramp, which had sustained considerable damage during the 1989 earthquake.

ALAMO SQUARE

Although San Francisco has a number of rows of charming Victorian houses, those most often seen on postcards are the "painted ladies" on Steiner Street beside **Alamo Square** ⑭, which is bordered by Fulton and Hayes streets at Scott. It's a pleasant little hillside park (although a place to be careful after dark), with a view not only of the brightly colored homes and Downtown's skyscrapers, but one also within sight of the Civic Center.

The neighborhood is an active one, with a well-attended flea market, usually held in August, and monthly movies shown during the summer months.

A *torii* gate marks the entrance to **Nihonmachi Mall**, a cobblestoned pedestrian shopping and eating area. The mall, designed by Ruth Asawa, resembles a small Japanese village. Silk-embroidered kimonos, books on Japanese art, tea ceremony utensils, and calligraphy scrolls are among the treats on sale.

Just south of Japantown is the **Western Addition** ⑫.

Hayes Valley ⑬ has also undergone gentrification and transformation

Boutiques in Hayes Valley.

HAIGHT-ASHBURY AND GOLDEN GATE PARK

Haight-Ashbury is the nexus of the hippie trail, but it also attracts post-millennium modernists in search of cutting-edge boutiques. Golden Gate Park is for everyone.

For many, a visit to San Francisco wouldn't be complete without a trip to **Haight-Ashbury** ❶.

In the 1960s, personal freedom and enlightenment dominated life in the Haight, with a growing spirit of kinship. Kids lived in communes, started neighborhood organizations, and ran grocery store cooperatives. In 1967, the nation's first non-religious health clinic was founded here. The Haight Ashbury Free Clinic remains a vital part of the community; there is one location on Clayton Street near Haight Street and another in the Mission.

Haight Street is really two parts: Upper Haight, bright, shiny, and closest to Golden Gate Park and the famous spot where Haight Street and Ashbury Street intercets, and Lower Haight, seedier, funkier, and to some people more exciting. The Upper Haight has the hippie legacy; the Lower Haight is more hip-hop than hippie.

UPPER HAIGHT

The Upper Haight is a good shopping destination, with great boutiques and second-hand shops. Some of the best vintage stores are **Relic Vintage** (1605 Haight Street; tel: 415-255-7460; www.relicvintagesf.com), Buffalo Exchange (1555 Haight Street; tel:

415-431-7733; www.buffaloexchange.com), and Held Over (1543 Haight Street; tel: 415-864-0818). **Wasteland** (1660 Haight Street; tel: 415-863-3150; www.shopwasteland.com) is the biggest and most extensive clothes store, featuring new and used togs for all genders and gender-benders. There are heaps of shoe stores, T-shirt shops, and one of the city's few McDonalds is at Haight and Stanyan sts.

At the end of the street is San Francisco's Taj Mahal of record stores, **Amoeba Music** (1855 Haight Street;

Street food.

The Haight is the place for sounds – the recorded kind. Amoeba Music at 1855 Haight Street started in Berkeley and now has three locations; it's good for vinyl and CDs. For something a little older, a little jazzier, don't miss Jack's Record Cellar, 254 Scott Street.

tel: 415-831-1200; www.amoeba.com). Housed in a former bowling alley, Amoeba has a vast range of new and used CDs and vinyl, in addition to vintage and modern music posters. Prices are great at Amoeba, but you might have trouble keeping the volume down.

Then and now

Haight-Ashbury's 1960s Psychedelic Shop hawked concert tickets and rolling papers, and is now a pizza parlor. Diggers, a street theater commune, is an organic food cafe. At the center of what was once the hippie universe – the corner of Haight and Ashbury streets, where Joplin, the Airplane, and the Dead performed – a t-shirt store, a burger joint, and a Ben & Jerry's ice-cream parlor are the primary attractions. Aside from the non-stop sideshow of street people, of course.

Not everything has changed. There are still ample head shops, where a

Street scenes in Haight-Ashbury.

variety of druggy paraphernalia can be bought, and the Haight continues to offer in abundance the tolerance that it proposed in 1967. The denizens of the post-millennium years owe something to the 1960s mind-expansion movement – in addition

Victorian building, hippie style.

HIPPIES & THE HAIGHT

For several hot months in the first Summer of Love, 1967, life became a costume party in a wonderland setting of brightly painted Victorian buildings. The neighborhood was a swirl of colors as flower children painted store fronts, sidewalks, posters, cars, vans, and, of course, themselves, with Day-Glo. The days and nights were filled with sex, drugs, and a pot-laced breeze, with music provided by Janis Joplin, Jefferson Airplane, and the Grateful Dead – all of whom lived in Haight-Ashbury pads.

Things change, of course. Today there are more homeless than hippies on the streets, and the color scheme on most of the Victorians has been toned down. Bus-riding tourists snatch up Summer of Love T-shirts. Nevertheless, boutiques in the Upper Haight now draw shoppers to avant-garde fashions found nowhere else in the city, and the neighborhood is happening again.

to a hippie culture all its own, the Haight was in its time a haven for new ideas in alternative medicine, ecological preservation, conceptual art, and natural foods.

To relive all this, walking tours of around two hours' duration are offered by Flower-Power Haight-Ashbury (tel: 800 979 3370), with tours setting out at 10.30am Tuesday, Saturday and Friday at 2pm.. To continue the hippie trail on your own, follow Haight Street west where it runs into that famous playground of the 1960s: Golden Gate Park.

Lower Haight

The Lower Haight is somewhat different from the Upper Haight. Heading east on Haight Street, the two neighborhoods are separated by several residential blocks. From the Upper Haight, the transition is marked by **Buena Vista Park**, a steeply sloping urban space with beautiful stone masonry that recalls its long-gone glory days, when residents flocked to the top to watch the city burn. It still retains spectacular views, including a panorama of the downtown area from the two tennis courts and a view toward the west on the very top.

Walking the downward slope of Haight Street, some beautiful Victorian architecture can be admired, with more and more being restored all the time. In particular, the block between Divisadero and Scott streets displays opulent examples.

East of Scott Street marks the real beginning of Lower Haight, a ragtag huddle of cafés, bars, vinyl record shops, hair salons, and medical marijuana dispensaries

Cafés and beer

Cafés here are a far cry from the see-and-be-seen scene, anchored by Café International (508 Haight Street; tel: 415 552 7390) and **Cafe du Soleil** (200 Fillmore Street; tel:

415-934-8637). Here you can see people actually reading and writing, not just posing and sipping soy chai lattes on their lunch hours.

If you're in need of more robust libation, beer is the norm in the Lower Haight, and Toronado (547 Haight Street; www.toronado.com) leads the pack with a menu of brews from all around the world. Mad Dog in the Fog (530 Haight Street) is a semi-British establishment that broadcasts non-American football games most of the time.

The bar at Toronado.

Janis Joplin in Golden Gate Park.

All you need is love – and music.

GOLDEN GATE PARK

Adjoining Haight-Ashbury and leading all the way to the Pacific Ocean, **Golden Gate Park** is eight blocks wide and 52 blocks long, covering an enormous 1,040 acres (420 hectares). This outdoor playland of lush green was the project of the park's designer, William Hammond Hall. His dream was to create a public space using natural topography rather than imposing artificial forms. With a combination of deep-rooting sea grasses, lupine, and trees, he began the arduous task of creating a park by tacking down the sand dunes in the eastern park.

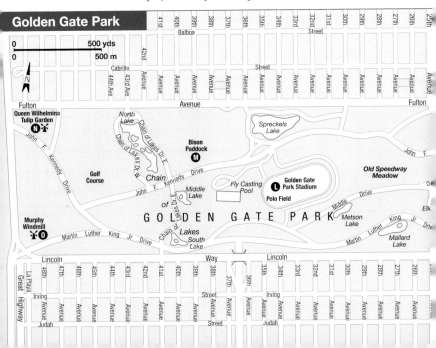

Reliving the Summer of Love in Golden Gate Park.

Credit for his effort, however, eluded Hall, mostly because his work was overshadowed by his successor, the Scotsman "Uncle John" McLaren. From the little house at the park's eastern edge, **John McLaren Lodge** Ⓐ (501 Stanyan Street), the gruff Scot managed his outdoor empire. Off Kennedy Drive in the Rhododendron Dell is a life-size statue of **McLaren**, who detested the monuments that the city fathers insisted on placing; many of the statues in Golden Gate Park are virtually hidden by foliage.

The park is a busy place: a popular way to experience the diversity

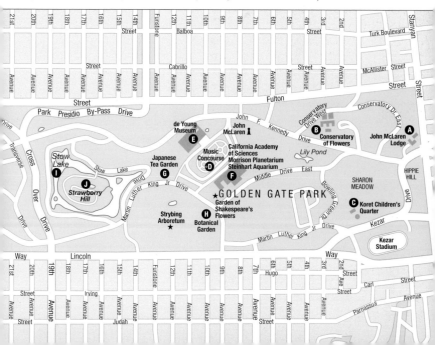

it offers is to rent a mountain bike. Start at the Panhandle (a narrow strip of parkland at the park's eastern edge bounded by Fell and Oak streets) and end at the ocean a few miles westward. Bicycle and in-line skate rentals are available along the park's periphery – and also at Stow Lake, if you want to start from the middle of the park. The following is a short tour of the park, starting from the east and ending in the west.

Conservatory of Flowers Ⓑ

Address: JFK Drive, Golden Gate Park; www.conservatoryofflowers.org
Telephone: 415-666-7001
Opening Hours: Tue–Sun 10am–4pm
Entrance Fee: charge
Transport: bus: 5, 7, 21, 33, 44, 71; metro: N

Conservatory Drive's most famous attraction had an extensive renovation program to repair the damage done in the winter storm that blew away 40 percent of its glass tiles. This glass "palace" is believed to have been modeled after a conservatory in London's Kew Gardens, and was the property of a San Jose businessman.

McLaren Lodge, built in 1896.

It opened to the public in Golden Gate Park in 1879. Housing wonderful collections of rare palms and other tropical flora, the atmosphere inside is one of color unleashed, and an energetic, vibrant mood pervades.

A seasonal flowerbed in front is a natural announcement to its entrance, and the grounds around the conservatory have fine collections of fuchsias and azaleas.

Oldest playground

Head west along Conservatory Drive to John F. Kennedy Drive and east to Kezar Drive, which curves by the **Koret Children's Quarter Ⓒ**, thought to be the oldest playground in a public park in America. After a major renovation and update in 2007, it is now one of the best in the city – with different levels of play areas for various ages. There's a sandbox for toddlers, climbing walls for older children, and swings for everyone. Fortunately, the concrete slide built into a hill was kept from the wrecking ball. Up the hill is a carrousel (Fri–Sun 10am–4.30pm, depending on the

Outside the de Young Museum.

Playing on the old fashioned concrete slide built into the hillside at the Koret Children's Quarter.

weather). Built in 1912, it has richly decorated steeds, a turning tub, rockers, and chariots for young Ben Hurs.

Hippie Hill, on the north side of the field opposite the Children's

Quarter, was renowned in the 1960s for gatherings of long-haired young flower people playing music and smoking pot. Some of that still goes on today, with a great deal of drumming thrown in for atmosphere.

Take MLK Jr Drive at the southwest corner of the playground, head west through the park, then north up to Concourse Drive. Take the second right to the cultural center of Golden Gate Park, where major museums flank the 20,000-seat outdoor **Music Concourse D**, a formal area of trees, fountains, and benches where musical performances are held in the summer.

de Young Museum E

Address: 50 Hagiwara Tea Garden Drive, Golden Gate Park; http://deyoung.famsf.org
Telephone: 415-750-3600
Opening Hours: Tue–Sun 9.30am–5.15pm, Fri until 8.45pm (mid–Apr–end of Nov), also open on selected Mon
Admission Fee: free on the first Tue of the month
Transport: bus: 5, 5L 7, 28, 33, 44; metro: N

Golden Gate Park's Conservatory of Flowers dates from 1879.

Enjoy afternoon refreshments in the Tea House, inside Golden Gate Park's serene Japanese Tea Gardens.

The botanical garden is free to enter.

Entrance to the Garden of Shakespeare's Flowers.

The area surrounding the Music Concourse has undergone massive reconstruction (see page 184). This started with the demolition of the existing de Young Museum because it was seismically unfit. The new de Young Museum is a bold, monolithic structure with a copper skin that will slowly oxidize and turn green, blending into the leafy park environment. The de Young Museum has an impressive collection of American paintings as well as art from Oceania, Latin America, Africa, and Meso-America. The tower at the northeast corner is

144ft (44 meters) high and has views of Richmond and Sunset all the way to Downtown and the Pacific Ocean.

California Academy of Sciences ❼

Address: 55 Music Concourse Drive, Golden Gate Park; www.calacademy.org
Telephone: 415-321-8000
Opening Hours: Mon–Sat 9.30am–5pm, Sun 11am–5pm
Admission Fee: free on four Sun per year
Transport: bus: 5, 5L, 7, 28, 33, 44; metro: N

Across the Music Concourse, the Academy of Sciences has also gone through interesting changes. Reopened as the greenest museum in the world, the Academy of Sciences now features live rainforest and coral reef exhibits, a two-acre (1-hectare) "living" roof of native grasses, porthole skylights, and solar panels that supply the museum's power. (See page 185.) The complex also includes the **Steinhart Aquarium** and the **Morrison Planetarium**.

Japanese Tea Garden ❽

Address: 7 Tea Garden Drive (at Martin Luther King Jr Drive); http://japaneseteagardensf.com
Telephone: 415-668-0909
Opening Hours: daily Mar–Oct 9am–6pm, Nov–Feb 9am–4.45pm
Admission Fee: free admission on Mon, Wed and Fri (before 10am), charge all other times
Transport: bus: 5, 7, 33, 44; metro: N

One of the most visited and loved sites in the park. Devised by George Turner Marsh, a successful dealer in Asian art, the garden was originally intended to represent a Japanese village. Marsh hired a renowned Japanese gardener, Makoto Hagiwara, who planted traditional dwarf bonsai conifers, elms, and cherry trees. Hagiwara also designed the winding brooks with their moss-covered rocks, irises, and carp pond.

A large bronze Buddha cast in Japan in the 1790s overlooks the garden. The Tea House offers rice cookies and green tea on its menu, while a wishing bridge, a wooden gateway, and a five-story pagoda complete the Japanese landscape.

San Francisco Botanical Garden

Address: 9th Avenue at Lincoln Way, Golden Gate Park; www.sfbotanical garden.org
Telephone: 415-661-1316
Opening Hours: daily summer 7.30am–6pm (till 4pm in winter)
Admission Fee: free daily 7.30–9am and the second Tue of every month
Transport: bus: 5, 7, 44; metro: N

On the other side of MLK Jr Drive is the Strybing Arboretum, with over 70 acres (28 hectares) of gardens, fountains, a bookstore, and a library. The Strybing is really a park within a park. The Garden of Fragrance is dedicated to the visually impaired, accompanied by the Succulent Garden and the Conifer Garden. The Biblical Garden grows plants that are mentioned in the Old and New Testaments. Visitors can also learn about planting techniques at the demonstration gardens, and classes, lectures, and "theme walks" are all available.

In the vicinity of Strybing is the **San Francisco Botanical Garden** (daily; guided walks at 1.30pm, meeting point at the main gate; free), containing some 7,500 varieties of plants from all over the world, including a number of varieties that are no longer found in their native habitats.

Not far away is the lovely, sweet-smelling **Garden of Shakespeare's Flowers**, with "lady-smocks," rosemary and 150 other species mentioned in Shakespeare's writings. The bust of the bard is one of only two copies cast in 1914 by George Bullock. Match the flora and the folio and compare your guesses with the botanical quotes on the plaques provided by the park.

Strawberry Hill

Exiting the arboretum at MLK Jr Drive, follow the road north, then west until you reach **Stow Lake** ❶, the largest of the park's 11 lakes, which offers boating, picnicking, and hiking. **Strawberry Hill** ❷ (459ft/140 meters), located in the center of the lake, is the highest point in the park. Anyone who climbs its slopes is rewarded with a spectacular view – on a clear day, you can see the Farallon Islands, 26 miles (42km) out to sea, and Mount Diablo, 30 miles (48km) inland to the east. Mount Tamalpais or "Mount Tam," can be seen to the north across the Golden Gate Bridge.

In addition to its many lakes, gardens, and millions of plants, Golden Gate Park offers sports-lovers of every kind a satisfying weekend workout (main park roads are closed to traffic on Sundays to make this easier). There are football, baseball, and soccer fields; bocce, basketball, tennis, and handball courts; and lawn bowling greens.

There are also horseshoe and barbecue pits, marble chess tables, a golf course, a running track, jogging, bicycle and bridle paths, and hiking trails.

Free tours of the grove are available between 9am and noon on the third Saturday of each month from March to October.

Relaxing in the park.

The San Francisco Botanical Garden has 7,500 types of plants gathered from all over the world.

Dog owners can let their pooches off the leash at the dog-run.

Swarms of in-line skaters take over much of the roadways and hold races during the summer, while others keep the lost art of roller disco alive. After-work or weekend games of ultimate frisbee are regularly in progress on the large grass fields. If fishing lures you, head for the charming and old-fashioned Fly Casting Pool (for details visit www.ggacc.org).

West of Transverse Drive is **Lloyd Lake** K, celebrated for its stately Portals of the Past. These six white marble columns formed the portico of the A.N. Towne home on Nob Hill before the big quake and fire of 1906, and they were brought here some time later to lend a dignified air to this part of the park.

Go west, young man

As sunset approaches, it's a good plan to end your visit to Golden Gate Park out by the ocean. It was this more secluded western end of the park that was the favorite gathering area for the outdoor, nature-loving hippies – notably for the huge Human Be-In during the famous "Summer of Love" in 1967.

A serene afternoon on pretty Stow Lake.

At the **Polo Field** L you might find an occasional polo match or a music concert, but the space is more likely to be occupied by joggers, or kids soccer clubs.

Heading west on JFK Drive, you'll come across a surprise. On the northern side of the road, evocative of the 18th century, is the **Bison Paddock** ⓜ. The buffalo here trace their lineage not to the Great Plains, but to the Bronx Zoo of New York City, where the species was bred in captivity and saved from extinction around 1900.

Following JFK Drive to the end, the **Old Speedway Meadow** is a lovely expanse of land at the western edge of the park. North is the **Queen Wilhelmina Tulip Garden** ⓝ, where the **North Dutch Windmill** and the renovated **Murphy Windmill** ⓞ stand. The former windmill also needs new repairs as its structure has been badly damaged by water, beetle and climate conditions.

These windmills once pumped water from the streams that flowed nearby; today they stand tall in the sun as it sets slowly over the ocean. Linger over the sunset awhile, or stroll back through the park to Haight-Ashbury.

GOLDEN GATE PARK HIGHLIGHTS

Take tea in dappled Japanese shade, tilt at windmills, admire art, and go on a tour of exotic tropical rainforests.

In this city of outdoor playgrounds, one of the most enjoyed is Golden Gate Park; the scene of hippie congregations in the 1960s remains a favorite spot for relaxation and fun. The renovated children's playground, the lush, green Japanese Tea Garden, the lovely San Francisco Botanical Garden, and the evocative windmills are all long-established and popular attractions. The California Academy of Sciences and the de Young Museum are also among the reasons San Franciscans come here to enjoy their time off.

Golden Gate Park is the setting for educational amusement as well, as at the Bison Paddock. The park offers tracks and trails for biking and roller-blading, and hosts several annual events like the exuberant Bay-to-Breakers foot race.

The de Young Museum stands perilously close to the San Andreas fault; the art gallery, with its fine collection of American paintings, was severely damaged in the 1989 earthquake. To withstand future seismic incidents, the new building is able to move up to 3ft (90cm).

The Essentials

Address: Great Highway (west); Stanyan St (east); www.golden-gate-park.com

Opening Hours: see page 176 for opening hours of most of the park's attractions

Transport: bus: 5, 5R, 6, 7, 7X, 18, 28, 29, 31, 33, 44

The rules of the road in Golden Gate Park.

The Conservatory of Flowers, opened in 1879, is reminiscent of the Palm House in London's Kew Gardens.

CALIFORNIA ACADEMY OF SCIENCES

Inside the aquarium.

Joining the Steinhart Aquarium and the Morrison Planetarium at the California Academy of Sciences is the four-story sphere called "Rainforests of the World." Pritzker Prize-winning architect Renzo Piano produced the ground-breaking design, which has been rapturously received. Topped by a living, planted roof the facility employs energy-efficient, environmentally sensitive building strategies that fit well with San Francisco's "green" credentials.

On one level, the living, indoor exhibit recreates the plant life and ecology of Borneo, exhibited with bats, flying snakes, scorpions, orchids, and frogs. The unique climate of Madagascar lays claim to innumerable species that are not found naturally anywhere else on earth; many creatures are both exhibited and preserved from extinction here. Macaws, parakeets, and butterflies are on the highest, canopy level of the dome, while in the basement is a flooded Amazonian rainforest with an enormous anaconda among the turtles and fishes.

Tip: the California Academy of Sciences can be visited for free every third Wednesday of the month.

Golden Gate geese have 11 lakes to swim in. Stow Lake is the largest, and can be explored by renting a boat.

The romantic five-story pagoda stands in one of the park's oldest features, the much-loved Japanese Tea Garden.

Mission Dolores Park, one of the sunniest spots in the city.

MISSION AND CASTRO

Gays, artists, tourists, and Latinos make a rich mix in these vibrant neighborhoods, where the music is loud and the residents are proud.

The Mission and the Castro districts of San Francisco are both vibrant elements of the city's culture. Their respective Latino and gay communities would seem to have little in common, but a visit to Dolores Park, the geographical meeting point of the two neighborhoods, shows how proximity has bred community: families gather for birthday celebrations alongside gay sunbathers, from whom the park gets its tongue-in-cheek nickname: Dolores Beach.

THE MISSION DISTRICT

The **Mission ❷** is San Francisco's Latino neighborhood, and "Latino" is as specific as anyone can get. The demographics of the area have changed in tandem with the politics of Latin America, as Central Americans fleeing political turmoil in their own countries joined Mexican immigrants here. In the latter part of the 20th century, thanks to accessibility and lower rents, artists and musicians moved in, too, earning the Mission its easy-going reputation for being the city's new bohemia.

With a wealth of good, reasonably priced restaurants, trendy cafés, and hip nightspots, the face of the

neighborhood has evolved from one that was predominantly Latino to include an energetic and eclectic mix of people.

The neighborhood's main strip is **Mission Street,** lined with discount shops, outlets for inexpensive clothes, pawn brokers, bars, diners, and produce stands. This is the place to check out the *cholos* cruising the neighborhood in low riders or to listen to salsa and lively folk songs blasting from the bars. Four blocks west of Mission Street is **Dolores Street,** a boulevard

Main Attractions
Mission Dolores
Galería de la Raza
Women's Building
Dolores Park
Harvey Milk Plaza
Castro Street
Castro Theater

Map
Page 196

The Mexican Baroque facade of this defunct theater on Mission Street dates from 1928.

TIP

Take the J-Church streetcar line from any stop in Downtown toward Noe Valley. Sit with your back to the driver and on the right-hand side of the car for incredible views at the top of Dolores Park.

Misson Dolores is the oldest building in San Francisco.

The beautifully crafted Misson Dolores.

Misson Dolores.

bordered by brightly painted homes with bay windows. Just off Dolores on Liberty Street, between 20th and 21st, are some of the city's beautifully restored Victorian houses. Nestled between Dolores and Mission streets is **Valencia Street**, the city's hip epicenter, lined with cafés, bars, and boutiques.

Mission Dolores

Address: 3321 16th Street (at Dolores Street); www.missiondolores.org
Telephone: 415-621-8203
Opening Hours: daily 9am–4pm

MISSION DOLORES

Captain José Moraga and Fray Francisco Palóu founded the mission with a handful of settlers in 1776, just days before the Declaration of Independence was signed on the opposite side of the country. The church was dedicated to San Francisco de Assisi, but became known as Mission Dolores, probably because of the small lagoon on which it was built, Nuestra Señora de los Dolores.

Over the centuries the stout mission building's 4ft (1 meter) -thick adobe walls have withstood numerous natural disasters. The original bells, cast in the 1790s, hang from leather thongs above the vestibule, and most of the original craftwork is intact. Over 5,000 unnamed Costanoan Indians are buried in the small cemetery adjacent to the mission, and along with them, a good number of luminaries from San Francisco's early years, including the first governor of Alta California and the first *alcalde* (mayor) of Yerba Buena.

Admission Fee: $5 donation suggested
Transport: bus: 14, 22, 26, 33, 49; metro: J; BART: all trains

San Francisco's oldest building and the sixth mission in a chain of Spanish settlements that stretched 650 miles (1,050km) from San Diego to northern California. **Mission Dolores** is also where the Mission District takes its name from.

Salsa and savvy people

The Latino community's identification with *la raza* (race, or the people) is reflected in the many **murals** scattered throughout the neighborhood: painted on bare walls, on buildings, and inside or outside restaurants. Of particular note is **Balmy Alley**, which has gained world recognition for its many political murals. It's worth strolling around the area just to see what you can see. Better still, take one of the guided walking tours that can take in 40 murals or more.

Galería de la Raza

Address: 2857 24th Street (at Bryant Street); www.galeriadelaraza.org

Hit a taqueria for the best burritos.

Telephone: 415-826-8009
Opening Hours: Wed–Sat noon–6pm
Admission Fee: free
Transport: bus: 9, 12, 14, 27, 33, 48, 49; BART: all trains

The **Galería de la Raza** has been hailed as one of the most important

Mural on the outside of the Women's Building, 18th Street.

SHOP

The Castro is a good place for shopping, as its residents are fond of independents and work hard to stop chain stores from moving in. Be sure to check out the food, wine, plant, and clothes stores, in addition to the adult-themed emporia.

Rainbow-colored crosswalk in the city.

Casting an eye over a Castro menu.

Chicano arts centers in the country, and presents a whole spectrum of exhibits, featuring both local artists and photographers. Also worth looking at is the **Women's Building** (3543 18th Street; tel: 415-431-1180; http://womensbuilding.org), which has its own set of inspiring murals.

Dolores Park is a sloping green square fringed at the top by a stately row of Victorian houses. This is one of the sunniest spots in the whole city. It also affords impressive views of the East Bay.

THE CASTRO DISTRICT

San Francisco is often referred to as the gay capital of the world, a title its residents wear with pride. The active lesbian and gay community that has made its home in the **Castro ❸** has contributed significantly to every area of San Francisco's culture: economic, artistic, and political.

Recent years have brought a calming effect on the once-turbulent community. Angry rhetoric has cooled as activists who once railed against the establishment have become a part of the establishment themselves. There are fewer raucous marches, as there are fewer local injustices for mass anger to be directed at – whatever the

take the Market Street trolley). Just outside the station in **Harvey Milk Plaza** is a plaque to the city's first openly gay politician, who was murdered in 1978 (see page 74).

Castro Street, between 17th and 19th streets, is the neighborhood's compact business section, and these two blocks have innumerable stores, bars, cafés, and restaurants with opportunities for an afternoon or two of browsing, imbibing, nibbling, or full-on dining.

Castro Theatre

Address: 429 Castro Street (at Market Street); www.castrotheatre.com
Telephone: 415-621-6120
Opening Hours: daily
Admission Fee: charge
Transport: bus: 24, 33, 35, 37; streetcar: F; metro: K, L, M

The Castro Theatre is a beautiful work of Spanish Baroque design. This Revival house features classic and cult films, film festivals, and sing-a-longs (*Sound of Music*, *Mary Poppins*, *Grease*), and sometimes a live organist plays on an ascending platform for a bit of nostalgia.

The Castro Theatre was built in 1922. On special evenings, an organist ascends from the stage floor.

situation in other parts of the world. And yet there are still struggles to overcome: equal rights and gay marriages are the perennial hot topics.

The entrance to all of this fun is the Market Street Muni station (or

The most significant building in the Castro.

TIP

Frameline (www.frameline. org), the non-profit organization that puts on the annual International LGBT Film Festival each June, also organizes free monthly screenings of socially relevant works at The Center, 1800 Market Street.

Another stroll, this time down Market Street between Castro Street and Church Street, also gives a feel for the vibrancy of the neighborhood.

The Charles M. Holmes Campus at The Center, locally known as **The Center** (1800 Market Street; tel: 415-865-5555; Mon–Sat), is located at the edge of Hayes Valley and is closer to the Mission than the Castro, but has become the nexus for community events, classes, support groups, and information regarding the local lgbt (Lesbian, Gay, Bisexual, Transgender) community. Stop on the third floor to check out the **Psychiatric Survivors Memorial Skylight,** dedicated to people who have suffered from damaging psychiatric treatment.

Fairs and festivals

By timing your visit, it's possible to catch one or more special events that are staged throughout the year. The International LGBT Film Festival in June, which began in 1977, receives worldwide attention each year for the films that are screened at the Castro Theatre, the Yerba Buena

Enjoying the sunny weather in the Castro.

Center for the Arts, and at other venues around town.

San Francisco Pride, also in June, attracts over half a million participants who answer its call to "Stand Up, Stand Out, Stand Proud." After a series of events, including a tea dance usually held at City Hall and the women's motorcycle contingent "dykes on bikes," the celebrations culminate in a parade of floats and high-stepping frivolity.

The Castro Street Fair (www.castro streetfair.org) takes place the first Sunday in October. While Halloween used to be a neighborhood mainstay with terrific costumes and a parade, violence in 2006 cast a shadow over the proceedings, and for the past few years Halloween revelry in the Castro has been cancelled. Former openly gay politician Harvey Milk's birthday is celebrated on May 22, while on November 27, a candlelight march is held to commemorate his murder in 1978.

A Castro couple.

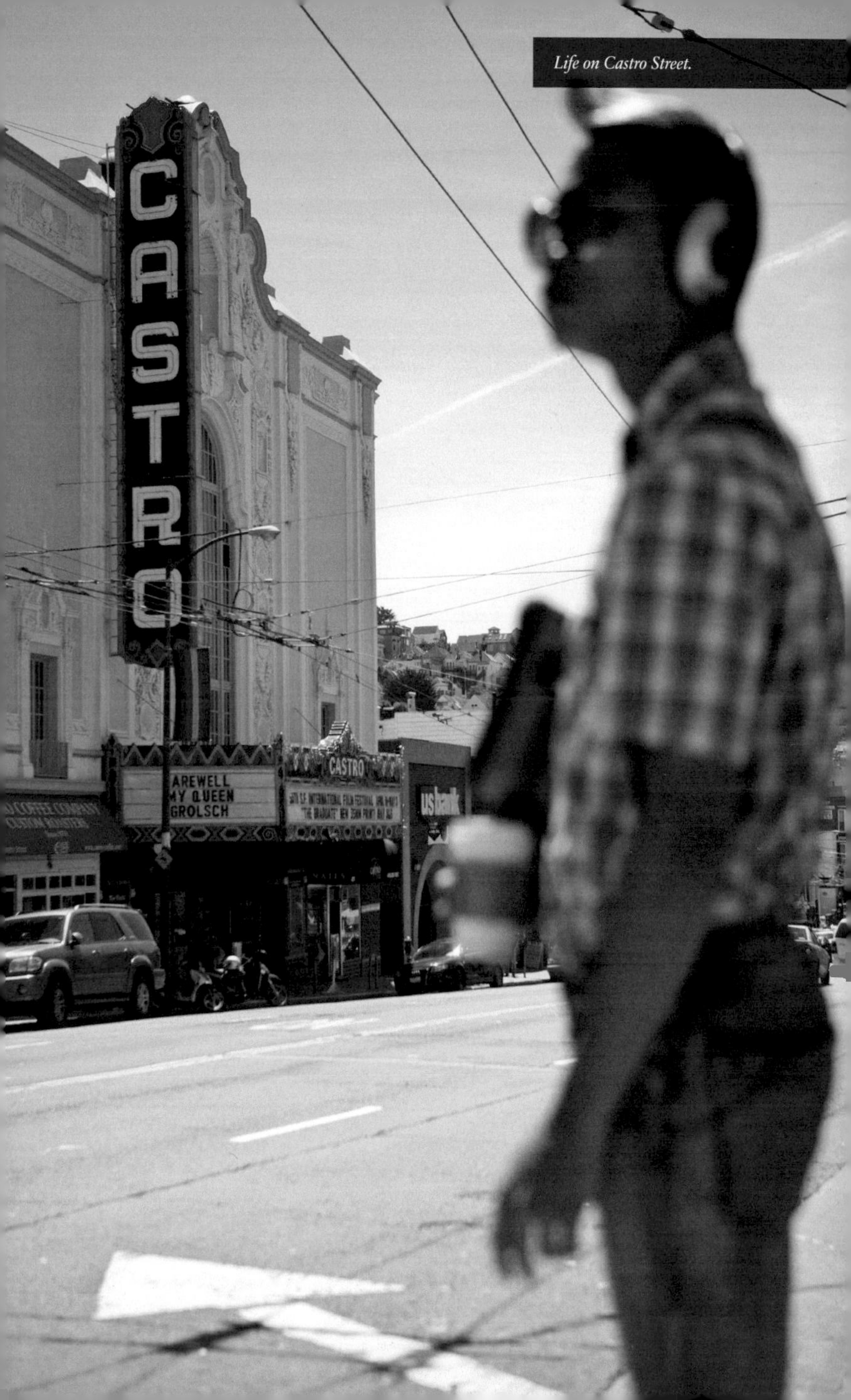

Life on Castro Street.

The Golden Gate Bridge, with the Palace of Fine Arts in the foreground.

AROUND SAN FRANCISCO

From bridge to shining bridge: a tour around
the city's outer fringes, from the Bay Bridge
in the east to the Golden Gate in the west.

More than their central cousins, San Francisco's outlying neighborhoods are reminders of the city's military and working-class foundations. Skirting the city's edges and highest peaks, they also offer some of the best views of the city, the ocean, and the natural landscape surrounding the Bay Area.

Although the Golden Gate Bridge is featured on all the postcards, many San Franciscans are particularly fond of its less glamorous counterpart, the **Bay Bridge ❹**. The Bay Bridge (correct title: San Francisco-Oakland Bay Bridge, although few refer to it as this) is one of the longest steel high-level bridges in the world, 8.25 miles (13.5km) in length. Built in 1936 with great difficulty (see page 48), it is two different types of bridge connected via a tunnel through Yerba Buena Island. The eastern span of the bridge was constructed to replace an unsafe portion of the Bay Bridge between 2002-2013 and is the most expensive public works project in California history, estimated to cost $6.4 billion.

TREASURE ISLAND

Just off the Bay Bridge, in the middle of the bay, is 403-acre (163-hectare) **Treasure Island ❺**. At the new

millennium, the former housing for officers and their families was rented out to the general public pending a redevelopment project – an interim between the US Navy's departure and the city's plans for renewal. The existing **Nimitz House** (which once housed naval top brass) is a venue for special events and to house important guests.

Man-made Treasure Island was created in the late 1930s and attached to the middle of the just-completed bridge, its purpose to house the

The fabulous view from Sutro's at the Cliff House.

Treasure Isle Marina, with the Bay Bridge in the background.

When the Navy left, the city inherited 1,011 housing units formerly occupied by Navy personnel, two vast hangars, a jail, movie theater, and marina, as well as sports fields, a bowling alley, and tennis courts. There is also a museum in the horseshoe-shaped **Administration Building**, with 20,000 items, and displays on the history of the Navy, marines, coastguards, the Bay Bridge, and the China Clipper flying boats.

SOUTH BEACH ❻

In the last decade, the city's eastern shore has had far-reaching developments in sight of the Bay Bridge. Along the Embarcadero, south of the Ferry Building, is a wonderful promenade, from the Financial District, under the Bay Bridge, all the way to AT&T Park.

For now (but maybe not for long), there are some throwbacks to the old waterfront days – a few sailors' bars and Red's Java Hut, where you can

Golden Gate International Exposition, which brought 17 million visitors in 1939 and 1940. The Expo's central landmark was a 400ft (122 meter) Tower of the Sun, designed by the acclaimed architect Arthur Brown Jr, who was also responsible for Coit Tower and much of Civic Center.

Around San Francisco

get a cheap burger and a beer, with one of the best views in the city. The area is often a sunny refuge from the fog-shrouded city, and it's easy to understand why this is fast becoming a popular spot for new housing developments, high-rises, and restaurants.

South of the Bay Bridge, the neighborhood of **South Beach** was transformed by the opening of a world-class baseball stadium.

AT&T Park

Address: 24 Willie Mays Plaza (at Embarcadero); http://sanfrancisco. giants.mlb.com/sf/ballpark/
Telephone: 415-972-2000
Admission Fee: charge
Transport: bus: 10, 30, 45, 47; metro: N, T

The park is home of the mighty San Francisco Giants who became world champions after winning the 2010 World Series and repeated that victory again in 2012 and 2014. The area is a great example of the marriage of

The opening of the baseball stadium revitalized the South Beach area.

old and new San Francisco. Formerly crumbling warehouses house fine restaurants, chic furniture galleries, and bookstores.

Desolate streets have been transformed into palm-tree-lined walkways, and a once-barren bay front is now **McCovey Cove** (named after Willie McCovey, baseball Hall

The opening of the baseball stadium revitalized the South Beach area.

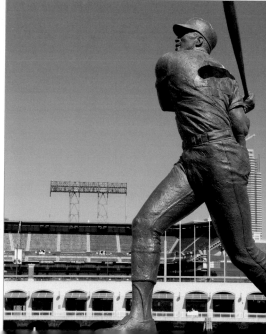

Noe Valley.

of Fame member and former San Francisco Giant). An historical **baseball** tour of the park and clubhouse lets foreign tourists into the mysteries of this sacred American pastime.

South Park, a small neighborhood between 2nd and 3rd, and Brannan and Bryant streets were, at the turn of the millennium, home of San Francisco's dot-com elite. (*Wired* and its web sibling *HotWired* began here.)

Now that most of those companies have come and gone, South Park is a lovely place to enjoy a meal at one of the cafés lining the park in the middle of the grand circle.

The gentrification of the South Beach area has spread down 3rd Street with the new Muni rail line. Forgotten districts, like **China Basin**, **Dogpatch**, and **Hunter's Point**, are now reachable by rail, and the social and cultural landscapes evolve again.

POTRERO HILL ❼

Southwest of Dogpatch is **Potrero Hill**, a former working-class neighborhood of colorful houses and utilitarian stores that has been discovered by the new gentry. Not far away is San Francisco's old and drafty sports park, Candlestick Park, where the Giants and the San Francisco 49ers football team both played. One of the reasons the 1989 mid-afternoon earthquake, which collapsed a section of the Bay Bridge, resulted in so few casualties is because most locals were either in the baseball park or at home watching the World Series, and not traveling on the bridge itself.

South of the **Mission** (see page 187) and the **Castro** (see page 190) is low-key **Noe Valley ❽** mothers pushing baby carriages. The street is like a miniature village with an array of offbeat stores and restaurants. Noe Valley is a pleasant place to stroll, away from most of the tourists, and is evocative of the city's residential neighborhoods, quite different in character from bustling **Haight-Ashbury** (see page 173).

TWIN PEAKS ❾

A winding scenic drive leads to the top of **Twin Peaks**, translated into Spanish as El Pecho de la Chola (the Bosom of the Indian Girl). The hills (910ft /227 meters in height),

A resident of the San Francisco Zoo.

dominated by Sutro Tower, offer a wonderful panorama of the city and surrounding bay. Parking and viewing points can be found along Twin Peaks Boulevard.

A pleasant way to reach the next destination overlooking the Pacific Ocean is to follow the **49-Mile Scenic Drive** as it meanders down Laguna Honda and 7th Avenue to and through Golden Gate Park. Alternatively, head west on Taraval through the **Sunset District** ⑩, and pick up the Great Highway northwest of **Lake Merced**.

At the far western end of Golden Gate Park is **Ocean Beach** ⑪. Although the beach has dramatic ocean views, only the hardiest souls dip their toes into the ice-cold water. Farther north along the coast is the **Cliff House** ⑫, now part of the Golden Gate National Recreation Area.

At **Seal Rocks** ⑬, sleek and playful sea lions frolic in full view, while up on the cliff are the **Sutro Baths**. Little remains of the original swimming complex, built to enchant the city's inhabitants when it opened in 1896, but the views are still as wonderful and it's fun to climb on the ruins and in the nearby cave.

The long and winding road to Twin Peaks.

LAND'S END ⑭

Near the Palace of the Legion of Honor is a path leading to **Land's End**, the wildest part of San Francisco's coast and one of the city's best urban hikes, with trails down to a labyrinth and a pocket beach and vista points pointing out where ships have sunk. This part of the Golden Gate National Recreation Area is next to **Lincoln Park** ⑮, where one of the city's three golf courses is located. It offers excellent, peek-a-boo glimpses of the **Golden Gate Bridge** ⑯ (see page 204).

The remains of Sutro Baths.

Golden Gate Bridge

Perhaps the biggest attraction in San Francisco and certainly one of the most iconic, the Golden Gate also has a long history.

Sailing under the Golden Gate Bridge today, it is interesting to consider that engineers once thought it impossible to span the Golden Gate Strait at this point, because of the depth of the water (318ft/97 meters, at its deepest point) and the powerful tidal rush.

The city authorized studies for a bridge in 1917, but it was 1933 before the first shovel turned under the gaze of master engineer Joseph B. Strauss (no relation to the famous waltz composer). Four years later the bridge opened, at a cost of $35 million and the lives of 11 construction workers. Today the bridge takes more than 40 million vehicles a year between the city and regions to the north.

Romantic as the bridge is, some people are more concerned about the hard facts: including its freeway approaches, the Golden Gate Bridge is 1.7 miles (2.7km) long, with the main suspended span stretching for 4,200ft (1,280 meters). The towers stand 746ft (227 meters) above the water. The total length of wire on both main cables is 80,000 miles (129,000km).

The bridge was built so sturdily that it has closed only three times due to high winds. Crews work continually from one end of the bridge to the other and back, sandblasting rust and repainting the bridge international orange – not red, as is often thought – using 10,000 gallons (38,000 liters) of paint a year.

With magnificent views and cooling, often frigid, breezes, the bridge is very popular with walkers, more than 200,000 of whom turned out to celebrate its opening in 1937. When it was again closed to motorists to honor its golden anniversary, four times as many pedestrians arrived – so many fans, in fact, that under their combined weight the bridge's central span sank measurably.

Legend has it that Alfred Hitchcock wanted to use the bridge for the final scene in *The Birds* (filmed in nearby Bodega Bay). He envisioned his heroine escaping toward San Francisco – only to find the Golden Gate Bridge covered in birds. It was thought too scary an ending to release.

The famous bridge is actually orange, not gold or red as it often appears in photographs.

California Palace of the Legion of Honor

Address: Lincoln Park, 100 34th Avenue (at Clement Street); http://legionofhonor.famsf.org
Telephone: 415-750-3600
Opening Hours: Tue–Sun 9.30am–5.15pm
Admission Fee: charge
Transport: bus: 1, 18, 38

The California Palace of the Legion of Honor opened in 1924 as a memorial to California's war dead. There is a peculiar and moving grandeur to the museum's architecture, with its courtyard and columns and porticoes. Inspired by the Palais de la Légion d'Honneur in Paris, it is also a showcase for European art. One of five original castings of Rodin's *The Thinker* cogitates in the palace's Court of Honor; and almost 70 more of his sculptures are on display in the **Rodin Gallery**, where weekend organ recitals are sometimes held. Also included in the museum's collection are El Greco's *St John the Baptist* and Monet's moody *The Grand Canal, Venice*. From the palace are some of the finest views of the city and the Golden Gate Bridge.

RICHMOND DISTRICT ⑱

The **Richmond District**, is a melting pot of Asian culture that is predominantly Chinese. Located between Golden Gate Park and the Presidio, Richmond was previously little but sand dunes stretching down to the Pacific Ocean. The well-known landscape photographer Ansel Adams used to play here as a boy, and a number of his photographs evoke the area as it looked around the end of the 19th century.

In the 1970s, second- and third-generation Chinese families began moving here from the crowded downtown Chinatown to settle next to the Greeks, Russians, and Irish who were already in residence. Today, the Richmond area is made up of

family dwellings, brick and cement row houses, and low-rise apartment buildings. The main avenue is Clement Street, crammed full of restaurants, bars, specialty shops, ethnic grocery shops and other funky shops tucked in between.

THE PRESIDIO ⑲

The **Presidio** housed the military guardians of the region for more than 200 years, and is one of the most desirable pieces of land in America, commanding the wooded heights overlooking the Pacific Ocean and the approach to the Golden Gate Bridge. It was decommissioned in 1993, amid endless discussions over its future.

The complex is managed now by the Golden Gate National Recreation Area, the National Park Service, and the Presidio Trust; the trust's aim has been to make the Presidio self-sustaining. One project is the massive **Letterman Digital Arts Center** next to the Lombard Street entrance, now housing filmmaker George Lucas's Industrial Light and Magic company as well as LucasArts. Recent years saw a flurry of activities aimed at

Rodin's The Thinker, outside the Legion of Honor Museum.

The beautiful Palace of Fine Arts was built in 1915.

The 49-Mile Scenic Drive passes near most of the city's best attractions. Look for the blue-and-white seagull signs.

revitalising the area. Former military barracks, hangars and warehouses have been converted into elegant restaurants, schools, museum and cultural centers . A $1 billon project to replace the old Doyle Drive viaduct with an eight-lane boulevard, two pairs of tunnels and a pair of elevated viaduct, is scheduled to be completed by the end of 2016. The Presidio Trust (www.presidio.gov/presidio-trust) poured $19 million into rehabilitation of hundreds of former military buildings including the Officers' Club which has been turned into a cultural and community center offering a great variety of free programmes such as archeological demonstrations, art walks, lectures, festivals live concerts and other performances. The club also houses the Heritage Gallery displaying ancient artifacts, photos, murals and texts. The entire Presidio area, especially the Crissy Field, is now crisscrossed with miles of hiking and bike trails and offers recreational activities including picnic areas and beach sports. Located in the renovated historic buildings near the Main Post is the **Walt Disney Family Museum** (Wed–Mon 10am–6pm; http://waltdisney.org) dedicated to life and legacy of Walt Disney.

The Legion of Honor Museum offers the perfect backdrop for wedding photos.

Windsurfer at the Presidio.

Interactive galleries, animations, movies, music and listening stations are equally entertaining for young and adult fans.

Palace of Fine Arts ⓴

At the Presidio's eastern end is one of the city's most admired buildings, whose domed rotunda and lagoon-reflected arches were designed by Bernard Maybeck for the 1915 Panama-Pacific International Exposition. The structure was modeled after the mysterious edifice in the painting, *The Island of the Dead* by Swiss artist, Arnold Böcklin.

The **Golden Gate Promenade** ㉑, which extends from the bridge past the palace and onward through the Marina District to Fisherman's Wharf, is a scenic way to approach Fort Point, at the northern end of the Presidio. **Fort Point National Historic Site** ㉒ (Thu–Tue 10am–5pm; tel: 415 556 1693) is a brick guardhouse, built around 1860, now run by the National Park Service (www.nps.gov). The fort was a base of operations for the construction of the Golden Gate Bridge.

The iconic Golden Gate Bridge.

THE GOLDEN GATE BRIDGE

The elegance of the structure and the beauty of the setting have stolen many hearts; crossing it is truly an exhilarating experience.

Costly. Ugly. Disruptive. Impossible. Critics, from City Hall to the Sierra Club, failed to weaken chief engineer Joseph B. Strauss's resolve to construct a suspension bridge spanning the Golden Gate Strait – where San Francisco Bay enters the Pacific. On opening day in 1937, the *San Francisco Chronicle* described the bridge as "a thirty-five million dollar steel harp." The distinctive orange vermillion color (which is clearly not gold) was chosen to harmonize with the setting and to stand out in the famous Bay fog. In the more than 75 years since, the bridge has weathered political detractors, powerful wind, and an earthquake. Unfortunately, Strauss did not live long enough to see it become one of the world's best-loved landmarks; the engineer died barely a year after completing the mighty task.

The famous orange color is known as International Orange, and was originally a sealant used to protect the structure.

Protesters in 2008 climb the bridge.

The Essentials

Website: www.goldengatebridge.org
Tel: 415-455-2000
Admission Fee: charge for vehicles; free for pedestrians
Transport: bus: 28

The bridge's vital stats.

Golden Gate in the Movies

2015 *Terminator: Genisys*
2011 *Rise of the Planet of the Apes*
2013 *Pacific Rim*
2006 *X-Men: The Last Stand*
2003 *The Core*
1994 *Interview with a Vampire*
1991 *Star Trek VI: The Undiscovered Country*
1986 *Star Trek IV: The Voyage Home*
1985 *A View to a Kill (James Bond)*
1978 *Superman*
1974 *Herbie Rides Again*
1958 *Vertigo (Alfred Hitchcock)*
1955 *It Came from Beneath the Sea*

THE HISTORY OF HARD HATS

A hard hat and a head for heights: indispensable requirements for all Golden Gate Bridge construction workers.

If you are driving 600,000 rivets into two soaring towers, you'd better make sure that all heads below are safely covered. Precisely that concern prompted the establishment of America's first "Hard Hat Area," on the Golden Gate Bridge's construction site. Compulsory protective headgear shielding against falling objects contributed to the project's remarkable safety record. San Francisco's E.D. Bullard Company manufactured the prototype hard hat worn by the bridge workers. The founder's son based the design on the Doughboy helmet worn by soldiers in World War I. Composed of steamed canvas, glue and an internal suspension device, this shiny black "Hard-Boiled Hat" evolved, through aluminum and fiberglass versions, into today's light, bright plastic model.

The first Pedestrian's Day, 1937.

The Golden Gate has reversible lanes so that most follow the flow of traffic during the busy rush hours. Carpools with a minimum of three people in them do not have to pay a toll.

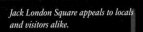
Jack London Square appeals to locals and visitors alike.

OAKLAND AND BERKELEY

Oakland has Jack London landmarks and speedy access to Silicon Valley, while Berkeley has long been a pioneer of social experimentation.

From the Black Panthers to Chez Panisse, the East Bay is as revolutionary as San Francisco. Built around the ports and the University of California, Oakland and Berkeley offer a slightly slower pace than their sister city, as well as craftsman-style homes, and leafy, winding neighborhoods. But don't mistake this for suburbia: the lively political culture, widely diverse demographics, museums, and intellectual centers make these cities thriving metropolitan areas with a distinctly urban edge.

OAKLAND

Despite author Gertrude Stein's infamous quip that "there is no *there* there," Oakland long ago emerged from the shadow of its older sister to the west. In fact, things are looking pretty good on Oakland – especially for women: according to recent data, Oakland ranks high as far as the number of businesses owned by women is concerned. More than half a century after Stein's disparaging observation, visitors would do well to reconsider: there really is a *there* here.

Jack London Square ❶

Address: Broadway at Embarcadero West; www.jacklondonsquare.com

The Oakland Museum covers the history and art of California.

Telephone: 510-645-9292
Tranport: AC Transit bus: 72M, 72R Alameda/Oakland

Oakland's version of Fisherman's Wharf is the restaurant and shopping pedestrian walk called **Jack London Square**. The Oakland native and author of *The Sea Wolf* and *The Call of the Wild* (see page 67), who died in 1916, might not be impressed to see the overpriced restaurants and souvenir stores, but he would be happy to munch crab, listen to good music, and watch the sailboats

Main Attractions
Jack London Square
USS Potomac
City Center
Paramount Theater
African American Museum
Lake Merritt
Oakland Museum
University of California
People's Park
Telegraph Avenue
Gourmet Ghetto

Map
Page 210

Oakland and Berkeley

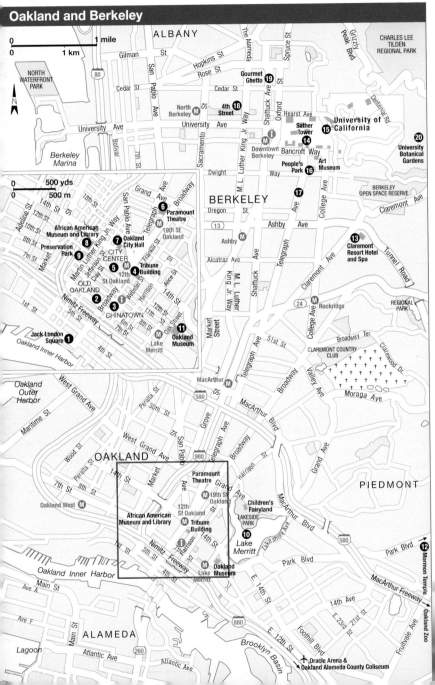

ALBANY

North Waterfront Park

Berkeley Marina

Oakland Outer Harbor

BERKELEY

Gourmet Ghetto ⑲

North Berkeley Ⓜ

4th Street ⑱

Downtown Berkeley Ⓜ

Sather Tower ⑭

University of California

People's Park ⑯ Art Museum

⑰

University Botanical Gardens ⑳

Claremont Resort Hotel and Spa ⑬

Rockridge Ⓜ

CLAREMONT COUNTRY CLUB

Moraga Ave

PIEDMONT

OAKLAND

Oakland West Ⓜ

Paramount Theatre

19th St Oakland Ⓜ

12th St Oakland Ⓜ

African American Museum and Library ⓘ Tribune Building

Children's Fairyland

LAKESIDE PARK

Lake Merritt

Oakland Museum ⑩

Oakland Inner Harbor

ALAMEDA

Lagoon

Mormon Temple ⑫

Oakland Zoo

Oracle Arena & Oakland Alameda County Coliseum

Inset:

Jack London Square ①

OLD OAKLAND ②

③

Tribune Building ④

⑤

CITY CENTER

Oakland City Hall ⑦

African American Museum and Library ⑧

Preservation Park ⑨

Paramount Theatre ⑥

19th St Oakland

CHINATOWN

Oakland Museum ⑪

Lake Merritt

The Tribune Tower.

Oakland attractions.

In the books Martin Eden (1909) and John Barleycorn (1913), Jack London wrote about the Oakland waterfront where he grew up.

pass by. The **First and Last Chance Saloon**, which London frequented, is popular with tourists, and nearby is his sod-roofed Yukon cabin, moved from Alaska to the waterfront, in tribute to the city's most famous son.

Moored in the harbor is the USS *Potomac*, President Franklin D. Roosevelt's "floating White House," and now a National Historic Monument (www.usspotomac.org; dockside tours Wed, Fri, and Sun 11am–2pm).

On Friday mornings, a **farmers' market** is held in the part of the city called **Old Oakland** ❷ (9th Street at Broadway; http://uvfm.org/old-oakland-fridays/), a neighborhood with stores, restaurants, and shops in its renovated buildings. Nearby, Oakland's **Chinatown** ❸ is more negotiable than its cousin across the bay.

Oakland's many landmarks include the **Tribune Building** ❹, with its distinctive tower, and **City Center** ❺, a mall with restaurants, jazz concerts, and art exhibits. The Art Deco palace, the **Paramount Theatre** ❻ at 2025 Broadway, is the home of the Oakland Ballet and the Paramount Organ Pops.

The theater also screens old movies, complete with newsreels.

Another Deco gem, the **Oakland Fox Theater** (www.thefoxoakland.com), located on Telegraph Avenue between 18th and 19th streets, has been saved by an eager band of

The First and Last Chance Saloon.

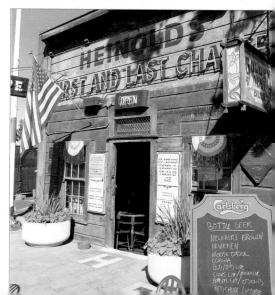

preservationists. It is now a concert venue showcasing major acts and indie music. The **Rotunda Building**, two years older than **Oakland City Hall ❼**, was built in 1912.

From City Hall, head back toward the harbor to visit the interesting **African American Museum and Library ❽** (659 14th Street and Martin Luther King Jr Way; tel: 510-637-0200; Tue–Sat noon–5.30pm; free; www.oaklandlibrary.org). Oakland has a special significance for black Americans; the Black Panther Movement was founded here in the 1960s. The Panthers' politics spread to college campuses around the country. Still closer to the harbor is pretty **Preservation Park ❾**, a restored Victorian village with 19th-century streetlamps and lush gardens.

On the eastern edge of town is a natural landmark, **Lake Merritt ❿**. The large saltwater lake and wildlife refuge, rimmed by Victorian houses and a necklace of lights, is the location of 10-acre (4-hectare) theme park **Children's Fairyland** (see box). The lake itself is popular all year round for sailing and picnicking.

Lake Merritt.

The Lionel Wilson Building.

Oakland Museum ⓫

Address: 1000 Oak Street; www.museumca.org
Telephone: 510-238-2200
Opening Hours: Wed, Thur 11am–5pm, Sat–Sun 10am–6pm, Fri 11am–10pm
Admission Fee: charge

Oakland also has its own, smaller Chinatown.

Transport: AC Transit bus: 72M, 72R Alameda/Oakland

Not far from the lake, the **Oakland Museum**, landscaped with terraces and gardens, and on three levels, is considered to be the finest museum in the state for California's art, history, and natural science. The **Cowell Hall of California History** has a huge collection of artifacts, and the **Gallery of California Art** is known for oil paintings.

Visible from the Nimitz Freeway, if you're driving toward the airport southeast of the city, is the **Oracle Arena and Oakland Alameda County Coliseum**, the home of the Oakland Athletic baseball team, the Oakland Raiders football team, and the Golden State Warriors basketball team, who won the NBA finals in 2015, claiming their first title in 40 years.

In the hills above Oakland to the east is the five-towered, white granite **Mormon Temple** ⑫, the second Church of Latter-day Saints temple to be built in California. From its heights are wonderful views of San Francisco Bay.

BERKELEY

On the approach to Berkeley from Oakland, two buildings catch the eye.

FACT

Currently, there are seven Nobel Prize-winners on the faculty at Berkeley. Since 1939, there have been a total of 29 Nobel laureates on staff.

CALIFORNIA CUISINE

The grand dame of California Cuisine, Alice Waters, never veered from her commitment to serving the freshest, locally grown and pedigreed ingredients. To achieve this, she built a network of specialized local suppliers that transformed the culinary landscape of Berkeley. Chez Panisse opened in 1971 and although it has inspired imitators, this is where California Cuisine began.

Menus change nightly, all meals are prix-fixe, and the selection (there are sometimes two main-course options, one fish or seafood, the other meat) may be made after securing a reservation, which must be confirmed a month in advance. The Café at Chez Panisse offers a more relaxed and moderately priced à-la-carte dinner menu. Chez Panisse is located at 1517 Shattuck Avenue, Berkeley, tel: 510-548-5525.

Sun-kissed in Berkeley.

On the hillside is a fairy-tale white palace, the **Claremont Resort Hotel and Spa**  (www.fairmont.com/claremont-berkeley/; tel: 510-843-3000), which, like San Francisco's Palace of Fine Arts, was finished just before the Panama Pacific International Exposition of 1915.

The other landmark is a pointed structure, a soaring bell tower. Its official name is the **Sather Tower** ⑭, but it is known to everyone simply as the "Campanile" because the tower is modeled after St Mark's Campanile in Venice, Italy.

The Sather Tower.

University of California, Berkeley ⑮

Address: Bancroft Avenue at Telegraph Avenue; www.berkeley.edu
Transport: AC Transit bus: 1, 7, 12, 1851B; BART: Richmond, Fremont

The Sather Tower belongs to the university, which is considered one of the country's finest. Berkeley grew from a humble prep school, operating out of a former fandango house in Oakland, to become part of the nine-campus University of California system.

The Free Speech Movement of 1964 put Berkeley on the map. At issue was a UC Berkeley administration order to limit political activities on campus. This touched off massive protests here and on campuses nationwide. For years the campus has been a center of political action.

In 1969, students took to the streets to stop the college expanding into an area they wanted for **People's Park** ⑯.

The Claremont Resort.

A sunny sidewalk in Berkeley.

They prevailed, despite the intervention of 2,000 National Guard troops, and violence that caused the death of an onlooker. Years on, People's Park drew more drug dealers and drifters from the city's homeless than it did students. But today, student unrest has turned more to rest and recreation, so the city has added basketball and volleyball courts to the park, which is also a site for festivals and concerts.

To get the feel of Berkeley at its liveliest, walk down **Telegraph Avenue** ⑰ from Dwight Way to the university. Students, townspeople, and visitors pick their way between stores harking back to the 1960s with jewelry and pottery, and those catering to modern students. Music fans head for Rasputin, one of the biggest independent record stores in the Bay Area. More shopping is found in the neighborhood north of University Avenue called **4th Street** ⑱, where boutiques sell bijou crafts, furniture, and designer clothes.

Gourmet ghetto

Shoppers in 4th Street often dine in Upper Shatuck Avenue, known locally as the **Gourmet Ghetto** ⑲.

Berkeley's climate (it can be foggy in San Francisco but sunny across the bay) produces sweet scents in the **University Botanical Gardens** ⑳ (tel: 510-643-2755; daily 9am–5pm; http://botanicalgarden.berkeley.edu; free on first Wed each month) in Strawberry Canyon. Over 12,000 species thrive in the research facility.

The famous Berkeley campus.

The view of Sausalito from across the Bay.

THE BAY AREA

From the high sequoias of Muir Woods to the high-tech spark of Silicon Valley, the Bay Area is happy, wealthy, and in constant flux.

Outside San Francisco are as many fascinating sights and delights as there are in the city. Mountains, redwood forests, and wonderful Pacific beaches beckon, as well as intriguing Silicon Valley. Travel is easy: several bridges span the bay; an underground train system (bart) links up the East and South Bay with the city; ferries crisscross the water; and trains run up and down the peninsula. Getting around by car, though, is the most attractive way to explore the coasts, hills, and valleys.

MARIN COUNTY

Starting north from San Francisco on US 101, the route to Marin County begins by crossing the fantastic Golden Gate Bridge. Directly ahead, the **Marin Headlands** are wild and lonely cliffs, standing in contrast to the metropolis left behind across the bay.

At the northern end of the bridge is the **Marine Mammal Center ❶** (www.marinemammalcenter.org; tel: 415-289-SEAL; daily 10am–5pm; free but donations welcome), a nonprofit organization that rescues sick or injured marine mammals stranded along the coastline. The Mammal Center is part of the Golden Gate National Recreation Area.

Stopping for a bayside breakfast.

The town of **Sausalito ❷**, accessible by ferry (tel: 415-705-8200; from Pier 39, Pier 41 or the Ferry Building; approximate 30-minute crossing) from San Francisco, is sometimes referred to as the "French Riviera" of the West Coast for its Mediterranean climate, art galleries, and restaurants. A stroll under the palm trees along the curved main street brings a sense of the changes of the past centuries in the gracious Victorian homes hugging the hill. In the 1870s, Californian fruit and vegetables were

Main Attractions
Sausalito
Bay Area Discovery Museum
Tiburon
Angel Island
Muir Beach and Woods
Mount Tamalpais
Palo Alto
Tech Museum of Innovation
San Jose Museum of Art
History San Jose Museum
Rosicrucian Egyptian
    Museum and Planetarium

Map
Page 218

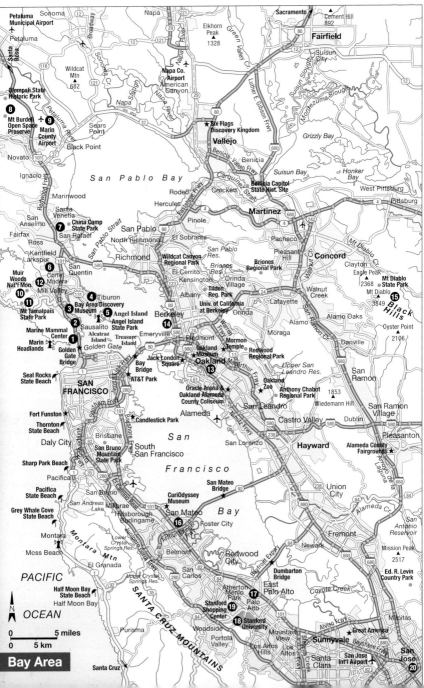

Houses in Sausalito.

Sailing past sunny Sausalito.

shipped to Europe, and English captains sometimes set up home here. Quaint, tree-lined walkways, small, manicured gardens, and specialty stores display the British influence.

When Sausalito became a vital shipping link between San Francisco and the rest of California, the main street sprouted saloons, brothels, and gambling houses, and the town was a base for bootleggers running hooch to supply the speakeasies of San Francisco.

Bay Area Discovery Museum ❸

Address: 557 McReynolds Road, East Fort Baker; www.baykids museum.org
Telpehone: 415-339-3900
Opening Hours: Tue–Sun 9am–4pm
Admission Fee: charge
Transport: No public buses go directly to the museum so the best way to get there is to drive or take a ferry from San Francisco (Ferry Building on Embarcadero or Pier 41 at

At home on a houseboat.

GREEN GULCH ZEN CENTER

Stop by the Green Gulch Zen Center near Sausalito (1601 Shoreline Highway; tel: 415-383-3134; http://sfzc.org/green-gulch), a meditation community offering a pastoral contrast to San Francisco, only 12 miles (19km) away. Extensive vegetable gardens, lovingly cultivated by Green Gulch residents, cater to the Zen Center's vegetarian restaurant, Greens, in San Francisco's Marina District.

Visitors are welcome to enjoy the tranquil grounds, to attend morning instruction, or simply to sample some home-baked bread with tea. The Zen Center offers classes in Buddhist philosophy, meditation retreats, and workshops, and holds special Sunday programs that are open to the public on a drop-in basis.

TIP

Ferries to Tiburon and Angel Island leave from Pier 39 on Fisherman's Wharf, home of the frisky sea lions. For more ferry information, see page 256.

One of the resident sealions.

Fisherman's Wharf) to Sausalito and then a cab.

Located just north of town, this museum has hands-on exhibits with children in mind, like Lookout Cove, Tot Spot, and art studios, focusing on natural sciences and art, with plenty of little-finger-friendly multimedia displays.

Tiburon

East of Sausalito, and also just a ferry ride from San Francisco, is **Tiburon ❹** – well known for **Ark Row**, a winding street of art galleries, restaurants, and specialty stores. Tiburon was not always so appealing. Before 1930 the town was a marsh, and people lived in rough and often shabby "arks." When entrepreneur Fred Zelinsky filled

Marin Civic Center in San Rafael was designed by Frank Lloyd.

in the swampy land, he built a street where people had to paddle to the grocery store. Tiburon is now a wealthy residential town, attracting San Franciscans who prefer the 20-minute ferry ride to freeway traffic jams. Robin Williams was a resident here for many years until his untimely death in 2014. The rainbow-hued Waldo tunnel that enters Marin from San Francisco was renamed in his honor.

Tiburon has been luring city dwellers for more than a century, since Dr Benjamin Lyford, a pioneering embalming surgeon, tried to start one of California's first utopian communities in the late 1800s. In his promotional brochure for Hygeia – named for the goddess of health – Doctor Lyford promised a community with "restrictions that will keep out the vices and vampires common to all communities." At the northern exit of town, his Victorian home and **Lyford's Tower**, once the gateway to the Hygeia, are reminders of this eccentric experiment.

ANGEL ISLAND

A ferry ride from Tiburon (or from San Francisco) reaches **Angel Island ❺**, an uninhabited isle of protected

Mill Valley.

parkland where deer and other wild animals graze. This triangular-shaped island draws picnickers to enjoy panoramic views of San Francisco and the Golden Gate Bridge. A stroll around the island's perimeter trails takes only about an hour, but an ambitious climb to the top of **Mount Livermore** delivers breathtaking views, literally.

Angel Island hides various secrets. It has been home to the Coast Miwok, to Spanish explorers, Russian otter hunters, American soldiers, and others. In the 1840s the island belonged to Antonio Osio, who grazed his cattle here and cut timber for the Presidio at Yerba Buena. In 1853, the United States assumed ownership and the island was used by the military.

First tagged *Isla de los Angeles* by the crew of the Spanish ship *San Carlos, for* thousands of Chinese immigrants interned here it became a dreaded "Ellis Island of the West." The stations used for processing immigrants and holding World War II prisoners have been renovated and are open for tours (tel: 415-435-3522). The buildings near the ferry landing were used as a quarantine station during a

19th-century smallpox epidemic. **Fort McDowell**, on the eastern side, was used to process soldiers as early as the Spanish-American War. Later, the fort became a missile base.

To the south, an area near the Coast Guard Station at Point Blunt was a favored dueling spot for San Franciscans. In 1858, a crowd of 1,000 came here to witness a duel between a state senator and a United States commissioner. These days people come to relax, sail, picnic, and mountain bike.

LARKSPUR AND SAN RAFAEL

Back in Tiburon, continue on **Paradise Drive**, which winds along the eucalyptus-scented **Ring Mountain Preserve** before opening onto lovely views of the bay. Paradise Drive leads to another bay town, **Larkspur ❻**, popular with commuters to San Francisco and the East Bay. Larkspur is quiet, nestled by the foot of Mount Tamalpais The downtown area is on the National Register of Historic Places.

Farther north is Marin County's largest town, **San Rafael ❼**, still only 17 miles (27km) from San Francisco. A main point of interest is the **Marin Civic Center** (tel: 415-499-6400; www.

Antipasta at Angelino's Italian, Sausalito.

Larkspur.

Muir Woods.

Dining on Main Street
in Marin County.

marincounty.org), designed by Frank Lloyd Wright for concerts, lectures, and performances, from symphonies to political and speaking programs. Straight up US 101, near the **Mt Burdell Open Space Preserve 8**, is the **Marin County Airport 9**.

MARIN COUNTY WEST

North of Sausalito, off Highway 1, are **Muir Beach and Muir Woods 10**. The beach is pretty and open, with sheltered coves for picnicking. A nude sunbathing area is protected from the wind by a cluster of rocks.

Both the beach and the woods are named for naturalist John Muir, and known for the grove of sequoia trees that thrive in the damp climate. Hikers and strollers set off on a paved walkway that winds through eucalyptus and tall columns of red-tinted trees, ultimately leading to a high, open path that drops to the ocean.

Steep Ravine, the rocky beach at the foot of the trail, offers the dramatic sight of the waves meeting the rock wedges head on, frothy spray bursting high in the air. Just past Muir Woods is Stinson Beach, the

Hiking to the top of Mt Tamalpais offers a rewarding vista.

most popular beach in the Bay Area. Students study and sunbathe, families picnic and build sandcastles, and brave souls splash in the chilly surf.

Continue north on Highway 1 for Point Reyes and Mendocino (see page 229). To stay local, turn right off Highway 1 onto Panoramic Highway and follow the signs to **Mount Tamalpais 11**. Once home to the Miwok tribe, Tamalpais has three peaks. The east one (2,571ft/784 meters) is popular for the trails to the fire-lookout tower at the summit. Cyclists enjoy the ride along **Corte Madera Creek** up to the top of Mount Tam.

At the foot of Mount Tamalpais is the little town of **Mill Valley 12**, on whose south side is Old Mill Creek. In 1836 John Reed built the US's first sawmill here. The streets of Mill Valley spread out from the old railroad depot and provide shady avenues for walking and shopping.

EAST BAY

The Bay Bridge leads to **Oakland 13** (see page 209) and **Berkeley 14** (see page 213). Over the Berkeley ridge and east of the town of Walnut Creek is **Mount Diablo 15**, a central landmark in California. The name

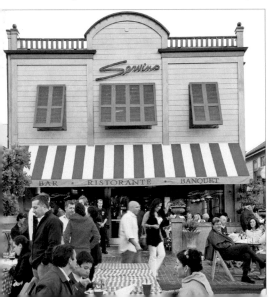

("mountain of the devil") stems from when the US Government tried to usurp it from the Native Americans, and a spirit was said to have intervened to scare away the troops. The peak's panoramic vista of the jarring, craggy summits of the Sierra Nevada mountains, bordering the fertile Central Valley, is unforgettable. In the shadow of Mount Diablo are some pretty, upscale communities.

SOUTH AND SILICON VALLEY

South of San Francisco, two other bridges cross the bay. The first is at **San Mateo** ⑯, a suburban residential community with a wildlife habitat and picnic facilities. **CuriOdyssey** (1651 Coyote Point Dr; Tue–Sun 10am–5pm; tel: 650-342-7755; http://curiodyssey.org) is a learning center to inspire environmental responsibility. Coyote Point has a huge walk-through aviary, which is home to more than four dozen native Californian bird species, in an up-close, natural setting, as well as an enlarged walk-through honeycomb display as part of a honeybee exhibit.

The second bridge, the Dumbarton Toll Bridge, is just before **Palo Alto** ⑰, the wealthy college town 33 miles (53km) from San Francisco. Palo Alto is a major player in the Silicon Valley tech scene, partly through its association with nearby **Stanford University** ⑱.

When the railroad tycoon Leland Stanford turned over the bulk of his fortune to the college in the 1890s, he included an 8,200-acre (3,320-hectare) horse farm that gave the campus its nickname, "the Farm," which is still in use. Frederick Law Olmsted (architect of New York's Central Park) had a hand in designing the campus, handsomely dotted with cloisters and yellow sandstone buildings with red-tile roofs. The university's first president wrote that the campus itself was "an integral part of a Stanford education."

The observation deck of the 250ft (76 meter) **Hoover Tower** (daily 10am–4pm; http://visit.stanford.edu/plan/guides/hoover.html) gives spectacular views of Silicon Valley, and rooms in the tower display documents from the Herbert Hoover presidency.

Also worth visiting are the **Rodin Sculpture Garden** (tel: 650-723-4177) and the **Stanford Linear Accelerator Center**, which generates high-energy electron beams. Six private tours are given every month by reservation

Stanford University's Hoover Tower.

Stanford has produced several tech zillionaires.

Silicon Valley

The home of technological evolution, Silicon Valley is where all the big guns made names for themselves, from Apple to Google to Facebook...

Silicon Valley stretches about 20 miles (32km) from the lower San Francisco peninsula to the town of San Jose. Google, Adobe, Cisco, Yahoo, Apple, Facebook, and Intel are just a selection of the famous IT names based here. A large part of any history of modern computing will be a list of Silicon Valley milestones.

Formerly known as Santa Clara Valley and settled by farmers in the mid-1800s, it is bounded to the east by San Francisco Bay and to the west by the Santa Cruz mountains. It embraces 16 cities, including Palo Alto, home of Stanford University. In 1938, two Stanford students, David Packard and William Hewlett, founded Hewlett-Packard on Palo Alto's Addison Street, now a State Historical Monument.

Testing a Google X self-drive car.

After receiving a Nobel Prize for the electronic transistor in 1956, Valley native William Schockley intended to build an empire, but the eight young engineers he hired all left to form Fairchild Semiconductor. It was here, in 1959, that Bob Noyce developed the miniature semiconductor set into silicon. Noyce, known to many as the mayor of Silicon Valley, co-founded Intel with Gordon Moore in 1968.

At 2066 Crist Drive in a Cupertino garage, the late Steve Jobs and Steve Wozniac turned out their first computer, and later formed Apple Computer. Apple's headquarters are still in the Valley town of Cupertino.

During the 1980s, personal computers replaced arcade games as the entertainment of choice. Then came email and the World Wide Web. At first these were mainly electronic noticeboards for tech geeks; now they are indispensable tools. When the internet started to catch on with an estimated 18 million users in 1995, a frenzy began. Entrepreneurs were eager to dig value from the emerging market, and people flocked to Silicon Valley, much as they had to the Sierras after gold 1848. This time, instead of picks and pans, they brought business plans and laptops. Through the tumult and excitement of the dot-com boom, many got burned and the industry suffered a huge crash in 2002.

Life rose from the rubble. The world discovered Google as a search engine. On its stock flotation Google overtook Time-Warner as the world's most valuable media corporation; eBay gobbled up many of the old "bricks and mortar" auction houses; and Apple Computer took a market out from under Sony, replacing the once-ubiquitous Walkman with the now-ubiquitous iPod.

Social media mania quickly became the next big phenomenon here with the rise of Facebook and Twitter. The communication, marketing, business, and political landscapes were forever altered by these seemingly innocuous but powerful media tools. A movie on the origins of Facebook, *The Social Network*, was nominated for a Best Picture Oscar at the 2011 Academy Awards.

With all these hard-working techies, the Valley must be the best place in the world to run a delivery pizza company.

Be amazed in Palo Alto.

only (visit www.slac.stanford.edu for tour schedules, or tel: 650-926-3300).

Between Stanford and **Menlo Park** is **the Stanford Shopping Center** ⓲, an upscale plaza of stores and eating places.

Tech central

About one hour's drive south of San Francisco on US 101 is the Silicon Valley capital of **San Jose** ⓴. Although the town has much to offer anyone in the tech industry, the attraction for casual visitors is its classy museums.

The Tech Museum

Address: 201 South Market Street (at Park Avenue); www.thetech.org
Telephone: 408-294-tech
Opening Hours: daily 10am–5pm
Admission Fee: charge
Transport: Caltrain; VTA bus: 63, 65, 64, 81, 168, 180, 181; light rail: Mountain View-Winchester, Alum Rock-Santa Teresa

This museum, which covers both bases, is known as "The Tech" to the geek community and other locals. It focuses on technology and the way it impacts on all aspects of society; how we work, live, learn, and play.

A huge space is packed with interactive exhibits, an imax theater, and an educational center for workshops and labs. Exhibitions range from the application of technology to the science of genetics to the art of robotics.

San Jose Museum of Art

Address: 110 South Market Street (at

The Tech Museum of Innovation in San Jose.

Exhibit from the Rosicrucian Egyptian Museum in San Jose.

San Jose Museum of Art.

Fernando Street); www.sjmusart.org
Telephone: 408-271-6840
Opening Hours: Tue–Sun 11am–5pm
Admission Fee: charge
Transport: bus: 63, 65, 64, 81, , 181, 168; light rail: Mountain View-Winchester, Alum Rock-Santa Teresa

Dedicated to 20th- and 21st-century art, and the diversity of the Bay Area, the collection houses nearly 1,500 works of art, new media, and installations. Among the treasures are glass sculptures by Dale Chihuly and photographs by Ruth Bernard.

The **History San Jose Museum** (1650 Senter Road; tel: 408-287-2290; daily noon–5pm; http://historysanjose. org) consists of 25 acres (10 hectares) on which are 27 original and reconstructed homes, businesses, and landmarks showing the history of San Jose and the Santa Clara Valley. The museum has paved streets, running trolleys, and an ice-cream parlor.

The **Rosicrucian Egyptian Museum and Planetarium** (1660 Park Avenue; tel: 408-947-3636; Wed–Fri 9am–5pm, Sat–Sun 10am–6pm; www. egyptianmuseum.org) is architecturally inspired by the Temple of Amon at Karnak and houses the largest collection of Egyptian artifacts exhibited in the western US. The collection includes tombs, mummies, and thousands of ancient objects. The "tomb tour" is a favorite with children. The planetarium in Rosicrucian Park at Park and Naglee avenues presents daily shows at 2pm and 3.30pm Sat–Sun.

Winchester Mystery House

Address: 525 South Winchester Boulevard; www.winchestermystery house.com
Telephone: 408-247-2101
Opening Hours: summer 9am–7pm, until 5pm rest of the year
Admission Fee: different tours available, charge
Transport: VTA bus: 23, 25

Up to her death in 1922, Sarah Winchester spent millions of dollars on bizarre building works. Staircases lead nowhere; doors open onto blank walls. All this construction was because she believed it was the only way to escape the spirits of all the people Winchester weapons had killed. The gardens are interesting – and the gift shop is huge.

NORTH TO MENDOCINO

With vineyards, whale watching, and traces of Sir Francis Drake, these California cliffs and beaches are a delight to discover.

San Francisco

California

Los Angeles

The four-hour drive from San Francisco to the lovely town of Mendocino can easily provide four full days of travel and delight. It starts at the Golden Gate Bridge, then hugs the coast on spectacular Highway 1 before turning inland to pass enticing wineries and towering redwoods. Pretty coastal towns, seductive diversions, and awe-inspiring scenery are here for the taking, mile after mile.

TOWARD POINT REYES

From Muir Woods (see page 222), the 45-minute drive to **Point Reyes National Seashore ❶** is particularly beautiful, especially the portion on Sir Francis Drake Highway, just off Highway 1. Drake landed here in 1579 and claimed the peninsula for the British, in the name of Queen Elizabeth I. He named the peninsula "New Albion" (New England), supposedly because he was reminded of the jagged cliffs and rugged shoreline of his homeland.

On January 6, 1603, Don Sebastian Vizcaino gave Point Reyes its current name, *La Punta de Los Reyes* (The Point of the Kings), in commemoration of the three Kings' visit to Jesus on the 12th day of Christmas. Like a blunted arrow, Point Reyes points

into the Pacific, the narrow finger of Tomales Bay at its base and Drakes Bay on its southern edge. Flocks of birds, a colony of sea lions and tide-pool creatures flourish in this 65,000-acre (26,000-hectare) natural showcase. Thirty-two thousand acres (13,000 hectares) of the National Seashore have been officially designated as wilderness.

Start at the delightful and innovative **Bear Valley Visitor Center** (daily 10am–5pm, longer hours during weekends in summer) for

Main Attractions
Point Reyes National Seashore
Bear Valley Visitor Center
Point Reyes Lighthouse
Bodega Bay
Russian River Valley
Mendocino

Map
Page 230

BEACH TRAIL

DOGS ON LEASH ONLY

DANGER

STRONG BACKWASH SLEEPER WAVES RIP CURRENTS

SURF UNSAFE NO LIFEGUARD

Beware the rip tides and backwash.

Stop off at the Bear Valley Visitor Center.

information and an introductory hike up to **Arch Rock** – from the trail a strange rock/statue can be seen jutting from the water – or **Sculpture Beach**, where waves crash into coastal caves and tunnels. Another hike is along the **Limantour Trail** leading to the Estero de Limantour, a quiet wetland protected by dunes and tall grass – a delightful picnic spot. **Drake's Beach**, where Drake once grounded his ships for repairs, is a little farther down the coast. Hemmed in by **Tomales Bay** on one side and the park on the other, the little town of **Inverness** provides a charming stop. On the way out of town, look for the miniature royal palace on the dock.

Oysters by the case

Just north of town is another place that might slow down your journey to Mendocino, the **Drake's Bay Oyster Farm** (formerly Johnson Oyster Company; 17171 Sir Francis Drake Boulevard) – especially if you're hungry. Oysters are sold by the case on the premises and to many Bay Area restaurants or – for instant gratification – in small, inexpensive cocktails.

The drive along the coast is magnificent, with grazed, smooth fields flanked by the ocean at one side and

Stop off at the Bear Valley Visitor Center.

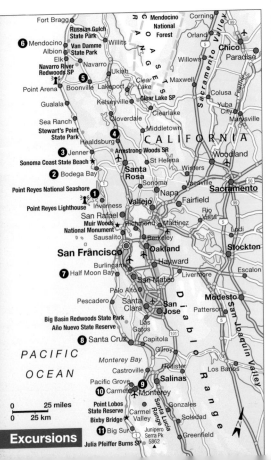

Capturing the coastline.

the commanding **Drakes Bay** on the other. At **Point Reyes Lighthouse**, gray whales can be spotted between December and May (peak period mid-Jan–Mar) as they head south toward warmer waters. The lighthouse, its revolving lens casting a powerful beam, was constructed in 1872 after 15 ships were destroyed off the point. It was built low on the precipice because winds at the top can reach 40mph (64kph). The beam is also visible beneath the frequent fog. Nearby is **Sea Lion Overlook**, where the sleek creatures sunbathe on rocks.

RUSSIAN RIVER VALLEY

Beautiful as the vistas are, not everyone has time to take Highway 1 all the way to Mendocino. Follow the coastal road through beautiful **Bodega Bay ❷**, named for the

Russian River Valley winery.

Housed in a beautiful historic church, Corners of the Mouth has operated as a collective since 1975.

Russia River Valley is perfect for camping and leisure activities.

Spanish explorer, Juan Francisco de la Bodega y Quadra. Then turn inland at **Jenner** ❸ to follow the equally gorgeous **Russian River Valley** across to US 101. Redwoods flank the Russian River, and the trees in 700-acre (284-hectare) **Armstrong Woods** reach suitably impressive heights.

Where the Guerneville River Road meets US 101 north of Santa Rosa, head north to **Healdsburg** 4, where three valleys meet – Alexander, Dry Creek, and Russian River. A beach on the river encourages swimming, fishing, and canoeing. There's also a tree-shaded, Spanish-style plaza dating from the 1860s. The **Healdsburg Museum** (www.healdsburgmuseum.org) on Mattheson Street, housed in the old Carnegie Library building, displays Pomo tribal artifacts and 19th-century exhibits from the region.

Vineyards and sheep

There are more than 60 wineries within a half-hour's drive of Healdsburg, and the industry's growth and the concomitant rise in tourism

Winding through the redwood forests.

FROM SAN FRANCISCO	
Time by car to/miles/km	
Carmel/Monterey	
2–3 hours/133/214	
Hearst Castle	
3–4 hours/197/333	
Lake Tahoe	
3.5 hours/211/340	
Los Angeles	
11 hours (coast)/437/703	
8 hours (inland)/389/626	
Mendocino	
4 hours/156/251	
Napa/Sonoma	
1 hour/44/71	
Santa Cruz	
2 hours/74/119	
Yosemite	
4 hours/210/338	

have been bringing almost a million visitors a year to this pretty town. Opposite the 130-year-old **Belle de Jour Inn** (www.belledejourinn.com) on Healdsburg Avenue is the tasting room of the **Simi Winery** (daily 10am–5pm; tours at 11am and 2pm; www.simiwinery.com). One entry in the 1942 guestbook is by Alfred Hitchcock, who drew a sketch of himself and noted "The port here is far too good for most people." There are numerous other wineries in the area, especially in the picturesque **Alexander Valley**, east of US 101.

State Highway 253 snakes westward from US 101 just south of Ukiah to join northbound State Highway 128 at Boonville. This narrow, often-wooded country road meanders through the valley past grazing sheep, vineyards, and orchards all the way to **Navarro** and beyond to the coast.

Definitively a roadhouse

Wine-making first began here more than a century ago, when many frustrated seekers after gold settled and planted vineyards. **Boonville ❺** is a

This church featured in Hitchhock's The Birds.

Memorable details of Mendocino architecture.

delightful little place. You can eat well and stay comfortably at the **Boonville Hotel** (tel: 707-895-2210; www.boonvillehotel.com), which calls itself a roadhouse: in *Funk & Wagnall's* dictionary, "an inn or restaurant in a rural locality which caters especially to transient pleasure seekers."

Other worthwhile stops include the **Anderson Valley Historical Society Museum** (www.andersonvalleymuseum.org), in a red, one-room schoolhouse north of Mountain View Road, and the **Buckhorn Saloon** and **Anderson Valley Brewing Company** (tours daily 1.30pm; https://avbc.com). The selection of microbrews is made using water from its own well. There are coffee shops here, too.

FACT

Between December and April, this portion of the California coast is part of the migratory path for whales. Whale-watching trips can be organized from Point Reyes or Mendocino.

Mendocino is lovely and low-key, but avoid the crowds at weekends.

Candy & Kites store, Bodega Bay.

Highway 128 accompanies the Navarro River all the way to the coast, skirting glorious **Redwoods State Park**, before heading up through tiny **Albion** – named by a British sea captain, who in 1853 built a sawmill. The estuary here, one of half a dozen in the county that mark the transition between freshwater rivers and the sea, is popular with kayakers. Along with the legends of Sir Francis Drake roaming the coast are tales that he built a fort here.

MAGNIFICENT MENDOCINO

Fortunes in Mendocino.

Mendocino ❻, 156 miles (251km) north of San Francisco, is a cultured town with an active year-round arts center and many galleries. Gingerbread houses cling to windswept headlands. There are white picket fences and ancient wooden water towers. It's a lovely, low-key place, much of the pleasure coming from just strolling around. But with more than 20 bed-and-breakfast inns, the town becomes crowded on weekends.

Among the homes dating from the middle of the 18th century, the **Ford House** (http://mendoparks.org) on Main Street and the **Kelley House** (www.kelleyhousemuseum.org) on Albion Street have been turned into historical museums. Blair House (www.blairhouse.com) on Little Lake Road will be familiar to TV viewers of *Murder, She Wrote*, and the Hill House also appeared on the show. Both offer bed and breakfast.

Mendocino was all but deserted in the early 20th century, but saw a cultural renaissance in the 1950s as artists and musicians moved in. That popularity continues. The town holds a Whale and Wine Festival in March, when migratory whales are seen off the coast, and a Music Festival in July. Just don't be fooled into thinking it will be hot in July; Mendocino and San Francisco have similar temperatures in the summer months.

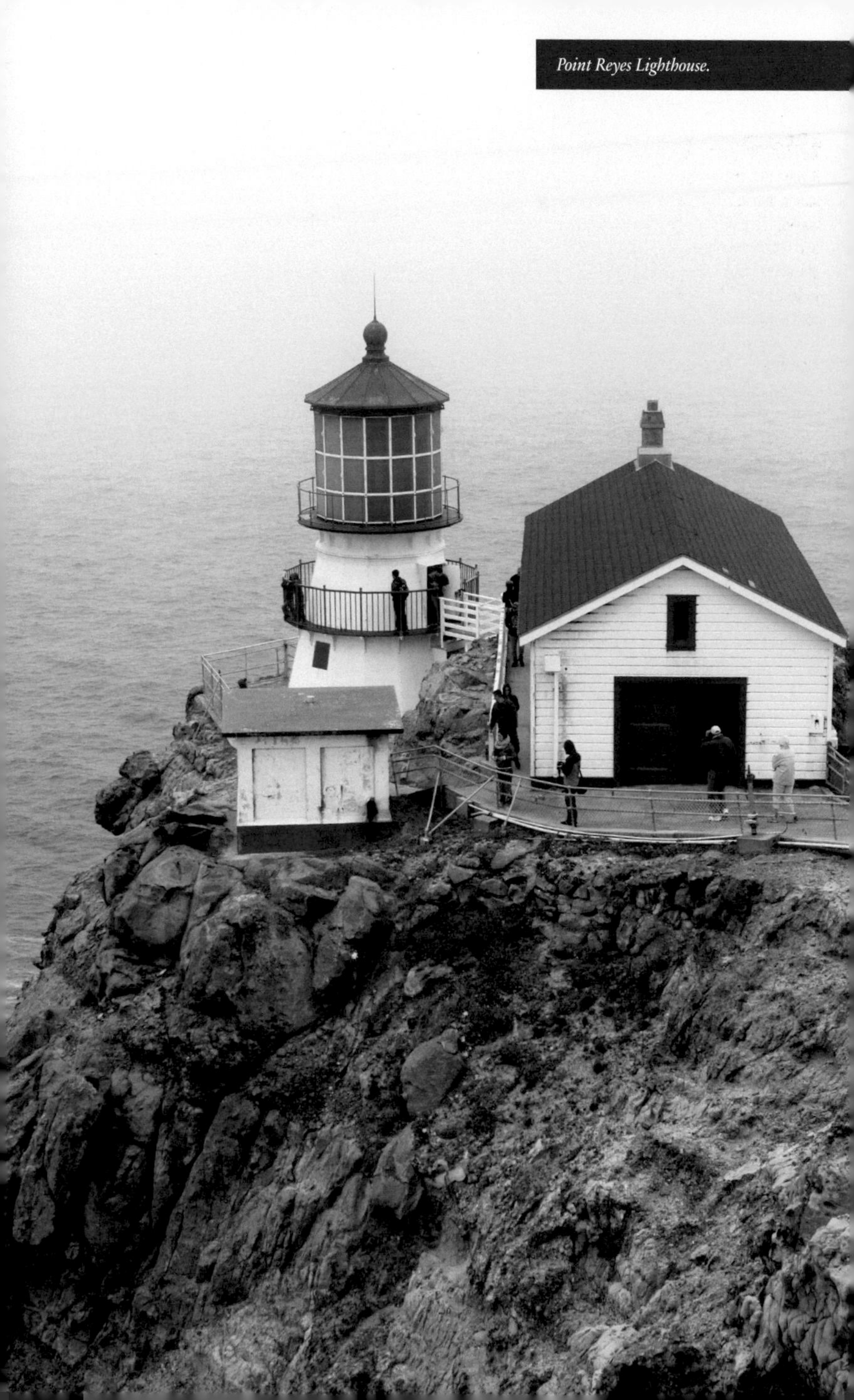

Point Reyes Lighthouse.

Julia Pfeiffer Burns State Park.

SOUTH TO BIG SUR

The stretch of Highway 1 from Santa Cruz to Big Sur is the most beautiful, with state parks, country inns, and great spots to surf.

Highway 1 south from San Francisco may be the most spectacular route in America. A series of razor-sharp switchbacks hug hills, plunge into valleys, and skirt the coast the entire way. Steep, rugged mountains loom on the left of the road, while on the right is nothing but a sheer drop to wild, crashing waves below.

For a real West Coast experience, the best way to travel is by motorcycle, or at least a convertible. Either can be rented in San Francisco, with a drop-off point arranged farther south. This way you can smell the scents, feel the fog, and play cruising music very loudly. However you travel, the climate changes every few miles – from fog to rain to blinding sunshine. This is the real California.

CRUISING TO SANTA CRUZ

Assuming there are no traffic problems, around 35 minutes after leaving San Francisco, Highway 1 reaches **Half Moon Bay ❼**, a picturesque coastal town with a small-town feel and known for exceptional plants, flowers, and produce. This part of the coast has some lovely stretches of open space and unspoiled beaches with postcard-perfect views. Past the sleepy hamlets of **San Gregorio** and

Pescadero that time has seemingly forgotten, is the vibrant beach town of Santa Cruz, 74 miles (119km) from San Francisco.

At the northern end of Monterey Bay, the city of **Santa Cruz ❽** (population: over 62,000) is cool, green, and shimmering with redwoods. When the **University of California** opened a campus here in the mid-1960s, the academic activity transformed what had been a quiet backwater into an activist community. Santa Cruz rejuvenated, with excellent restaurants,

Santa Cruz – surf country.

Santa Cruz is home to one of the few monuments to surfers in the world.

The Beach Boardwalk turned 100 years old in 2007.

cafés, bookstores, and a multitude of stores catering to the needs of students and visitors.

The university campus plays a significant part in local life; it is responsible for the **Long Marine Lab**, a working marine studies laboratory (Tue–Sun 10am–5pm, July–Aug daily; http://seymourcenter.ucsc.edu); an arboretum with plants from around the world, plus an outdoor Shakespeare festival and a range of performing arts (tel: 831 460 6396, tickets: 831-460-6399; www.santacruzshakespeare.org).

Santa Cruz has sparkling clean air and is one of the sunniest spots around, usually unaffected by the fog and chilly winds that hover over the coast, north and south. Bring your swimsuit, and use plenty of sunscreen; the rays are strong. This is also a great place for surfing; the town has one of a very few – maybe the only – surfer monuments, on the promenade. For more on hanging 10, stop by the **Santa Cruz Surfing Museum** in the Mark Abbott Memorial Lighthouse (summer Thu–Tue 10am–5pm, winter Thu–Mon noon–4pm; www.cityofsantacruz.com).

Santa Cruz pier is the place for all things fishy – fish restaurants, fish markets, and good facilities for fishing. Next to the pier is a wide, white, sandy beach, and nearby the Beach Boardwalk (mid-May–early Sept daily, weekends only in winter; free; http://beachboardwalk.com), more than 100 years old, with a carousel only a little younger and the Giant Dipper rollercoaster built in 1924. Wednesday afternoons, rain or shine, the Downtown Farmers' Market is at the corner of Cedar and Lincoln streets, with stands overflowing with fruit, flowers, seafood, cheese, and olive oil.

Leaving Santa Cruz, Highway 1 follows the coast in a beautiful arc around Monterey Bay. During the springtime, the high sand dunes are covered in a carpet of marigolds. The road passes near the beach town of Capitola in a confusing manner, then dramatically chills out again. Peanut stands along the way make pleasant stops for picking up snacks.

MONTEREY

The city of **Monterey** ❾ (population: 27,000), at the northern end of

Life inside the aquarium.

the Monterey Peninsula, is a surprise after this peaceful journey. Thanks to writer John Steinbeck, a big attraction is the part of town known as **Cannery Row**. During World War II, Monterey was a major sardine capital, and in Steinbeck's words, was "a poem, a stink, a grating noise, a quality of light, a tone, a habit, a nostalgia, a dream."

When the boats came in, heavy with catch, the canneries blew their whistles, and the residents streamed down the hill to take their places in the canning plants, amid rumbling, rattling, squealing machinery. When the last sardine was cleaned, cut, cooked, and canned, the whistle blew again, and the workers trudged back up the hill, wet and wreathed in the smell of fish.

After the war, whether from over-fishing, changing tidal currents, or divine retribution, the sardines disappeared from Monterey Bay and all the canneries went broke.

But, as Steinbeck pointed out, it was not a total loss. In the early years of the industry, the beaches were so deeply covered with fish guts, scales, and flies that a sickening stench covered the town. Today, the beaches are bright and clean, and the air is sparkling fresh. Cannery Row, located along the waterfront on the northwest side of town just beyond the Presidio, has become an impressive tourist attraction, the old buildings now full of bars, restaurants, a wax museum, stores, a carousel, and food vendors.

Monterey Bay Aquarium

Address: 886 Cannery Row; www.montereybayaquarium.org
Telephone: 831-648-4800
Opening Hours: daily, 9.30am–6pm
Admission Fee: charge

A trip to Cannery Row affords a visit to one of the world's premier aquariums. The enormous building, with indoor dolphin tanks and outdoor pools overlooking the sea, stands on the site of what was Cannery Row's largest cannery, the Hovden Cannery. More than 100 galleries exhibit more than 350,000 sea creatures, from sea otters, leopard sharks, bat rays, and giant octopuses, to towering underwater kelp forests.

In downtown Monterey, the main visitor attraction is **Fisherman's Wharf**. Fisherman's Wharf is alive with restaurants, stores, fish markets, and sea lions swimming noisily around the pilings.

FACT

Since San Francisco Radio began the event in 1958, the Monterey Jazz Festival has brought world-class and ground-breaking music among the oaks of the Monterey fairground, with the purpose of raising funding for jazz education programs around the United States. At the first jazz festival, Billie Holiday sang the blues, just nine months before Lady Day's last goodnight.

Sea creatures from the Monterey Bay Aquarium.

TIP
If possible, time your visit to the Monterey Bay Aquarium to be there at feeding time, when keepers in wet suits climb into the glass tanks and talk to spectators through underwater microphones.

Vintage signs.

The Path of History

To see the rest of Monterey, a 3 mile (5km) walking tour, called The Path of History (www.seemonterey.com), leads past the more important historical buildings and sites. These include the **Customs House**, the oldest public building in California, now part of the Monterey State Historic Park; **Pacific House**, a two-story adobe with a Monterey balcony around the second floor; and impressive historical exhibits from the Spanish, Mexican, and early American periods.

Other attractions include **Colton Hall**, a two-story building with a classical portico, the site of the state's first (1849) constitutional convention; **Stevenson House**, a former hotel where the romantic (and sickly)

Clowning around in Monterey.

Robert Louis Stevenson stayed while courting his wife; and the **Royal Presidio Chapel**, in constant use since 1794. US President Herbert Hoover's wedding was held here.

The **Presidio**, founded in 1770 by Gaspar de Portolá, now serves as the **Defense Language Institute Foreign Language Center**. Other points of interest are the **Allen Knight Maritime Museum**, with relics from the era of sailing ships and whaling, and the **Monterey Museum of Art** (559 Pacific Street; www.montereyart. org; tel: 831 372 5477; Thur–Mon 11am–5pm).

In mid-September, the **Monterey Jazz Festival** (see page 239) attracts many of the biggest names in music to the Monterey Fairgrounds. It was here that Jimi Hendrix came to the attention of the United States.

Kayaking on Monterey Bay is growing in popularity, offering a delightful opportunity to get out among the otters and sea lions. A local company operates tours out to see the gray whales on their migration between Alaska and Baja California, down Mexico way.

THE 17-MILE DRIVE

The 17-Mile Drive meanders in a three-hour tour around the Monterey Peninsula, via the **Del Monte Forest**, to Pacific Grove. Close to the **Ghost Tree Cypress**, a big stone mansion looks like something seen in a lightning flash that cleaves the midnight darkness of the Scottish moors. The **Lone Cypress**, a single gnarled and windswept tree near the top of a huge wave-battered rock, is a much-photographed site.

The drive's famous attraction is the **Pebble Beach Golf Links** (www. pebblebeach.com), site of some of the most prestigious tournaments in the US, and usually rated by *Golf Digest* as the number one public course in America. The 17-Mile Drive is undeniably beautiful, but the attitude of

Lone piper on Pebble Beach.

the Pebble Beach Company toward tourists is somewhat condescending. Motorcyles are not allowed, and the landscape is littered with "no trespassing" signs punishable by a fine and imprisonment. All the roads in the Del Monte Forest are privately owned, so anyone traveling on the road owes a fee to the company.

The 17-Mile Drive is probably worth your time, even if you aren't an ardent golf fan. The many beaches and parks along the drive are lovely,

but watch out for runners and cyclists along the road; there's not much of a shoulder.

CHARMING CARMEL ⓾

The southern gateway to the Monterey Peninsula is the town of **Carmel**. A few chance factors made Carmel what it is today – starving writers and unemployed painters in flight from the devastation of the 1906 San Francisco earthquake, and canny property developers who, to reduce their taxes, covered the treeless acres of the local landscape with a thick, lush carpet of shady Monterey pine trees. The result is one of the most charming seaside towns on the West Coast. When the evening fog rolls in, the lights inside the cozy houses, combined with the faint whiff of wood smoke from roaring fires, give Carmel the peaceful feeling of a 19th-century European village. Its best-known attraction is the peaceful Carmel Mission.

Carmel Mission

Address: 3080 Rio Road; www.carmelmission.org
Telephone: 831-624-1271

TIP
Be aware that there is a charge to take the 17-Mile Drive around the Monterey Peninsula. No motorcycles are allowed on this private road, and you should watch out for golfers. The drive takes approximately three hours.

Carmel.

QUOTE

"The face of the earth as the Creator intended it to look."

Henry Miller on Big Sur

Opening Hours: daily 9.30am–7pm
Admission Fee: charge

The **Carmel Mission** dates from 1771. Masses are still conducted daily, and self-guided tours or docent-led tours of the church and the grounds are available. The fees that are collected support the church's ongoing restoration program.

Cowboy mayor

Although some 3 or 4 million people visit the town each year – Carmel's popularity was boosted substantially when actor Clint Eastwood became mayor for a couple of terms – it has resisted the glare of neon signs, or the clutter of cheap souvenirs. The plazas and little shopping malls attract pedestrians to wine shops and antiques stores, art galleries, and boutiques. The local market stocks fresh artichokes and has racks and racks of wines. At night, a dozen couples might be dining quietly by candlelight behind dark restaurant windows. Streets meander casually through the forest, sometimes splitting in two to accommodate an especially praiseworthy specimen of pine.

The Carmel Mission dates from 1771.

Local residents.

Having said all this, the town is not to everyone's taste. Its sweetness and pretension can cloy, and its plethora of gift shops is just a little too removed from real village life to digest without irony. But Carmel beach, at the bottom of the hill and within easy walking distance of the town, is still sandy and stunning.

South of Carmel is **Point Lobos**

State Reserve (www.parks.ca.gov), a rocky park overlooking the sea. Nature trails crisscross the reserve, and big natural rock pools are home to lolling sea lions. Be sure to take water and a picnic: there are no food facilities.

Highway 1 south of Point Lobos begins to swoop and curve in dramatic fashion. The San Lucia Mountains rise steeply to the left; the foamy sea to the right changes shape and color constantly. Only the two-lane road separates the two, which means the curling ribbon of road has its own distinct weather pattern (read: fog). Although the sun may be shining brightly on the other side of the mountains, and can often be seen through the trees, Highway 1 can be distinctly chilly, and the fog comes on quickly, obliterating the world for unexpected moments, which can be alarming on this narrow road.

BIG SUR

This is a suitably theatrical entrance to **Big Sur** ⓫, arguably California's most beautiful stretch of coastline. One of its most popular photographic subjects is **Bixby Bridge**, north of Big Sur Village, spanning the steep gorge of Bixby Canyon.

The Henry **Miller Library** (www.henrymiller.org; tel: 831-667-2574; 11am–6pm), near the **Nepenthe** restaurant (www.nepenthebigsur.com) where many gather for sunset, has works by and about this local hero. **Big Sur Village** is little more than a huddle of stores and a post office. Places to stay here are scarce, and if you plan a weekend visit, book very early.

There are a couple of campgrounds, a few motels, and rustic inns, like the **Big Sur River Inn** (tel: 831-667-2700, toll free: 800-548-3610; www.bigsurriverinn.com), and some luxurious hot-tub- and fireplace country inns. Notable among these are the **Ventana Inn and Spa** (tel: 831-667-2331; www.ventanainn.com) and the **Post Ranch Inn** (tel: 831-667-2200; www.postranchinn.com), which was designed by local architect Mickey Muenning.

South of Big Sur Village, Highway 1 winds past several state parks, all worth visiting. One of the most beautiful is **Julia Pfeiffer Burns State Park**, with twisting nature trails and a silvery waterfall.

The Carmel Mission is designed in a typical Spanish Mission style, and includes several stunning Azulejo tiles.

The Bixby Bridge spans Bixby Creek.

Sonoma County.

WINE COUNTRY

Only a couple of hours' drive from the streets of San Francisco are Napa and Sonoma, and some of the most attractive wineries in America.

Before Napa comes Sonoma, geographically and historically. *Sonoma* is a Patwin tribal word meaning "Land of Chief Nose," and may honor a chief with a distinctive snout. Founding father Mariano Vallejo romanticized Sonoma Valley as the "Valley of the Moon," and Jack London took up the name, as the title of a book about urbanites rejuvenated by country living.

Sonoma County is a patchwork of country roads, orchards, hills, ridges, and small towns. US 101, the wine country's only freeway, runs the length of the county north to south, entering near the town of **Petaluma ❶**. State Highway 12 runs through Sonoma Valley to Santa Rosa, passing the towns of Sonoma, Glen Ellen, and Kenwood.

SONOMA COUNTY

Father Altimira founded beautiful **San Francisco de Solano Mission**, California's last mission, in 1823, in this fertile region. General Mariano Vallejo set up the town of **Sonoma ❷** in 1835, making it the northernmost outpost of a Catholic, Spanish-speaking realm that, at its peak, extended to the tip of South America. Sonoma was briefly a

republic after the Bear Flag Revolt in 1846, when Americans stormed Vallejo's home, but Count Agoston Haraszthy's innovations at Buena Vista Winery about a decade later showed the area's vinicultural potential.

The town is pleasant, relaxed, and well-heeled, and dominated by **Sonoma Plaza**. Restored adobe buildings line the plaza and nearby streets, including the mission, Vallejo's old house, **Lachryma Montis**, and the **Sonoma Barracks**.

Main Attractions

Sonoma
Napa
Napa Valley Wine Train
St Helena
Silverado Museum
Culinary Institute of America
Old Faithful Geyser
Silverado Trail

Map

Page 246

The Napa Valley Barrell Auction draws wine aficionados from all over the world.

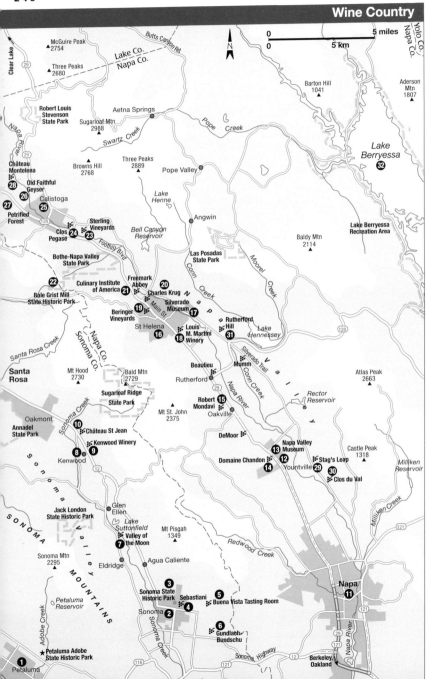

A sunny day at a Sonoma winery.

Sonoma State Historic Park ❸

Address: 363 3rd Street West, Sonoma; www.parks.ca.gov
Telephone: Mission: 707-938-9560, Vallejo's Home: 707-938-9559, Barracks: 707-939-9420
Opening Hours: daily 10am–5pm
Admission Fee: charge

Two blocks away is the **Sebastiani Vineyards ❹** (tel: 707-933-3230; www.sebastiani.com), on lands once cultivated by the people of the San Francisco de Solano Mission. The winery is still owned by the Sebastiani family.

East of Sonoma, the **Buena Vista Winery Tasting Room ❺** (tel: 800-926-1266; www.buenavistawinery.com) retains connections with Count Haraszthy. The Gundlach and Bundschu families were involved with wine for more than 125 years, and **Gundlach-Bundschu ❻** (tel: 707-938-5277; www.gunbun.com) wines are exported around the globe. Nearby is the Fairmont Sonoma Mission Inn and Spa (tel: 707-938-9000; www.fairmont.com/sonoma).

North on State 121, the Valley of the Moon Winery ❼ (tel: 707-939-4500; www.valleyofthemoonwinery.com) occupies part of George Hearst's 19th-century vineyards (George was the father of tycoon William R. Hearst). North on State 1 is the town of **Kenwood ❽**. **The Kenwood Winery ❾** (tel: 707-282-4228; https://kenwoodvineyards.com) features Zinfandel, Cabernet Sauvignon, and Chenin Blanc. Chardonnay-lovers head for **Château St Jean ❿** (tel: 707-257-5784; www.chateaustjean.com), for excellent white wines.

NAPA COUNTY

Wineries, delicatessens, restaurants, and country inns lie close together in **Napa Valley** and the little town of **Napa ⓫**. Although rural, the valley's socialites, titled Europeans, and semi-retired Hollywood directors and producers give **Napa County** a genteel, wealthy, if slightly slick, aura.

A 30 mile (48km) thrust of flatland between the Mayacamas Mountains and the buff-colored Howell Mountains, Napa Valley is pinched off in the north by **Mount St Helena**. The vineyards are broken up by farmhouses, stone wineries, and towns stretched along **State Highway 29**.

Napa Valley Wine Train

Address: 1275 McKinstry Street, Napa, CA; www.winetrain.com

The Napa wine train.

A WINE PRIMER

Winemaking begins at the crusher, where juice is freed from the grapes. White wine is made from the fermentation of the juice alone. Yeast is added, and fermentation occurs in stainless-steel vats. For red wines the grape skin and pulp are fermented, yeast is added to turn the sugar into alcohol, skins are pressed for more juice, and the wine then ages in steel or wooden vats. The wine is clarified, and aged further before bottling. Leaving in the yeast makes dry wines; controlling the yeast makes sweeter wines. Sparkling wines like Cava, Prosecco, and Champagne undergo a second fermentation in the bottle. Carbon dioxide is trapped inside, creating the heady bubbles.

Most wineries open daily 10am–4pm; some by appointment only. Contact Napa Valley Tourist Information at www.napavalley.com, or Sonoma Valley Visitors Bureau, 453 1st Street E., www.sonomavalley.com, tel: 707-996-1090.

TIP

If no one wants to be the designated driver, you may want to consider renting a limo and driver for the day. And not just any limo – how about a 1947 white Packard convertible? For a treat you'll never forget, go to: www.ccwinetours.com.

Telephone: 707-253-2111, 800-427-4124
Opening Hours: daily
Admission Fee: charge

A one-of-a-kind fine-dining experience paired with exceptional locally sourced Napa wines awaits the passenger on this popular Wine Country attraction. Imagine feasting on delicious, made-to-order seasonal fare while sipping wines from one of the premier wine destinations in the world as you kick back in lavishly restored 1915 Pullman dining and lounge cars. Velvet drapery, mahogany paneling, and plush banquettes lend an air of opulence to this tasteful journey.

The train whizzes past wineries along 36 miles (58km) of track in the heart of the Napa Valley during the three-hour tour. The tracks run parallel to Highway 29 and through the towns of Yountville, Rutherford, and Oakville.

The Wine Train operates year-round and offers a variety of packages – from champagne brunch to a moonlight escape. Special trains operate on all holidays, and they offer wine-makers' dinners and murder mystery rides. Optional excursions

Touring Sterling Vineyards near Calistoga.

The place to buy Napa Valley and Sonoma County small label wines.

include tours of Domaine Chandon Winery and Grgich Hills Estate.

The town of Napa is mainly an administrative center; wine country begins in earnest at **Yountville** ⑫, where vineyards abut the village's historic buildings. Yountville's city park is across from George Yount's grave at the Pioneer Cemetery. One of General Vallejo's beneficiaries, Yount gained his huge land grant for roofing Vallejo's Petaluma adobe in one of history's better contracting deals.

A chance to learn about wine is at the **Napa Valley Museum** ⑬ (55 President's Circle; tel: 707-944-0500; Wed–Sun 11am–4pm; http://napavalley museum.org). **Domaine Chandon Winery** ⑭ (tel: 707-944-8844; www. chandon.com) just west of town is French throughout. The winery makes sparkling wine in the *méthode champenoise*; fermented in the bottle, but not called "Champagne," as the name is only for products of the French Champagne region. North of **Oakville** is the **Robert Mondavi Winery** ⑮ (tel: 707 226 1395; www.robertmondavi winery.com), a sleek operation, as befits the famous name. Guided tours only.

St Helena ⑯

St Helena has historic stone buildings, picnic parks, chic stores, upscale restaurants, country inns, and about 40 wineries.

Silverado Museum ⑰

Address: 1490 Library Lane, St Helena; www.silveradomuseum.org
Telephone: 707-963-3757
Opening Hours: Tue–Sat noon–4pm
Admission Fee: free

The Silverado Museum has Robert Louis Stevenson memorabilia such as first editions of his work and souvenirs of the author's global jaunts. South of town, the **Louis M. Martini Winery** ⑱ (tel: 800 321 9463; www.louismartini.com) is run by one of the valley's oldest wine-making clans, and offers reasonably priced wines in a relaxed setting. Two wineries lie just north of St Helena. Brothers Jacob and Frederick started the **Beringer Vineyards** ⑲ (tel: 707 257 5771; www.beringer.com) in 1876, modeling the Rhine House (1883) after their ancestral estate in Mainz, Germany. Today's winery, owned by Nestlé (the chocolate people), features Fumé Blanc and Cabernet Sauvignon in the tasting room. The building of the **Charles**

Krug Winery ⑳ (tel: 707 967 2229; www.charleskrug.com) dates from 1874.

Culinary Institute of America ㉑

Address: 2555 Main Street, St Helena; www.ciachef.edu
Telephone: 845-452-9600

The lavish **Greystone Mansion** was the world's largest stone winery when it was erected in 1889 by William Bourn, and now forms part of the Culinary Institute. In this beautiful setting, the school offers a variety of programs, from conferences to classes in cooking, baking, pastry, management, and wine.

For a break from eating or drinking, go for a walk in **Bale Grist Mill State Historic Park** ㉒ (open Jul and Aug Fri–Sun 10am–5pm; tel: 707 963 2236), only a couple of miles north of St Helena.

Between Bale Grist and the town of Calistoga are two excellent stops: **Sterling Vineyards** ㉓ (tel: 800-726-6136; www.sterlingvineyards.com) reigns over the upper valley on top of a knoll. A tram whisks visitors 300ft (91 meters) up on to the hill for a self-guided tour. The tram fee is redeemed from the cost of Sauvignon

EAT

The Culinary Institute of America's (www.ciachef.edu/cia-california) Wine Spectator Greystone Restaurant is open to the public, with tasty tidbits, meticulous service, personally selected wines, and up-and-coming chefs guaranteed; just call 707-967-1010 to make a reservation. Open Tue-Sat lunch and dinner.

Interactive cooking demonstration at the Culinary Institute of America.

There are more than 400 wineries and tasting rooms scattered across the Napa Valley.

Blanc or other wines. **Clos Pegase 24** (tel: 707-942-4981; www.clospegase. com) is close by. Designed in 1986 by architect Michael Graves in a sleek, modern style, Clos Pegase is known for its art collection almost as much as for the wines.

The one-street town of **Calistoga 25** is a gem; wooden hangings shade storefronts for a Wild West feel. Calistoga is a spa town, rich in mineral springs and hot, therapeutic mud. Low-key treatment centers all around town make beautiful Californians even more beautiful.

Old Faithful Geyser 26

Address: 1299 Tubbs Lane, Calistoga
Tel: 707-942-6463
Opening Hours: daily, 8.30am–7pm
Two miles (3km) north of Calistoga, boiling water jets into the sky. Tickets are expensive, but tables in the little waiting area make for a pleasant picnic while waiting on the geyser. To the west is the disappointing **Petrified Forest 27**, where fallen redwood trunks turned to stone millions of years ago.

Calistoga is surrounded by too many wineries to mention, but one has a historic (1882) lakeside setting. **Château Montelena 28** (tel: 707-942-5105; http://montelena.com) produces Chardonnay and Cabernet Sauvignon and has picnic sites on Jade Lake; booking essential.

THE SILVERADO TRAIL

Running alongside State Highway 29 between Napa and Calistoga, the **Silverado Trail** joins the highway as the route into Lake County's resort and wine region.

Stag's Leap 29, a rocky promontory near Yountville where a Roosevelt elk once plunged to its death, overlooks the award-winning *Stag's Leap* **Wine Cellars** (tel: 707-261-6410; http://stagsleap.com) and **Clos du Val 30** (tel: 707-261-5251; www.closduval.com). Toward St Helena is the ark-like **Rutherford Hill Winery 31**, (tel: 707-963-1871; www. rutherfordhill.com) and picnic grounds, as well as the warm-water paradise of **Lake Berryessa 32**. Take State 128 from St Helena or State 121 from Napa to the lake's beautiful shoreline. Bring along a few bottles of your favorite vintage and enjoy your wine in a picnic setting.

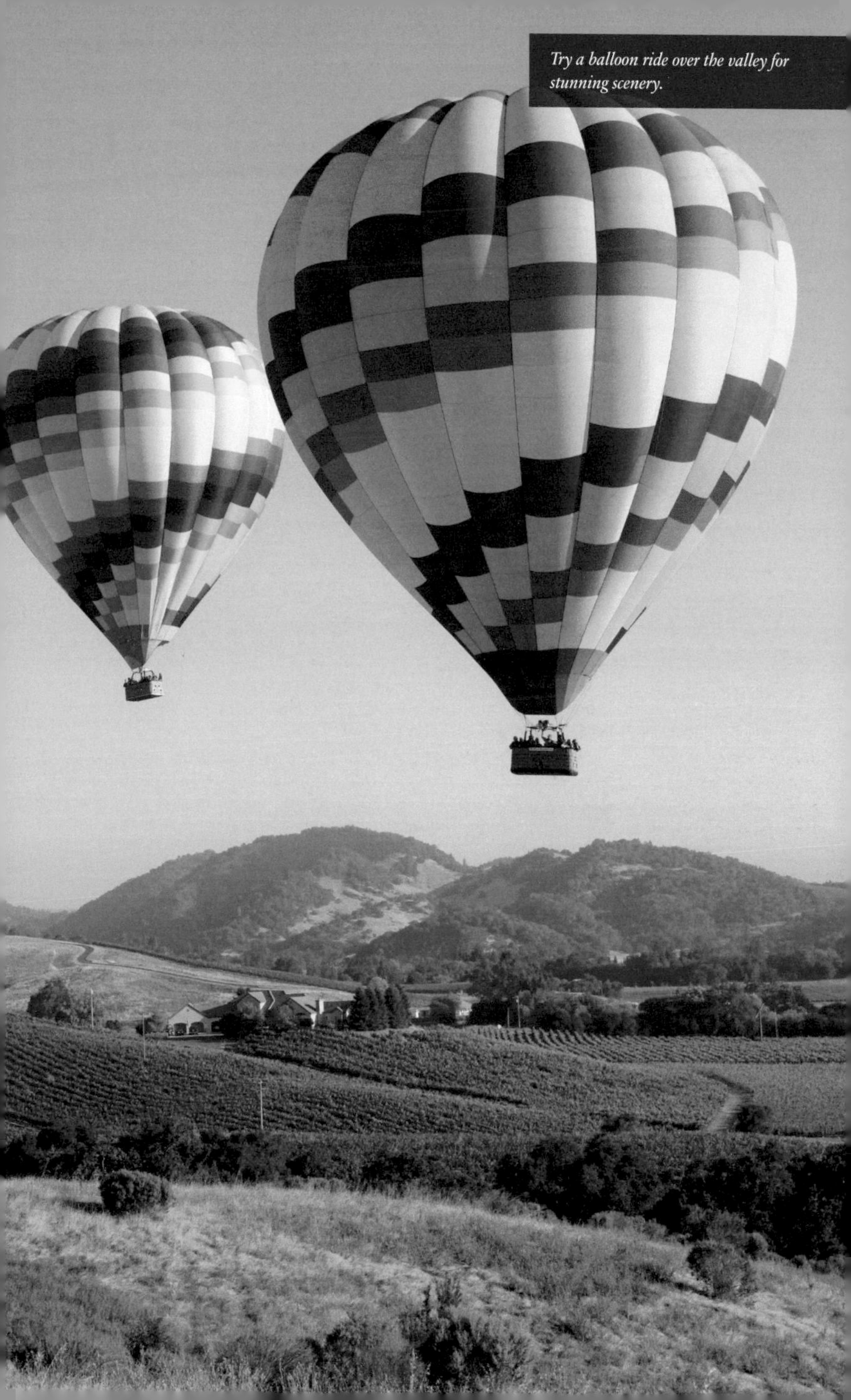
Try a balloon ride over the valley for stunning scenery.

Sailboat in Sausalito with Alcatraz in the background.

INSIGHT GUIDES TRAVEL TIPS

SAN FRANCISCO

TRANSPORTATION

GETTING THERE AND GETTING AROUND

San Francisco is surrounded by water on three sides, and its broad boulevards are arranged on a grid system. An exception to all this orderliness is Market Street, which cuts through on a diagonal. Although often referred to as the City of Seven Hills, there are actually more than 40 hills within its boundaries. San Francisco is only 7 sq miles (11 sq km), and can easily be explored on foot, by bicycle, bus, trolley, and cable car. Remember, the hills really are steep; it isn't a Hollywood myth, so wear comfortable shoes.

GETTING THERE

By Air

San Francisco International Airport (sfo), tel: 650-821-8211, www.flysfo.com, just 14 miles (23km) south of the city, near the town of San Mateo, is the major gateway for foreign travel. Most of the international airline companies that serve northern California land at SFO.
Oakland International Airport, tel: 510-563-3300, http://oaklandairport.com is much smaller and less crowded than SFO. A shuttle takes passengers to the Bay Area Rapid Transit (BART) station for a 30-minute

AIRLINES

US airlines that fly regularly into San Francisco include:
Alaska Airlines
www.alaskaair.com
American Airlines
www.aa.com
Delta Airlines
www.delta.com
Jet Blue
www.jetblue.com
Southwest
www.southwest.com
United Airlines
www.united.com
Virgin America
www.virginamerica.com

ride through the underwater Transbay Tube to downtown San Francisco. Airport buses, taxis, shuttles, and AC Transit provide transportation as well.
One hour south of the city is **San José International Airport**, tel: 408-392-3600, www.flysan jose.com, served by the carriers Alaska, America West, American, Continental, Delta, Jet Blue, United, and United Express.
Most airports are served by **Airport Commuter Limo & Sedan Service**, tel: 650-876-1777 or 888-876-1777, www.airportcommuter.com; **SuperShuttle**, tel: 888-888-6025, www.supershuttle.com.

By Train

Amtrak: all trains come into a depot across the Bay Bridge in Oakland, where free bus service is provided into San Francisco itself. Passes for unlimited travel on Amtrak are available and very good value, but they can only be bought from a travel agent in a foreign country. Information about Amtrak's train services is available by calling the toll-free number: 800-USA-RAIL or online at www.amtrak.com.
Emeryville depot, 5885 Horton Street, Emeryville (across the Bay Bridge next to Oakland), tel: 510-450-1087.

By Sea

Cruising into San Francisco Bay is a luxurious way to arrive. "Vagabond"cruises, which feature a limited number of passengers on cargo steamships, are less common than they once were, but check with the **San Francisco Port Authority** (tel: 415-274-0400; http://sfport.com) or your travel agent to determine which line has a current scheduled stop. Cruise ships representing four major lines dock regularly at Pier 35 in San Francisco. These are **Holland America, Princess Cruises, Royal Caribbean,** and **Crystal**.

TRANSPORTATION

A – Z

By Bus

Greyhound-Trailways provides bus services to San Francisco (www.greyhound.com). The buses arrive at the terminal on San Pablo Ave 2103 (near 20th St.) not far from downtown. BoltBus and Megabus (terminal at 1451 7th St, near West Oakland BART) offer services to Los Angeles. Due to demolition and reconstruction of the Transbay Terminal, the temporary arrival and departure location is on the block bounded by Main, Folsom, Beale, and Howard streets. Bus systems using this terminal include **AC Transit** (East Bay), **SamTrans** (San Mateo County and the peninsula) and city tour-bus lines, including **Gray Line**.

Remember that the bus terminals are located in downtown areas and require caution for personal safety. Bus travelers should avoid walking alone at night, and use cabs or city buses to get to and from the terminals.

The **Green Tortoise** (tel: 800-TORTOISE; www.greentortoise. com) is a great alternative to Greyhound. Trips often make stops at national parks or other points of interest, and for maximum comfort, the buses have communal areas that convert to reclining sleeping quarters at night. The headquarters, in North Beach at 494 Broadway (tel: 415 834 1000), is also the site of the Green Tortoise hostel.

By Car

Major land routes into San Francisco are: US Highway 101, over the Golden Gate Bridge, from the north; Interstate 80 over the Oakland Bay Bridge from the east; and US Highways 1, 101, and 280 up the peninsula, when traveling from the south.

North–south travelers who are in a hurry use Interstate 5 to connect with I-80. Travelers from Los Angeles can cut three hours off their trip to San Francisco by taking I-5. The slower coastal routes are more scenic and pass through small towns.

GETTING AROUND

From the Airport

Signs in the airport mark the way to the internal AirTrain **Red Line**, which stops at all terminals, and BART (Bay Area Rapid Transit), which provides a metro rail service within the Bay Area station. bart now offer services to San Francisco and Oakland airports (tel: 415-989-2278; www.bart.gov). The longer **Blue Line** links a rental car center with stops for terminals, garages, and the BART rail system. Service runs 24 hours a day.

There are also door-to-door shuttles – **Quake City Shuttle**, tel: 415-255-4899; www.quake cityshuttle.com, and **Super-shuttle**, tel: 800-BLUE VAN (258 3826); www.supershuttle.com, are the most prominent and compete for passengers on the upper level of the SFO terminal at specially marked curbs. Supershuttle operates 20 hours a day, with vans circling the upper terminal area every 20 minutes, or less often at peak periods. Call from the terminal or simply walk out to the marked curb on the roadway island and wait. The price is marked on the window of each van. Tipping of around 15–20 percent is encouraged.

The shuttles are harder to come by late at night, particularly after 1am, and after midnight it's safer to call a cab. A line of cabs waits outside the luggage terminal marked by a yellow column. Be sure to ignore hotels suggested by the drivers, and have the fare quoted up front first. Limousine service is available by using the toll-free, white courtesy phones in the terminal.

The **Marin County Airporter Coach** (tel: 415-461-4222, www.marinairporter.com) services are more expensive than the shuttles. **SamTrans**, San Mateo County's bus system, makes stops between the airport area and downtown San Francisco and is very cheap. KX, 140, 292, 397, 398 lines serve San Francisco and nearby areas. For details visit www.samtrans.com. a.

Airport Buses

Buses connect SFO with several hotels in San Francisco. For a full list visit www.flysfo.com/to-from/ hotel-shuttles.

Public Transportation

Many locals only use their cars for trips outside the city. There are two good reasons for this: the city streets are narrow and congested, and the public transportation network is excellent.

A map is published by Muni (San Francisco Municipal Railway) and is available at drug- and book-store counters all over the city. For further information, refer to www.sfmta.com.

Hop on and hop off cable cars.

For help in navigating the public transit system anywhere in the Bay Area, call **511**, or look online at www.511.org. The people behind this service can offer assistance with planning trips using public transportation, traffic, and drive time information, tips for traveling with bicycles, and links to various municipal transit agencies.

By Muni and Bus

For getting around in the city, San Francisco Muni is your best bet. Muni is responsible for all buses, streetcars, trolley cars, and cable cars in San Francisco. Vintage trolleys, collected from all over the world, trundle up and down Market Street; these are a delight as well as a regular form of transportation, unlike the tourist-laden cable cars. You must have the exact change to ride.

Muni visitor passports (one-, three- or seven-day) offer unlimited rides on public transportation, or a CityPass (www.citypass.com/san-francisco) gives seven consecutive days on Muni, plus reduced admissions to some attractions in the city. Discounts are available on Muni tickets for children, the disabled, and those over 65.

If you don't have a pass, ask for a transfer when you board; valid for any Muni service (except cable cars) for at least 90 minutes, but no more than two hours, from the time of issue.

Bus stops are marked by the words "Coach Stop" on the street, a long rectangle of wide, white lines, by a bright yellow marking on a telephone or light pole, and/or by an orange and brown route sign mounted on a bus-stop pole. Service is frequent and some Muni lines run 24 hours.

For information, tel: 415-701-2311, www.sfmta.com. If you know your starting point, your destination, and the time of day for travel, the Muni operator can plan your route for you. Some buses are equipped for wheelchairs.

AC Transit

To travel east from San Francisco, AC Transit (Alameda-Contra Costa Transit) provides daily services from the Transbay Terminal to most cities in the East Bay area. Fares vary by distance, and the exact fare is required. Many buses are wheelchair-accessible. For more information, tel: 510-891-4700, www.actransit.org.

Golden Gate Transit

To travel north of the city, Golden Gate Transit buses and ferries connect San Francisco with Marin and Sonoma counties. Buses stop where green, blue, and white signs are posted on the bus-line poles. The exact fare is required and fares vary according to distance traveled. Golden Gate Transit buses are wheelchair-accessible. For information, tel: 415-455-2000 or 511 (toll free), www.goldengate.org.

Samtrans

To travel south of San Francisco, SamTrans buses run seven days a week, connecting with ac Transit and Golden Gate Transit at the Temporary Transbay Terminal (a new terminal replacing the old one is scheduled to be operational in 2017). SamTrans also connects with BART at the Daly City and Hayward stations. Stops include the San Francisco International Airport, Southern Pacific Caltrain station, and the Greyhound depot. Fares vary according to distance traveled and you need to have the exact fare when boarding. Most buses are wheelchair-accessible. For information, tel: 800-660-4287, www.samtrans.org.

By Train

Bay Area Rapid Transit (BART)

BART is one of the most modern, efficient, and automated regional transportation systems in the country. The sleek, clean, air-conditioned cars carry hundreds of thousands of commuters each day at speeds approaching 80 miles (129km) an hour. BART serves 45 stations in three counties, from San Francisco to Millbrae and throughout Alameda and Contra Costa (the East Bay), Mon–Fri 4am–midnight, Sat 6am–midnight, Sun 8am–midnight. Some of the BART tracks are underground, others are on the surface, or elevated.

Tourists can ride BART for a special reduced fare which entitles you to stay on board for up to three hours. You must enter and exit BART from the same station. Commuters crowd the cars from 7am to 9am and 4pm to 6pm on weekdays. For current information, tel: 415-989-2278, www.bart.gov. BART now offer services to and from the San Francisco and Oakland airports.

State-owned **Caltrain** and **Samtrans** run passenger trains between San Francisco and San José with several stops along the peninsula. Used by many commuters, the service is most frequent northbound in the morning and southbound in the afternoons. Caltrain operates from a terminal at 4th and Townsend streets. For information, tel: 800-660-4287, www.caltrain.org and www.sam trans.com. The terminal is served by many Muni bus lines, and it is easy and fun to take a sightseeing train excursion down the peninsula. Main San Francisco depot: 700 4th Street.

By Ferry

For commuters and sightseers alike, ferryboats are a convenient and scenic way to cross the bay. Golden Gate Ferry services are offered from the original Ferry Building at the foot of Market Street to Sausalito and Larkspur. Two lines run from the Fisherman's Wharf area: the Red & White Fleet has tours around the bay, as well as ferry services to Sausalito, Tiburon, Angel Island and Alcatraz Island. The Blue & Gold Fleet also operates narrated bay cruises from the Wharf.

It's worth checking the fleet and pier before arriving for a crossing, as they are dependent on the weather and may vary:

Blue & Gold Fleet, Pier 39 Marine Terminal, The Embarcadero at Beach Street, tel: 415-705-8200, www.blueandgoldfleet.com. Angel Island, Sausalito, Tiburon, Oakland, Alameda.
Golden Gate Ferry, tel: 415-455-2000 or 511, www.goldengate.org, leaves from the Ferry Building to Sausalito and Larkspur.
Red & White Fleet, Pier 43, ½ Fisherman's Wharf, tel: 415-673-2900, www.redandwhite.com. Round-the-Rock and Golden Gate Bridge tours.

Private Transportation

Taxis

San Francisco is compact, and taxis can be a convenient alternative to walking or public transportation for short distances or if you're in a hurry. In busy downtown areas, cabs can be hailed from the sidewalk, but they can be scarce in other areas. Use the numbers below to book in advance. San Francisco cab drivers are known for their helpfulness, and the city is so small, it's difficult to get lost.
Arrow, tel: 415-648-3181.
Flywheel, tel: 415-970-1300; http://flywheeltaxi.com.
Green Cab, 415-626-4733; www.greencabsf.com.
Luxor, tel: 415-282-4141; www.luxorcab.com.
Pacific Cab, tel: 415-596 6666; http://pacificcabs.com.
National Veterans, tel: 321-TAXI; http://sfnationalcab.sftaxischool.com.
Yellow Cab, tel: 415-333-3333; http://yellowcabsf.com.

Driving

Car Rentals

There are dozens of automobile rental agencies at the airports

and in San Francisco. Rates vary; insurance is extra and varies in price and coverage. Check your own auto policy before you leave home to see if you really need the extra coverage. Read the rental agreement before you sign. Most companies offer unlimited mileage and special weekend rates. Shop around for the best rates and service. Often, smaller local rental companies offer better deals than national firms. Reservations are advised.

Most rental agencies require you to be at least 21 years old (sometimes 25), to hold a valid driver's or international driver's license, and a major credit card. Drivers are required to abide by local and state traffic regulations.

If you are an auto club member in another country, National Automobile Club will extend emergency cover, information, and other services to you. The California State Automobile Association may extend services – you must check first. Contact www.csaa.com.

Car Rental Companies

Alamo, tel: 800-462-5266, www.alamo.com.
Avis, tel: 800-331-1212, www.avis.com.
Budget, tel: 800-527-0700, www.budget.com.
Dollar, tel: 800-800-3665, www.dollar.com.
Enterprise, tel: 800-261-7331, www.enterprise.com.
Hertz, tel: 800-654-3131, www.hertz.com.
National, tel: 800-227-7368, www.nationalcar.com.
Thrifty, tel: 800-367-2277, www.thrifty.com.

Motorcycles & Scooters

Dubbelju Motorcycle Rentals, 274 Shotwell Street, tel: 415-495-2774, www.dubbelju.com.
Eaglerider Motorcycle Rental, 488 8th Street, tel: 415-503-1900, www.eaglerider.com.

HOW TO PARK

Much of San Francisco's parking space is on steep hills. The law requires wheels to be "curbed" on these inclines, to help prevent runaways. Turn your front wheels into the curb on a downhill slope and away from the curb if facing uphill. Be sure to set the emergency (hand) brake. Not only are fines issued for cars that are not curbed, but there's also the possibility of finding your car at the bottom of the hill.

Motohaven, 160 Ford Way, Novato, tel: 415-898-5700,.

Bicycles

It is possible to tour San Francisco and never struggle uphill. Both Golden Gate Park and Golden Gate Bridge have designated weekend bicycle routes. Rental shops can be found on Stanyan Street, at the park's entrance, and in the Marina area and Fisherman's Wharf. Many shops have route maps, too. Rental places include:
Bike and Roll, 899 Columbus Avenue, tel: 415-229-2000, www.bikeandroll.com/sanfrancisco.
Blazing Saddles, 1095 Columbus Avenue, tel: 415-202-8888, www.blazingsaddles.com. Other locations in Fisherman's Wharf.
Golden Gate Park Bike and Skate, 3038 Fulton Street, tel: 415-668-1117, https://goldengatepark.com.
Wheel Fun Rentals, next to Stow Lake boathouse, Golden Gate Park, tel: 415-668-6699, www.wheelfunrentals.com

Rideshare Apps

Ridesharing is a service that arranges one-time shared rides on generally very short notice and is usually arranged through a smartphone app.
Uber, www.uber.com
Lyft, www.lyft.com

A – Z

AN ALPHABETICAL SUMMARY OF PRACTICAL INFORMATION

A

Admission Charges

Most of San Francisco's large museums charge entrance fees – typically $15 to $30. The California Academy of Sciences is the most expensive at $34.95, with discounts for teenagers, students and seniors. Call or check the website of an attraction for any days on which admission is free or for special circumstances where charges might be lowered. Many museums offer free entry on a given day during the first week of every month.

B

Budgeting for Your Trip

For a hotel or Airbnb room with a minimum level of comfort, cleanliness, and facilities, a reasonable starting point for a double room is $99 in budget-class; upping the budget from there to around $185 makes a significant difference in quality. Between $185 and $300 a range of options opens up, from bland business traveler stops to hip little boutiques in the heart of Union Square. Beyond this, is deluxe

territory; though "discreet celebrity hideaway" status doesn't start until $500 and above.

Food costs range from $7–15 for a perfectly acceptable sandwich, burrito or Asian delicacy, to $50 for a two- or three-course meal at a cute California cuisine-type restaurant. Expect to pay $70–125+ at a fine restaurant.

Getting around by public transportation (bus, MUNI, bart, and cable car), within city limits, can cost as little as $17 a day. A day pass on public transportation might be significantly cheaper than paying individual fares (currently $2.25) for each trip. Cab fares for journeys in the city center can range from as little as

$8 to as much as $25, depending on the distance. A cab to the airport should cost $42–62, while a shuttle to the airport will cost $15–20, excluding tip.

C

Climate

Summers in San Francisco can be foggy and chilly; in wintertime, expect rain. September and October are the warmest months, when temperatures occasionally reach 80°F (32°C). See www.sf gate.com/weather for daily weather reports.

What to Wear

San Francisco is a city best explored on foot, so bring a comfortable pair of walking shoes. Also keep in mind that fog and wind can conspire to make summer days wintery. Even if you visit in summer, bring warm clothes, a windbreaker, and a coat. Dress in layers, since temperatures are known to drop considerably, especially when the fog rolls in.

San Franciscans do dress up, but in a more casual way than in New York or Europe. Some restaurants employ a dress code, so men should bring a jacket and tie if you plan to dine out.

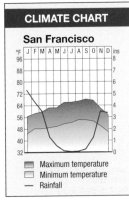

CLIMATE CHART

San Francisco

°F	J	F	M	A	M	J	J	A	S	O	N	D	ins
96													8
88													7
80													6
72													5
64													4
56													3
48													2
40													1
32													0

■ Maximum temperature
□ Minimum temperature
— Rainfall

TRANSPORTATION

Crime and Safety

It is safe to walk the streets during the day in most parts of the city, but use special caution in the following areas, especially at night: the Western Addition (bordered by Gough, Divisadero, Geary, and Golden Gate streets – between Golden Gate Park and Civic Center); Hunter's Point (the peninsula just north of Monster Park); the small streets of the Mission District (unlit passages between Dolores, Potrero, 10th, and Cesar Chavez streets); the Tenderloin (bordered by Bush, Powell Market, and Polk streets, which is near the Theater District and is commonly frequented by tourists).

Most safety precautions are common sense. If possible, and particularly at night, travel with another person while sightseeing or shopping. Do not walk in deserted or run-down areas alone. If driving, keep your door locked when moving. Auto theft can be a problem in San Francisco, so take a few simple precautions to protect your vehicle. Never leave luggage, cameras, or other valuables in view, either when driving or parked. Put them in the glove compartment or trunk to avoid any break-in. With regard to personal belongings, you should never leave luggage unattended. Never leave money or jewelry in your hotel room, even for a short time.

Report any theft or criminal activity to the nearest police station or call **911**.

Customs Regulations

If you are 21 or over, you are allowed to bring in 200 cigarettes, 100 cigars, or 3lb (1.3kg) of tobacco, 1 US quart (1 liter) of alcohol and gifts up to a value of $800. You are not allowed to bring in food items, seeds, plants, or narcotics.

There is no limit to the amount of money you can bring in or out, but if the amount exceeds

$10,000, you must fill out a report at the airport or on the plane. Anything you have for your personal use may be brought in duty- and tax-free. **Duty-free shopping** is available to those who are leaving San Francisco for a destination in another country. You must show your flight number and date of departure, then you can purchase retail goods duty-free at the San Francisco airport.

D

Disabled Travelers

Access Northern California is a non-profit organization geared toward helping those with disablties travel comfortably in the Bay Area. Their website, www.accessnca.org, has information on hotels, restaurants, and activities plus tips on renting accessible vehicles.

For those eager to get out and get some exercise, the **Janet Pomeroy Center** at 207 Skyline Boulevard near Lake Merced offers an adapted gymnasium, sports and physical fitness area, a therapeutic warm-water swimming pool, and three outdoor par golf courses. For more information call 415-665-4100 or visit www.janetpomeroy.org.

E

Electricity

The standard electric current in the US is 110–120 volts, which requires a voltage converter and adapter plug for European appliances. Some of the bigger hotel bathrooms have plugs for electric shavers that work on either current.

Embassies and Consulates

Australia: 575 Market Street, Suite 1800
Tel: 415-644-3620

Canada: 580 California Street, 14th floor
Tel: 415-834-3180
Great Britain: 1 Sansome Street, Suite 850
Tel: 415-617-1300
Ireland: 100 Pine Street, Suite 3350
Tel: 415-392-4214
New Zealand: One Maritime Plaza, Suite 700
Tel: 415-399-1255

Emergency Telephone Numbers

Police, Fire, and Ambulance
Tel: 911
Victims of Crime Resource Center
Tel: 800-842-8467
Red Cross Hotline
Tel: 888-443-5722
Poison Control Center
Tel: 800-222-1222
General information and services
Tel: 311

G

Gay and Lesbian

San Francisco is known as one of the world's most welcoming places for gay men and lesbians. No one really agrees on what made it into the current thriving, politically influential gay community it is today, but it doesn't matter. Resources for gay, lesbian, and transgender travelers include www.onlyinsanfrancisco. com/gaytravel, a virtual visitor's bureau for the gay community. The best source for up-to-date information on new clubs, shows, films, events, and gay news are the free newspapers, notably the Bay Times (http://sfbaytimes.com) and the Bay Area Reporter (BAR; www.ebar.com), found in cafés or street-corner boxes. The Center, at 1800 Market Street, www.sf center.org, has become a vital nexus for the lgbt (lesbian, gay, bisexual, and transgender) community and has numerous

A – Z

Party responsibly.

flyers and listings for city-wide events.

The Women's Building, www.womensbuilding.org, houses non-profit organizations, and newspapers, bulletin boards, and information are here too. The *SF Weekly* (www.sfweekly.com) has useful listings and information.

H

Health

Being sick in the United States is costly. It is essential to be armed with adequate travel medical insurance and to carry identification and/or policy numbers at all times. If expense is a concern, neighborhood clinics offer good service and may not charge a fee. If you need immediate attention, go directly to a hospital emergency room. If you have to be treated, make sure your insurance company is informed within 24 hours.

Medical Services

Referrals and other medical-related assistance can be obtained from the San Francisco Department of Public Health, www.sfdph.org.
San Francisco Medical Society Referral Service, tel: 415-561-0850

San Francisco Dental Society, tel: 415-928-7337
ucsf Physician Referral Service, tel: 888-689-8273, www.ucsfhealth.org.

Hospitals

Some larger hospitals with 24-hour emergency services are: the **California Pacific Medical Center** (www.cpmc.org), with buildings at 3700 California Street, Castro & Duboce, 3555 Cesar Chavez Street and 2333 Buchanon Street. For information, tel: 415-600-6000.
24-hour medical services are also provided at the **San Francisco General Hospital** (www.sfgh.surgery.ucsf.edu), 1001 Potrero Ave, tel: 415-206-8000.
Other hospitals include:
Children's Hospital Oakland (www.childrenshospitaloakland.org) 747 52nd Street, Oakland
Tel: 510-428-3000
Kaiser-Permanente Medical Center (https://healthy.kaiserpermanente.org) 2425 Geary Boulevard
Tel: 415-833-2000
St Francis Memorial Hospital 900 Hyde Street (www.dignityhealth.org/saintfrancis)
Tel: 415-353-6000
St Luke's Hospital (www.cpmc.org)

Working on the move.

3555 Cesar Chavez Street, at Valencia Street
Tel: 415-600-6000
St Mary's Medical Center (www.dignityhealth.org/stmarys) 450 Stanyan Street, at Hayes Street
Tel: 415-668-1000
UCSF Parnassus Campus (www.ucsf.edu) 505 Parnassus Avenue
Tel: 415-476-1000
UCSF Mount Zion Campus (www.ucsf.edu) 1600 Divisadero
Tel: 415-567-6600

Outpatient Clinics

San Francisco is good at low-cost outpatient clinics. These provide good care but the wait can be long.
Centers include:
Integrated Care Center 1735 Mission Street
Tel: 415-746-1940
Haight-Ashbury Free Medical Clinic 558 Clayton
Tel: 415-746-1950
Health Care Center at St Lukes 1580 Valencia Street
Tel: 415-611-6996
Women's Options Center 1001 Potrero Ave
Tel: 415-206-8476

Pharmacies

Certain drugs can only be prescribed by a doctor. Most drugstores stock a variety of drugs and have a pharmacist on duty. These stores are often open 24 hours.

Walgreen Drugs: there are over 60 locations throughout the city. Some Walgreens drugstores (pharmacies; www.walgreens.com) stay open 24 hours a day; in others, pharmacists are available until midnight. Check with your hotel: you may find that some medicines obtainable over the counter in your home country are available only by prescription in the US, and vice versa. CVS Pharmacy (www.cvs.com) is another drugstore chain with numerous locations.

USEFUL WEBSITES

www.sfgate.com: the *San Francisco Chronicle*'s website reproduces the daily newspaper online and has archives of information on everything from restaurant reviews to events listings.

www.sfweekly.com and www.sfbg.com: both of the free weeklies have corresponding websites with entertainment, arts, and cultural events listings.

www.craigslist.org: a community site with a cult-like following.

www.sfstation.com: a hip, comprehensive site dedicated to food, entertainment, and activities in San Francisco.

www.citysearch.com: another informative guide to the city.

www.sanfrancisco.travel: the Convention and Visitors Bureau site is packed with tons of useful information for travelers.

www.yelp.com: a site for people to review all manner of restaurants, bars, shops, cafés, and services. Valuable insight can be gleaned here.

www.transit.511.org: useful information for all forms of Bay Area transportation.

www.wunderground.com/US/CA/San_Francisco.html: detailed short- and long-range local weather forecasts.

www.mistersf.com: a quirky collection of San Francisco anecdotes, history, contemporary culture, and characters.

I

Internet

It's easy to get online in San Francisco and there are many ways to do it. Wireless hotspots are in abundant supply. A very helpful site, www.openwifispots.com, has a searchable list of spots across the US, and can help you find a location in San Francisco. A free public WiFi service is available in selected areas and parks of the City. For details go to http://sfgov.org/sfc/sanfranciscowifi. Some cafés ask you to pay a minimal service fee for use of their wireless router. Others, like Starbucks, offer it free of charge. Another good resource is www.yelp.com, which also has listings for internet cafés and WiFi hotspots throughout the city.

The California Welcome Center, and Cyber Café, Pier 39 – Upper Level – Building P, Beach Street and The Embarcadero, tel: 415-981-1280, www.visitcalifornia.com, is open seven days a week and has a computer available for $5 every 30 minutes. A cheaper option is the Public Library, 100 Larkin Street at the Civic Center plaza, tel: 415-557-4400. Free terminals are on the first floor and are available for 15 minutes on a first-come, first-served basis.

Most hotels have dataports in the rooms; the more expensive offer high-speed internet connections and the use of a laptop for at least an hour at a time, while many cheaper hotels have at least one computer for guests' use.

L

Left Luggage

As security has tightened recently, leaving luggage has become trickier. No airports have lockers, but larger hotels may allow you to leave bags with them. Or use this agency: Airport Travel Agency (www.airporttravelagency.org), tel: 650-877-0422, in SFO's international terminal.

Lost Property

Lost property is handled by the SF police department, and found items are held at the Property Clerk's Room for 120 days. To report lost property, phone a local police station, or from Mon–Fri 9am–4pm, call the Property Clerk, tel: 415-553-1392, fax: 415-553-1555. Faxing serial numbers, descriptions, or photos of items may aid in recovering lost or stolen valuables.

Restaurants, taxicabs, nightclubs, stations etc. are not responsible for your personal property, but you might have luck calling up and asking for lost and found. Be friendly and patient, and you may have a reunion.

M

Maps

If you find yourself confused and mapless, look for a Muni bus shelter, which often has a detailed map of the city, including a close-up map of Downtown. *Insight FlexiMap: San Francisco* is a laminated map, and has text and photographs of sites; it's good in San Fran's wet weather. Some corner shops and gas stations also sell maps.

A comprehensive map of the city's streets and public

RADIO STATIONS

Formats are often subject to change, but the most popular local radio stations include:

AM
560 **KSFO**: talk
680 K**NBR (NBC)**: sports, talk
740 **KCBS (CBS)**: news, sports
810 **KGO (ABC)**: news, talk, and sports
960 **KNEW**: talk
1260 **KSFB**: Christian
1450 **KEST**: general
FM
88.5 **KQED**: PBS, NPR, news

89.5 **KPOO**: soul, blues
91.1 **KCSM**: jazz
94.9 **KYLD**: urban, top 40
95.7 **The Woff**: country
96.5 **KOIT**: lite rock
97.3 **KLLC**: rock, top 40, alternative
98.1 **KISQ**: soul, R&B, urban
102.1 **KDFC**: classical
103.7 **KKSF**: smooth jazz
104.5 **KFOG**: rock, alternative
105.3 **KITS**: alternative
106.1 **KMEL**: urban, hip-hop
107.7 **KSAN**: classic rock

transport system is sold by MUNI, the San Francisco Municipal Railway. Free tourist magazines usually include maps of the popular areas. For interactive maps, visit www.san francisco.travel/maps.

Media

Television and Radio

The major television stations in the San Francisco area include channels 2 (**KTVU**), 4 (**KRON**), 5 (**KPIX-CBS**), 7 (**KGO-ABC**), 9 (**KQED-PUBLIC TELEVISION**), and 11 (**NBC**). There are also foreign-language stations, mainly Spanish and Chinese. Dozens of other cable channels are available through the city's local cable company, **Comcast**. Complete TV listings appear daily in the *San Francisco Chronicle* newspaper.

Newspapers and Magazines

The major daily newspaper is the *San Francisco Chronicle* (www.sf chronicle.com). The San *Francisco Examiner* (www.sfexaminer.com) is a free daily paper that specializes in local news. The Sunday *Chronicle* includes special sections, such as the "Pink Pages," which is a comprehensive guide to various current sports, entertainment, cultural, and artistic events.

Free weekly paper *SF Weekly* (www.sfweekly.com) features coverage and commentary on everything from arts to city politics and include film, music, and arts listings. Sidewalk racks and cafés carry a variety of other free magazines, from real-estate publications to neighborhood papers and literary journals.

Besides the English-language publications, various communities publish daily and weekly papers in foreign languages. These are available at a number of places, including: **Juicy News**, 2181 Union Street, tel: 415-441-3051; **Fog City News**, 455 Market Street, tel: 415-543-7400; and **Smoke Signals**, 2223 Polk Street, tel: 415-292-6025.

Money

Current dollar exchange rates are usually listed in the travel section of the *San Francisco Chronicle* Sunday edition.

Exchange: the airport is the most convenient place to change currency (though fees could be steep), since only certain banks perform this service for customers who do not have accounts. In the city, you can exchange currency at **Currency Exchange International**, 343 Sansome Street, tel: 415-677-4040; **Bank of America**, 345 Montgomery Street, tel: 415-

913-5891; and **The San Francisco Mechanics Bank**, 343 Sansome Street, tel: 415-677-4040.

Cash: most banks belong to a network of ATMs (automatic teller machines) that dispense cash 24 hours a day. ATMs are found on the street, inside some stores, in lobbies of buildings, and outside of banks. With a debit card you will be able to get cash back with purchases at all major grocery and drugstores. (If the card is issued in a foreign country, this may not be the case.)

Credit cards: not all credit cards are accepted at all places, but most places accept either **Visa**, **American Express**, or **MasterCard**. Major credit cards can also be used to withdraw cash from atms. (Look for an atm that uses one of the banking networks indicated on the back of your credit card, such as Plus, Cirrus, and Interlink.) There will be a charge for this transaction.

O

Opening Hours

Shopping hours differ from one neighborhood to another. In Union Square and Fisherman's Wharf, business hours are 9am–6pm, seven days a week, with extended hours at night for the larger chains. Smaller boutique shops in surrounding areas may open as late as noon and close as late as 9pm. Banking hours vary; some branches offer a Saturday service.

P

Photography

Many museums and galleries do not allow pictures, and flash photography is seen as rude and disruptive during public perfor-mances. The use of tripods is also restricted in many public places.

For photographic equipment or services in the downtown area, avoid the shops along Grant and Kearny. Fireside Camera in the Marina (2117 Chestnut Street; tel: 415-567-8131; www.firesidecamera.com) sells all the major camera brands, as well as offering digital print services and camera supplies.

Postal Services

The **United States Post Office General Mail Facility** is located far away at 1300 Evans Avenue, tel: 415-550-5001. Many of the city's 50 postal stations are open for extended hours on weekdays and limited hours on Saturday. For current postal rates and other information, visit www.usps.com.

You can have mail addressed to you care of "General Delivery" at the post office of your choice. You will need the zip code of the station and you must pick your mail up in person.

Stamps may be purchased from the post office or from vending machines in hotels, stores, supermarkets,

Yosemite National Park in fall.

transportation terminals, and the post office.

The Art Deco **Rincon Center Post Office**, 180 Steuart Street, is the jewel of the city's postal history, with beautiful murals and a philatelic center. The building makes "doing the mail" a pleasant experience. Stop in to take a picture and send a postcard.

Public Holidays

Most banks, post offices, government buildings, and some large businesses are closed on the following major holidays:
New Year's Day: January 1.
Martin Luther King's Birthday: January 15.
Presidents' Day: third Monday in February.
Memorial Day: last Monday in May.
Independence Day: July 4.
Labor Day: first Monday in September.
Columbus Day: second Monday in October.
Veterans' Day: November 11.
Thanksgiving: fourth Thursday in November.
Christmas: December 25.

Public Toilets

San Francisco has over 25 public pay toilets scattered about the city in an experimental effort to help travelers caught out and also to deter homeless people from using the city streets for relief. The toilets are painted green and gold and cost 25 cents to use. Most are acceptably clean, but avoid public toilets in the Tenderloin district, especially at night, as they are notorious for illicit activity. The new trend is for open air urinals which can be found in Dolores Park.

Many restaurants discourage anyone but patrons from using their facilities; your best bet is to try a department store, hotel, gas station, or fast- food chain restaurant. The fine for urinating in public is $500.

S

Senior Travelers

Senior citizens (over 65) are entitled to many benefits, including reduced rates on public transportation and reduced entrance fee to museums. Seniors who want to study should write to **Roadscholar,** call toll-free 800-454-5768 or visit www.roadscholar.org, for information on places that provide both accommodation and educational classes. The Bay Area has a number of Roadscholar locations.

Smoking

San Francisco's famed tolerance for alternative lifestyles does not extend to smokers. California state law bans smoking in bars, clubs, restaurants, within 25ft (7.5 meters) of playgrounds or sandboxes, and within 20ft (6 meters) of all public buildings, even though the former governor of California, movie star Arnold Schwarzenegger, had a "smoking

Connected at North Beach.

tent" of his own on the grounds of the Capitol.

San Francisco law also prohibits smoking in all city-owned parks, plazas, and public sports facilities. Even in blues bars and the city's famed coffee houses, smoking isn't tolerated, despite the beatnik heritage. It can also be difficult to reserve a hotel room where smoking is permitted; be sure to check at the time of booking.

Student Travelers

Most museums and movie theaters offer discounts to students with a valid student identification card from their university or school.

The café at the San Francisco Art Institute (www.sanfrancisco artinstitute.com) at 800 Chestnut Street is open to the public and is known for inexpensive vegetarian meals and one of the best views of the city.

T

Telephones

The number of telephones located in hotel lobbies, bars, restaurants, and other public places has dwindled as more

TELEPHONE CODES

415/628: San Francisco, Sausalito, Larkspur, Mill Valley, Tiburon.
510: Oakland, Berkeley.
650: San Mateo, SFO airport, Palo Alto.
707: Napa, Sonoma, Mendocino.
408: San Jose.
831: Monterey, Carmel, Santa Cruz.

people carry cell phones. California is adding to its existing telephone codes extremely fast, and area codes can change with little warning; if in doubt over an area code, contact an operator. The main San Francisco area code is 415 or 628.

Long-distance rates can vary, but discounts are available at specific times; check the telephone directory or dial 0 for operator assistance for both local and international calls.

Toll-free numbers for various services or businesses are indicated by an **800** or **888** prefix. The **Directory** for toll-free numbers is 800-555-1212. To call the **Information Operator** for all other numbers, dial **411**. Note: there is a charge.

To dial another country from the United States, use the prefix **011** before the country code and number. To call another area code within the US, simply add the prefix **1**.

Cell phones

If you have a tri-band cellular phone, contact your service provider to set up international roaming. To rent a cellular phone in San Francisco (it may be cheaper than roaming charges), try AllCell Rentals; tel: 877-724-2355, www.allcellrentals.com. They are open 24 hours a day.

Time Zone

California is in the Pacific Time Zone, which is two hours behind

Chicago, three hours behind New York City, and eight hours behind London. The US begins Daylight Saving Time at 2am local time on the second Sunday in March and reverts to Standard Time at 2am local time on the first Sunday in November.

Tipping

The accepted rate for porters at airports is $1 or so per bag. Hotel bellhops and porters usually expect the same. A doorman should be tipped if he or she unloads or parks your car. Tip your chambermaids at the end of your hotel stay; a few dollars per day should be sufficient. Depending on the quantity and quality of service rendered, 20 percent of the bill before tax is the going rate for most other help such as cab drivers, barbers, hairdressers, waiters, waitresses, and bar persons. In some restaurants, the tip or a service charge will be included in the bill if it is for a large group; be sure to check with the restaurant first.

Tour Operators and Travel Agents

There are many tour operators in San Francisco offering a variety of options. The best place to start is

Don't forget to tip service staff!

at the **San Francisco Visitors and Convention Bureau**. They can be extremely helpful when choosing activities and operators. You can call or visit the centrally located offices at Hallidie Plaza, Powell and Market streets, Mon–Fri 9am–5pm, Sat–Sun 9am–3pm, tel: 415-391-2000.

The website www.sanfrancisco. travel offers a number of listings for hotels, restaurants, and tour operators. Translations are available in French, German, Italian, Korean, Spanish, Mandarin, and Japanese.

The San Francisco Chamber of Commerce is also a helpful resource with links to various business and tourism professionals. For more information, contact them at 235 Montgomery Street, tel: 415-392-4520, or visit https://sfchamber.com/.

V

Visas and Passports

Visitors coming to the United States must have a valid passport, visa, or other documentation. However, in an effort to attract more tourists, the US initiated the Visa Waiver Program for those coming on vacation for a maximum of 90 days. With 36 countries participating, the program allows for travelers to enter the US with only a machine-readable passport.

The terrorist attacks of September 11, 2001 have caused an increase in security measures taken by the Department of Homeland Security. It now requires all VWP participants to apply with the Electronic System for Travel Authorization. Done online, authorization does not take much time and can occur at any point before entry into the US; try to apply as early as possible to minimize complications. There is a $14 application fee, payable over the internet.

To check your eligibility for the Visa Waiver Program, and for complete and up-to-date information for all travelers and travel entry requirements, visit the US State Department at https://travel.state.gov/content/visas/en.html.

Extending Your Stay

A foreign visitor who comes to the US for business or pleasure is admitted initially for a period of not more than six months. Extensions of stay are likewise limited to 90 days. Visitors may not accept employment during their stay. Check with your consulate for more details.

W

Weights and Measures

The US uses the Imperial system of weights and measures. Some conversions:

1 inch = 2.54cm
1 quart = 1.136 liters
1 foot = 30.48cm
1 gallon = 3.8 liters
1 yard = 0.9144 meters
1 ounce = 28.40 grams
1 mile = 1.609km
1 pound = 0.453kg

TOURIST OFFICES

San Francisco Visitors and Convention Bureau
900 Market Street, San Francisco, CA 94103
Tel: 415-391-2000
www.sanfrancisco.travel
Berkeley Convention and Visitors Bureau
2030 Addison Street, #102, Berkeley, CA 94704
Tel: 510-549-7040
Toll-free: 800-847-4823
www.visitberkeley.com
Carmel Chamber of Commerce
PO Box 4444, Carmel, CA 93921
Tel: 831-624-2522
Toll-free: 800-550-4333
www.carmelcalifornia.org
Marin County Visitors Bureau
One Mitchell Boulevard, Suite B, San Rafael, CA 94303

Tel: 415-925-2060
www.visitmarin.org
Monterey Peninsula Chamber of Commerce
243 El Dorado Street, Suite 200, Monterey, CA 93940
Tel: 831-648-5350
www.montereychamber.com
Napa Valley Destination Council
600 Main Street Napa, Napa, CA 94559
Tel: 707-251-5895
www.visitnapavalley.com
Oakland Convention and Visitors Bureau
481 Water Street, Oakland, CA 94607
Tel: 510-839-9000
www.visitoakland.org
Sausalito Chamber of Commerce
1913 Bridgeway, Sausalito,

CA 94965
Tel: 415-331-7262
www.sausalito.org
San Jose Convention and Visitors Bureau
408 Almaden Boulevard, Suite 1000, San Jose, CA 95110
Tel: 408-295-9600
Toll-free: 1-800-SAN-JOSE
www.sanjose.org
Sonoma County Tourism Bureau
400 Aviation Boulevard, Suite 500, CA 95403
Tel: 707-522-5800
Toll-free: 800-576-6662
www.sonomacounty.com
Sonoma Valley Visitors Bureau
453 First Street E., Sonoma CA 95476
Tel: 707-996-1090
Toll-free: 866-996-1090
www.sonomavalley.com

FURTHER READING

GENERAL

You Can't Win by Jack Black. A favorite of Beat writers, Black's autobiography details his life of crime in San Francisco at the turn of the 20th century. It is a fascinating and entertaining look at the city, particularly its seedy underbelly.
The Best of Herb Caen by Herb Caen, A collection of the quintessential chronicler of San Francisco culture from 1960–75.
Stairway Walks of San Francisco by Adah Bakalinsky. A delightful new edition of Bakalinsky's previously out-of-print guide to 27 urban hikes up and down some of the city's 350 stairways.
Above San Francisco by Robert Cameron and Arthur Hoppe. A gorgeous book of aerial photography of the City by the Bay.
Infinite City: A San Francisco Atlas by Rebecca Solnit. An extraordinary atlas including essays and maps concerning Monarch butterflies, Hitchcock;s films, blues clubs etc. As one critic put it, it's "a terrific guide to the city's possibilities".

FICTION

The Maltese Falcon by Dashiell Hammett. A noir classic that tells the tale of Sam Spade, a hardboiled SF detective, hired to solve the mystery of a missing gold statuette for which he must dodge villains and beautiful women alike.
Tales of the City by Armistead Maupin. Originally a serial in the San Francisco Chronicle, Maupin's novel stitches together the lives of residents of the fictitious Barbary Lane told with delightful candor.

On the Road by Jack Kerouac. In what became the bible of the Beat generation, the iconoclastic writer chronicles his jazz and drug-fuelled travels and travails crisscrossing the United States and Mexico in the 1950s.
The Joy Luck Club by Amy Tan. The award-winning first novel of local lit darling Amy Tan, chronicling the lives of daughters of Chinese immigrants in San Francisco and the challenges of being modern American women with old-world parents.
Telegraph Avenue by Michael Chabon. The title is a reference to the avenue that runs through the cities of Oakland and Berkeley in the Bay Area. This multi-generational comic novel set in the mid-2000s explores and challenges, among others, America's attitudes to race.

MEMOIR

Oh the Glory of it All by Sean Wilsey. This amusing and poignant memoir by the son of wealthy San Francisco socialites was met with controversy due to Wilsey's revelations about his extended family, who happen to be the city's power elite.

HISTORY

The Great Earthquake and Firestorms 1906 by Philip L. Fradkin. An amazingly compelling and insightful account of the destruction, corruption, and fortitude that defined the city during that terrible week in April over one hundred years ago.
Imperial San Francisco by Gray Brechin. Brechin offers an alternative history of San Francisco, as seen through its myriad statues and monuments, and one in which the city is a global power player.
The Electric Kool-Aid Acid Test by Tom Wolfe. A classic of "New Journalism" finds the author immersed in the psychedelic adventures of Ken Kesey and his band of Merry Pranksters as they "turn on" first San Francisco, then America, with LSD.
Gimme Something Better: The Profound, Progressive, and Occasionally Pointless History of Bay Area Punk from Dead Kennedys to Green Day by Jack Boulware and Silke Tudor. An oral history of the Bay Area punk scene from the '70s into the '00s, warts and all: an exciting and sometimes skanky treasure trove of insider info.
The Mayor of Castro Street: The Life and Times of Harvey Milk by Randy Shilts. Perhaps the quintessential biography of the first openly gay man elected to office in America, from his triumphant election and ground-breaking championing of gay rights, to his tragic assassination and the subsequent rioting upon the light sentence of his killer.

OTHER INSIGHT GUIDES

Insight Guides cover the breadth of the US, from Alaska to Hawaii and New England to Florida. Within the United States, the City Guide series covers NYC, Las Vegas, SF, Boston, and Seattle.
Other *Insight* series include Experience, Explore and *Insight: FlexiMaps* of New York City, San Francisco, and Orlando.

SAN FRANCISCO STREET ATLAS

The key map shows the area of San Francisco covered by the atlas section. An index of street names and places of interest shown on the maps can be found on the following pages. For each entry there is a page number and grid reference

Map Legend

=====	Freeway (under construction)
=====	Divided Highway
─────	Main Road
─────	Secondary Road
─────	Minor Road
▬ ▪ ▬	International Boundary
─────	State Boundary
─ ● ─	National Park/Reserve
─────	Ferry Route
✈ ✈	Airport
✝ ✝	Church (ruins)
✝	Monastery
▟ ▨	Castle (ruins)
Ω	Cave
★	Place of Interest
☼	Viewpoint
⌐	Beach
─────	Freeway
─────	Divided Highway
─────	Main Roads
─────	Minor Roads
─────	Footpath
▬▬▬	Railroad
▭	Pedestrian Area
▭	Important Building
▭	Park
Ⓜ	Metro
🚌	Bus Station
❶	Tourist Information
✉	Post Office
✝	Cathedral/Church
✡	Synagogue

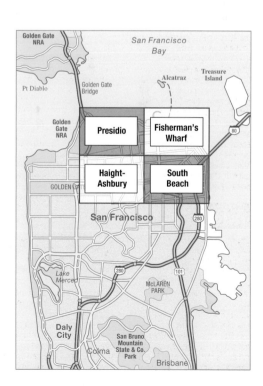

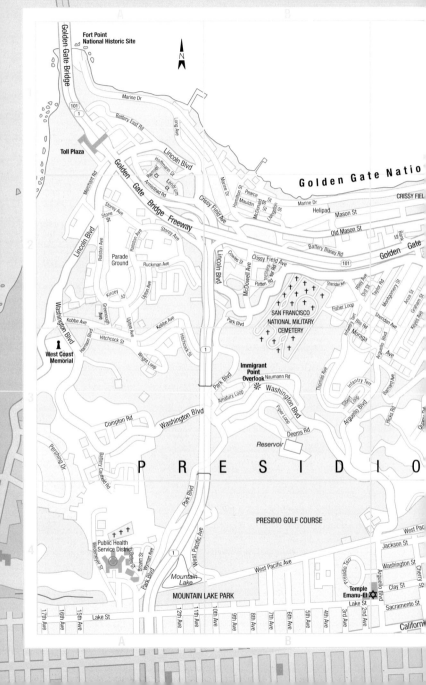

D

E

0   400 yds

0   400 m

Wave Organ

Marina Small Craft Harbor

Golden Gate
Yacht Club

*East
Harbor*

**Fort Mason
Center**

Yacht Rd

Marina Green Dr

MARINA GREEN

West Harbor

**Museo
ItaloAmericano**

reation Area

Marina Blvd

Marina Dr

Marina Blvd

Marshall St

Jauss St

Allen St

Mason St

Doyle Dr

Exploratorium

Gorgas Ave

Birmingham Rd

Thornburg Rd

Eddie Rd

101

**Palace of
Fine Arts**

Lagoon

Kennedy Ave

**Letterman
Digital
Arts Center**

Richardson Ave

Letterman Dr

Lyon St

Baker St

Jefferson St

Beach St

Broderick St

North Point St

Bay St

Francisco St

Chestnut St

Scott St

Prado St

Avila St

Cervantes Blvd

Pierce St

Divisadero St

MARINA

Casa Way

Rico Way

Pablo St

Jefferson
St

Beach St

North Point St

Capra Way

Mallorca

Alhambra St

Toledo Way

Avila St

Way

Jefferson
St

Beach St

North Point St

Buchanan St

Laguna St

Bay St

FUNSTON PLGD

Chestnut St

Magnolia St

Lombard St

101

St

Greenwich St

Webster St

Buchanan St

Lombard St

Baker St

Broderick St

Divisadero St

Scott St

Pierce St

Steiner St

Moulton

Pixley

Fillmore St

Filbert St

✡ **Former
Vedanta
Temple**

Presidio Blvd

Lombard St

Sherman Rd

Simonds Loop

Simonds Loop

Shafter Rd

**COW HOLLOW
PLGD**

Greenwich St

Filbert St

Union St

Green St

Vallejo St

Union St

PACIFIC HEIGHTS

Green St

Summer Ave

Norton St

Clark St

Liggett Ave

Sanches St

Sibley Rd

West Broadway

Baker St

Broadway

Rayliff
Terr

Pacific Ave

Jackson St

Washington St

Clay St

Broderick St

Divisadero St

Normandie
Terr

**Casebolt
House**

Vallejo St

Pierce St

**Smith
House**

**James Irvine
House**

Scott St

**ALTA PLAZA
PARK**

Clay St

Sacramento St

Perine Pl

**Convent of the
Sacred Heart**

Vallejo St

Steiner St

Fillmore St

Bromley
Pl

Jackson St

**Flood
Mansion**

Broadway

**Bourn
Mansion**

Pacific Ave

Webster St-Historic District

Washington St

**Pacific Medical
Center**

California St

FILLMORE

Webster St

Orben St

PRESIDIO HEIGHTS

Pacific Ave

Presidio Ave

Locust St

Laurel St

Walnut St

Lyon St

**PRESIDIO
HEIGHTS
PLGD**

Sacramento St

California St

Jackson St

Washington St

Clay St

Pierce St

California St

Pine St

Bush St

Wilmot St

Cottage
Row

LAUREL HEIGHTS

Mayfair Dr

Pine St

**S.F. Fire Department
Museum**

Sutter St

D

E

Alcatraz

0   400 yds
0   400 m

Pier 35
Pier 33
Pier 31
Pier 29
Pier 27
Pier 23
Foreign Trade Zone
Pier 19
Pier 17
Pier 15
Pier 9
Pier 7
Pier 3
Pier 1

Montgomery St
Winthrop St
Lombard St

TELEGRAPH
Coit
Tower

HILL

Alta St
Calhoun Terr
Montgomery St
Castle St
Sonoma St

Levi's
Plaza

Union St
Commerce St
Green St

Battery St

The Embarcadero

Sansome St
Front St
Davis St
Vallejo St

N.E. Waterfront
Historic District

Kearny St
Dunnes Alley
Prescott Ct
Crowell
Osgood Pl

Broadway

Beat Museum
Nottingham Pl

Columbus Ave

Gold St
Jerome Alley
Bartlett
Beckett St

Pacific Ave

SIDNEY
WALTON
PARK

Maritime
Plaza

Custom-
house
Jackson
Square
Hist. Dist.

Jackson St

Buddha's
Universal
Church

Chinese
Culture
Center

Transamerica
Pyramid

Washington St

Justin
Herman
Plaza

World Trade
Center

Ferry Plaza
East

Ferry Building

Tin Hou
Temple

Portsmouth
Square

Merchant St

Clay St

Ferry
Building
Marketplace

Pier 2

CHINA
TOWN

Commercial St

Wells
Fargo
Bank
History
Room

Embarcadero Center

Sacramento St

Hyatt
Regency
Hotel

Old St Mary's
Roman Catholic
Church

Montgomery St

Battery St
Sansome St
Front St
Davis St

Halleck St

California St

Federal
Reserve Bank

Steuart St

FINANCIAL

Embarcadero M

Pine St

The Embarcadero

Promenade

Chinatown
Gate

55 California St
(former Bank of
America Building)

Quincy St
Belden St
Claude

Bush St

Market St
Fremont St
Beale St

Mission St
Main St

Rincon
Center

Rincon St

Folsom
Station

Transbay
Terminal

Kearny St

Harlan Pl
Hardie Pl

Hallidie
Bldg

Sutter St

Trinity St
1st St
Ecker St
Jim Alley

Howard St

Pier 24

Bay Bridge

DISTRICT

Crocker
Galleria

Post St

Lick Pl

Spear St
Steuart St

Ricon
Point

Pier 26

Campton Pl

Maiden Lane

Montgomery
New Montgomery
2nd St
Anna St

Minna St

Natoma St

Sterling Alley

Beale St
Zeno Pl
1st St

Folsom St

Main St

Harrison St

80

Pier 28

Geary St
Grant Ave

Sheraton
Palace Hotel

Cartoon Art
Museum

Tehama St

Fremont St

Bryant St

Pier 30

Market St
Stevenson St
3rd St

California
Hist. Soc.
Museum of the
African Diaspora

San Francisco
Museum of
Modern Art

Clementina St
Lansing St

Pier 32

Exploratorium

Golden Gateway
Center

Wells Fargo Bank
History Room

Union St

Mayfair Dr
Collins St
Laurel St
Euclid Ave
Iris Ave
Mayfield Ave
Heather Ave
Manzanita Ave
Blake St
Cook St
Wood St
Emerson St
Lupine Ave
Masonic Ave
Presidio Ave
S.F. Fire Department Museum
Bush St
Lyon St
Baker St
Broderick St
Divisadero St
Scott St
Pierce St
Sutter St
Post St
Japan Center
Sutter St
Post St
Ericson
Garden St
Mt Zion Hospital

L. HILL PLGD

Geary Blvd
Geary Expressway
KIMBELL PLGD
Steiner St
Fillmore Auditorium
Fillmore St

Kaiser-Permanent Medical Center
Terra Vista Ave
Anza Vista Ave
Barcelona Ave
Encanto Ave
Fortuna Ave
Vega St
Nido Ave
Anza Vista Ave
O'Farrell St
Ellis St
Eddy St
Pacific Coast Hospital
Beideman St
St John Coltrane

Farrell St
S.F. College for Women
Ewing Terr
Masonic Ave
Baker St
St Joseph's Ave
Broderick St
Divisadero St
Scott St
Pierce St
WESTERN ADDITION

University of
Turk Blvd
Kittredge Terr
Rossiyn Terr
Tamalpais Terr
Annapolis Terr
Atalaya Terr
Hennway Terr
Loyola Terr
Turk St
Central Ave
Golden Gate Ave
Turk St
Elm St
Golden Gate Ave
Sprnca St

Parker St
Tarnescal Terr
Chabot Terr
San Francisco
St Ignatius
McAllister St
McAllister St
HAYES VALLEY

Schrader St
Grove St
Cole St
Clayton St
Ashbury St
Masonic Ave
Central Ave
Fulton St
Grove St
Lyon St
Baker St
Broderick St
ALAMO SQUARE

Hayes St
Hayes St
Fell St
Oak St
Fell St
Oak St

Fell St
ak St
PANHANDLE
Oak St
Page St
Divisadero St
Scott St
Pierce St
Steiner St

HAIGHT-
ASHBURY
Cole St
Clayton St
Ashbury St
Central Ave
Haight St
Haight St
Waller St
Buena Vista Ave East
Waller St
Lloyd
Carmelita
Page St
Haight St
Waller St
DUBOCE PARK
Duboce Ave

Waller St
Schrader St
Cole St
Belvedere St
Clayton St
Downey St
Delmar St
Ashbury St
Masonic Ave
Java St
Buena Vista Ave West
BUENA VISTA PARK
Duboce Ave
Alpine Terr
Buena Vista Terr
Divisadero St
Ralph K. Davies Medical Center
Sanchez St
Waller St
14th St

Beulah St
Frederick St
Cole St
Belvedere St
Clayton St
Downey St
Delmar St
Piedmont St
Upper Terr
Roosevelt Way
Buena Vista Ave East
Roosevelt Way
15th St

Carl St
Stanyan St
Parnassus Ave
Grattan St
Belvedere St
Ashbury St
Clayton St
Ashbury Terr
Clifford Terr
Mt. Olympus
Upper Terr
Levant St
Ord Ct
Museum Way
CORONA HEIGHTS PLAYGROUND
Randel Museum
STATES PLGD
States St
Flint St
15th St
15th St
Beaver St
16th St
Market St
16th St
Prosper St
Pond St
Noe St

Alma St
Rivoli St
Cole St
Upper Terr
Roosevelt Way
Temple St
Saturn St
Lower Terr
Vulcan Stairway
Douglass St
Castro St
Harvey Milk Plaza
★ 17th St
M Castro
Castro St
Noe St
Pond St
Ford St

17th St
Stanyan St
Schrader St
2nd Ave
Carmel St
Deming St
Belvedere St
Corbett Ave
Market St
Eureka St
Diamond St
Collingwood St
Castro St
Castro Theatre
18th St
Hartford St

TANK HILL PARK
Clayton St
Burnett Ave
Upper Terr
18th St
Clover St
Caselli Ave
Caselli Ave
EUREKA VALLEY PLAYGROUND
Eureka St
Douglass St
CASTRO

Contemporary Jewish Museum
San Francisco Museum of Modern Art
Center for the Arts
Metreon
Yerba Buena Square
Moscone Convention Center South
Childrens' Creativity Musuem
Moscone Center West
Hall of Justice
Upper Deck
Bayside Village Pl
Brannan Station
Pier 32
Pier 34
Pier 36
Pier 38
Pier 40
South Beach Harbor
SOUTH PARK
2nd & King Station
AT&T Park
McCovey Cove
Pier 48
Newsprint Terminal
Mission Rock Terminal
Pier 50
Mission Rock Station
Boat Launch Ramp
Pier 52
San Francisco Caltrain Depot
4th & King Station
UCSF Mission Bay Station
Pier 54
Pier 64
AGUA VISTA PARK
Mariposa Station
20th St Station
JACKSON PARK

SOUTH OF MARKET

CHINA BASIN

POTRERO

James Lick Skyway
Southern Embarcadero Freeway
Mission Creek Marina
The Embarcadero
Terry A. Francois Blvd
China Basin St
James Lick Freeway
San Bruno Ave

STREET INDEX

ART AND PHOTO CREDITS

Cover Credits

INDEX

ABOUT THIS BOOK

INSIGHT GUIDES
SAN FRANCISCO

Editor: Kate Drynan
Author: Lisa Dion
Head of Production: Rebeka Davies
Update Production: AM Services
Pictures: Tom Smyth
Cartography: original cartography Berndtson & Berndtson, updated by Carte

Following her thirst for travel and adventure, **Lisa Crovo Dion** left Boston after college to drive across country with two girlfriends in an '87 Chevy. She camped in Bryce Canyon, drank whisky at a topless bar in Kansas City, and got a tattoo in Phoenix. Eventually she made it to San Francisco and never left. Today, she works as a travel writer/blogger and a marketing copywriter while raising two children, and chronicling her much tamer exploits on her blog, friscomama.com. She has contributed to Insight Guides for more than a decade and written for the San Francisco Chronicle, SOMA magazine, Uptake.com, SF Weekly, salon.com, Gayot's, San Francisco, and Via.

From previous editions, we would like to thank the following writers: Jen Dalton, Elizabeth Linhart Money, and John Wilcock. Thanks also to Helen Peters who indexed the copy.

Most of the photographs were taken by Richard Nowitz. David Dunai's on-the-spot shooting was also appreciated.

Distribution

UK, Ireland and Europe
Apa Publications (UK) Ltd
sales@insightguides.com

United States and Canada
Ingram Publisher Services
ips@ingramcontent.com

Australia and New Zealand
Woodslane
info@woodslane.com.au

Southeast Asia
Apa Publications (SN) Pte
singaporeoffice@insightguides.com

Hong Kong, Taiwan and China
Apa Publications (HK) Ltd
hongkongoffice@insightguides.com

Worldwide
Apa Publications (UK) Ltd
sales@insightguides.com

Special Sales, Content Licensing and CoPublishing

Insight Guides can be purchased in bulk quantities at discounted prices. We can create special editions, personalised jackets and corporate imprints tailored to your needs.
sales@insightguides.com;
www.insightguides.biz

Printing

CTPS-China

SEND US YOUR THOUGHTS

We do our best to ensure the information in our books is as accurate and up-to-date as possible. The books are updated on a regular basis using local contacts, who painstakingly add, amend, and correct as required. However, some details (such as telephone numbers and opening times) are liable to change, and we are ultimately reliant on our readers to put us in the picture.

We welcome your feedback, especially your experience of using the book "on the road". Maybe we recommended a hotel that you liked (or another that you didn't), or you came across a great bar or new attraction that we missed.

We will acknowledge all contributions, and we'll offer an Insight Guide to the best letters received.

Please write to us at:
Insight Guides
PO Box 7910, London SE1 1WE
Or email us at:
hello@insightguides.com